Illness and Health in the Jewish Tradition

*Writings from
the Bible to Today*

In this illustration, taken from an early twentieth-century book of stories for little girls, the angel Raphael is promoting the healthfulness of milk for children. The illustrator invokes the ancient and medieval Jewish lore that one of God's chief angels, Raphael, whose name means "God is healing," protected and cured the ill. Raphael is featured at length in the late second Temple period story "Tobit," which is not in the Hebrew Bible but is found in the Christian Bible. In this tale, Raphael restores sight to the good man Tobit and is said to have defeated the demon of diseases Azmodeus. According to the Rabbis, Raphael was one of the angels who appeared to Abraham after his circumcision, and in the Zohar, one of Raphael's tasks is to relieve suffering. *Courtesy of Rachel Raphaela Feingold*

ILLNESS AND HEALTH IN THE JEWISH TRADITION

Writings from the Bible to Today

Edited by
David L. Freeman, M.D.
and
Rabbi Judith Z. Abrams, Ph.D.

The Jewish Publication Society
Philadelphia
1999 · 5759

The Jewish Publication Society
1930 Chestnut Street
Philadelphia, PA 19103-4599

Design by Masters Group Design, Philadelphia
Composition by Book Design Studio II
Manufactured in the United States of America

00 01 02 03 04 05 06 07 08 10 9 8 7 6 5 4 3 2

Library of Congress Cataloging in Publication Data

Illness and health in the Jewish tradition : writings from the Bible
  to today / edited by David L. Freeman and Judith Z. Abrams.
      p.   cm.
    Includes bibliographical references and index.
    ISBN 0-8276-0673-7
    1. Medicine--Religious aspects--Judaism.   2. Health--Religious
aspects--Judaism.   3. Suffering--Religious aspects--Judaism.
4. Spiritual life--Judaism.   5. Medicine in the Bible.   6. Medicine
in rabbinical literature.   7. Jews--Medicine.   8. Ethics, Jewish.
I. Freeman, David L., M.D.   II. Abrams, Judith Z.
BM538.H43I45   1999
296.3'76--dc21   99-20744
                                                          CIP

For Amanda

—David L. Freeman

For my healers, with great gratitude

—Judith Z. Abrams

This anthology is dedicated in loving memory of
DR. ABRAM COHEN
אברהם בן יהודה ויסי
(1901–1998)

His commitment to God, his family, patients, and fellow human beings was a constant source of pride in all our lives. He showed us the way.

from his family:

Goldie Cohen (ז"ל)
Wife

Betty Ann (ז"ל) and D. Walter Cohen
Josephine Cohen
Children

Jane and Martin Millner
Amy S. Cohen
Joanne and Aaron Katz
Grandchildren

Rachel Millner
Lauren Millner
Michael Millner
Great grandchildren

The Divine Presence (Shekhina) rests above an invalid's bed.

—Talmud

He shall set his heart upon making his body perfect and strong so that his soul will be upright to know the Lord.

—Maimonides

To study (medicine) diligently is among the greatest acts of worship.

—Maimonides

Contents

Part III.
From Where Will My Help Come?

Preface

In this sourcebook of Jewish writings on health, illness, and recovery, writers reflect on the experience of being ill from a Jewish spiritual perspective. The authors address key questions devout Jews have confronted through the ages: whether suffering and loss have some larger meaning or lessons, whether extra-medical means such as prayer can alleviate pain and what the proper roles of secular and spiritual healers may be. Because illness is a human constant, words from Babylon to New York, written in Aramaic or English, in poetry, story, prayer, or essay will always have resonance. Being sick and returning to health are subjects on which every person is, or may eventually become, expert. Remembering an experience of illness from any time and any place is still valid and authentic; even the most ancient of texts may speak to us on this subject. A fundamental, even quintessential, Jewish impulse is to transform raw, inarticulate pain into written words and then to use those writings to guide and teach. We offer these passages to our readers in the belief that they will be begin to envision illness not just as a clinical, physical state but also as a spiritual challenge, thereby opening new avenues for alleviation of suffering.

The selections here were chosen to be inspiring, empowering, and provocative to people who have been ill, their loved ones, and caregivers. They were part of a monthly prayer service called *Refuat Hanefesh,* the healing of the soul, at Temple Israel in Boston. Since 1990, Temple Israel has conducted this special service to give participants a tranquil experience of prayer and reflection when coping with illness. The service's liturgy is made up of Jewish prayers, poems, and readings—much of it set to music. The service also incorporates a group discussion focusing on different readings about healing, all selected from Jewish texts, new and old. They may come from classic Jewish sources, such as the Bible or the Talmud, or they may be written by contemporary rabbis, physicians, and other health professionals, or people grappling with illness. The search for such material has uncovered a vast lode, which lends itself well to the spirit of *Refuat Hanefesh.*

This sourcebook reflects the quest of people touched by illness. How can one cope? What does illness mean? What might it teach? What are the relevant Jewish prayers? What makes for a good healer? What can a rabbi do for someone who is suffering? What is expected of the community and of the ill person in Jewish law and custom? Everyone will, in some way, someday, confront the challenge of being a patient, a loving companion, a healer, a teacher, or a member of a supportive community.

While some commentary is added, it is hoped that readers will find their own meaning and context in these selections. One overarching theme that impressed the editors is the emphasis throughout on the healing effects of human relationships. Jewish thought stresses the therapeutic effects of human interaction: visiting, empathic support, reinforcement of love in relationships, and a return to communal life. Healing, whether emotional or physical, is not something one achieves alone, but always together in synergistic connection to family, friends, community, physician, rabbi, and others. Even prayer, which is akin to meditation, is not envisioned merely as a mantra or an antidote to anxiety, but rather as a private form of self-reflection on one's relationship to God and others, taking place within a supportive communal setting.

The literature on Jewish healing is much too vast to be placed in a single book, so this anthology must of necessity be selective. The editors used several criteria for their choices. First, the passages all deal with physical illness. Healing here refers narrowly to recovery from the effects of disease, and not, as it often means, to a sense of spiritual wholeness applicable to the physically healthy as well as the sick. Second, these excerpts are unambiguously Jewish. Either they come from Jewish religious texts, or they take a Jewish religious perspective on the subject, or they are derived from a singularly Jewish experience, such as the Holocaust, or they describe an experience that is viewed through the context of Jewish culture, as in Yiddish literature. Third, entries were chosen to spotlight a particular literary tradition or a revered scholar. For example, a passage from Julius Preuss's *Biblical and Talmudical Medicine* demonstrates Preuss's outstanding scholarship. In a similar vein, the works of Maimonides, Rosner, Friedenwald, and Jakobovits exemplify their contributions to this field. We also took into account stylistic considerations such as lucidity in writing, whether an excerpt could be lifted out of context and still be understood, and whether a piece added something new to the anthology.

We have divided the book into seven sections, which reflect topics of concern to people who are ill. Within each section passages are organized roughly chronologically—from the biblical era, through the second Temple period, to the talmudic, medieval, and modern eras. Much good material has been omitted, but a list of additional readings at the end of the book should offset these omissions, in part. Many valuable writings in Hebrew and diaspora languages, not translated into English, are absent. Several contemporary literary currents, including writings on modern Jewish medical ethics, Jewish medical history, and the involvement of Jews in modern medicine, are so extensive as to merit separate books.

Finally, Jewish tradition points to a number of ways in which we can better care for people who are ill. We must create new forms of prayer and ritual to reach Jews unfamiliar with traditional forms. The concept of visiting the sick must be reshaped to conform to the chronic illnesses that are so common today. Furthermore, as the hospital increasingly becomes a place limited to short-term, acute, intensive care, we will need to devise new systems of spiritual support in clinics, health centers, community centers, and places of worship—wherever people go for help. Because so much of modern care is out of individual hands and has become the responsibility of large hospitals, HMOs, and nursing homes, we need to readapt medical ethics to fit within institutional and governmental medical ethics. Modern constructs of empathy, or "treating the patient as a person," will be no more than superficial, mannered, and hollow forms unless we find ways to bolster long-term relationships between patients and health professionals.

We pray that this anthology will prove useful to people who now suffer from major illness, and for their loved ones, linked with them in distress. May they find consolation and food for thought in these pages. For chaplains, this volume may serve as a useful sample of classical and modern Jewish literature on the subject of illness. We hope that caregivers, seeking to examine their actions and attitudes in light of Jewish ethics and models, will gain valuable insights. Finally, anyone interested in the interconnection of medicine and religion will find much to ponder here. What emerges from these diverse selections is a holistic Jewish understanding of the healing of conjoined body, mind, and spirit through loving human relationships, communal support, and individual will.

The editors acknowledge their own limitations in the search for a literature of healing drawn from Jewish sources. Undoubtedly, we have missed much, especially among works not translated into English. This is not a scholarly or, in any way, complete work; it is meant to be inspirational and to point out the traditional concern that Jews have had for health and illness. We invite scholarship in a field that has been examined only on the surface. We have included selections from every branch of Judaism, and hope that our own biases have not seriously distorted the teachings of those branches to which we do not belong. We welcome suggestions for additions and amendments for any future editions.

There is a hunger in modern society for a spiritual understanding of illness. Without a better grasp of our own literature and history, we are left vulnerable to spiritual beliefs and practices foreign to our own tradition. We hope that this book, and others on health to be published by the Jewish Publication Society, will begin to address this current need.

Acknowledgments

Many people have helped to bring this sourcebook to fruition. It would never have been conceived without the guidance of the clergy of Temple Israel in Boston—Rabbis Bernard H. Mehlman, Elaine S. Zecher, Ronne Friedman, and Ruth Alpers, and Cantor Roy B. Einhorn. Others who gave inspiration, support, and insight are Dr. David Gordis, the late Rabbi Roland Gittlesohn, Rabbi Nina Beth Cardin, Professor Marc Z. Brettler, Dr. Aaron J. Feingold, Dr. Leonard S. Gold, Dr. Seth Jerchower, librarian Ann Abrams, and Rabbi Meir Sendor. The library of Temple Israel—a rich source of Jewish writings translated into English—was invaluable. Special thanks are due to Professor Carol Myers and Rabbi William Cutter for their original essays. Laurena A. Rosenberg, Muriel Morris, and Diane Frankel Schoenfeld helped to prepare the text. Dr. Ellen Frankel, editor-in-chief at JPS, provided much guidance and encouragement. Rabbi Judith Z. Abrams was instrumental in giving the material a coherent form and organization. The people affected by illness and the caregivers who have attended the Temple Israel service have tested many of the ideas in this volume. I am grateful to them all.

—David L. Freeman

First of all, I would like to thank David L. Freeman for so many things. He allowed me the pleasure of co-editing this volume with him. He has tirelessly brought this volume through the book-creation process. His erudition has been astounding but not intimidating. More than that, though, he has been the personification of kindness to me as I went through my own journey toward illness and then away from it. For this, he holds a special place in my heart.

Secondly, I would also like to thank the people at the Jewish Publication Society, Ellen Frankel in particular, who have helped this book come to be. They have been wonderfully supportive and insightful, and I appreciate their professionalism and their personal commitment to the study of Jewish healing practices.

Naturally, my greatest sources of inspiration are my family: Steven, Michael, Ruth, and Hannah. They are the most potent forces for healing anyone could ever love.

—Judith Z. Abrams

General Introduction: Judaism and Healing

Illness wounds the spirit as it injures the body. Disease is more than a fever, a lump, overwindedness, or some other physical symptom. It is, in part, the paralyzing fear when an HIV test is positive, the debilitating discouragement of Parkinson's disease, or the loneliness and confinement brought on by multiple sclerosis. The pain of a back injury is sometimes compounded by loss of employment, impoverishment, and tremendous family stress. After a heart attack, can one be the same mother, father, spouse, professional, sports enthusiast, collector, musician, lover, or dreamer as before?

Illness begins with the symptoms that impel us to see a doctor, but soon after it disrupts other dimensions of our psyche and life. Constant worry leads to heartache, sleeplessness, and fatigue, for often lurking behind a physical symptom is the unexpressed primal fear of death, decline, and future pain. When we are confined to home, hospital, or nursing home, boredom may erode our sense of joy in life. Specific losses of body function—such as vision, hearing, and mobility—or failure of memory and specific skills may affect our independence, appearance, or sexuality. We may feel sadness or worse, an emptiness of emotional feeling, obsessive worry, or utter hopelessness. We may become angry, bitter, envious, and frustrated. Family, friends, and companions participate in, internalize, and unwittingly reinforce the burgeoning distress, as they are cast in the role of grievers and caregivers, sometimes for a loved one whose very personality or even personhood may have been transformed.

Suffering from any illness, even a minor sickness, has a spiritual component. If the disease is life threatening, spiritual needs are more acute, urgent, and easily defined. When illness is chronic, the spiritual component of the suffering becomes inseparably intertwined with physical and emotional symptoms, and it may distort the person's basic temperament and social behavior. Spiritual wounds are poorly articulated, deeply felt, varied in their expression, inadequately recognized by patients and loved ones, and often difficult to resolve.

Mitigation of spiritual distress requires not medicine but, rather, human assistance. What is needed are solace, hope, companionship, perspective, guidance, engagement, redirection, encouragement, and a renewed sense of self-worth. To ameliorate spiritual wounds, people from all cultures and in all times have turned to prayer, ritual, magic, and spiritual healers in whom they have faith.

Every organized religion has attempted in some way to relieve suffering brought on by illness and to complement medical care. Ancient religions in Egypt and Mesopotamia had healing rituals, shrines, shamans, sorcerers, and diviners drawing on beliefs in benign and demonic supernatural forces. Greco-Roman temple ruins throughout Mediterranean lands testify to the popularity of the cult of Asclepius, a priesthood devoted exclusively to ritual healing. The ancient sufferer normally would have used both priest and lay healer, and there was much overlap in what the two offered. Similar notions and practices, re-shaped in monotheistic form, entered the religion of the ancient Hebrews.

Through its evolution over three thousand years, the Jewish religion has developed its own unique, pluralistic, multifaceted approach to illness. There is no singular Jewish dogma for healing, no one set of prayers or practice, and no simple intellectual constructs to help us heal. Jewish thought from each period has bequeathed a different mode of alleviating suffering, and Jews from every subsequent period have added or enhanced some elements of healing, de-emphasized others, and borrowed ideas from contemporary non-Jewish sources. In every age, one finds relics of the beliefs of prior ages, which are re-cast and given new meaning. Traditional Jewish sacred texts, the Bible, the Babylonian Talmud, Maimonides' *Mishneh Torah,* and the Shulḥan Arukh, each express a distinct perspective on the nature and alleviation of illness. As a result, the Jewish approach to healing is empirical, eclectic, complex, and without order or hierarchy, some elements at times in conflict with others. In a classic example of prior doctrine being altered for the sake of healing, magical chants were accepted in the Talmud despite the prohibition against magic in the Bible because, the Sages said, saving life is the higher priority. What the Jewish approach(es) to healing lacks in intellectual consistency, it makes up for in diversity, flexibility and adaptability. To be specific, how does traditional Judaism view illness and healing?

The most ancient mode of alleviating suffering in Judaism has been through prayer and ritual. The deepest hope of anyone suffering from illness is for a miraculous cure. The Bible unambiguously declares that God has the ultimate power over life and death, health and illness. Responding to the prayer of Moses, "O God, pray heal her," God cures Miriam of a cursed skin condition.

Similarly, the prophets Elijah and Elisha revive dead children upon the entreaties of their mothers. Following a prayer to God, King Hezekiah is cured of a debilitating illness. King Hezekiah prays also to express gratitude for his recovery. Among Judaism's greatest gifts to mankind has been the solace of biblical prayer.

Following biblical times, regular, frequent praying has been a central element of Jewish healing religiosity. The *Amidah,* a prayer recited thrice daily and dating from the early years after the Jews returned from Babylonia to Jerusalem, includes the plea, "Heal us O Eternal One and we shall be healed." The *mi shebeirakh,* a prayer composed in the early Middle Ages and recited at each weekday synagogue service, calls on God to heal any particular individual. Two selections in this sourcebook testify to the existence of healing liturgy in the Jerusalem Temple and among the Dead Sea Scrolls. In the Middle Ages, Jewish women composed tekhines, personal prayers to express their concern for the trials of pregnancy and childbirth. Since its earliest periods, traditional Judaism has compassed a concern for the ill with everyday personal and communal liturgy.

Prayer, like song lyrics, can be appreciated for its poetry, but it is meant to be experienced in its own milieu. Much of Jewish prayer is conducted in the presence of others and is a part of the spiritual tapestry of a Jewish service. In the novel, *East River,* excerpted in part 1, Sholom Asch captures the transcendent effects of communal prayer on his ill character Moses Wolfe. Moses returns to the Hasidic prayerhouse of his childhood. There, surrounded by old friends, familiar melodies, cadenced davening, and the charisma of an old rabbi, he is for the moment lifted into a dreamlike, hypnotic state. Mysteriously, much of his anxiety over illness and dying disappears. Worried thoughts find subliminal resolution. In the words of Rabbi David J. Wolpe, he has had a "normal mystical experience," in which he "feels God in an acute way."

If prayer can be said to be the heritage of the Bible, visiting the sick and folk medicine stem from rabbinic literature. The rabbinic Sages made visiting the sick a moral imperative, virtually an additional commandment. "He who does not visit the sick," said Rabbi Akiba, "is like a shedder of blood." The sacredness of this obligation is underscored by the declaration that "the Divine Presence rests above an invalid's bed." Midrashic literature contains numerous stories of rabbis visiting and offering healing to other rabbis. This emphasis on visiting, connecting to, and communicating with the sick person, the rabbis said correctly, contributes to healing. Illness isolates; from isolation comes depression; and from depression comes a worsening of disease. The Sages knew that visiting is more than a social courtesy; it is therapeutic.

Talmudic duties to visit the sick were refined in later centuries and made part of the Jewish religious code. Maimonides distilled talmudic discussions into a short set of rules. In turn Joseph Caro incorporated Maimonides' rules with little change into the Shulḥan Arukh, considered by Orthodox Jews a sacred canon. Consequently, for centuries visiting the sick has been an important facet of Jewish culture. *Bikkur Holim* societies have existed since the early Middle Ages to ensure that the obligation to visit the sick—at home and in the hospital—is carried out. Modern rabbis visit the sick as part of their professional responsibilities. The practice is aptly portrayed in an exhibit of a traditional shtetl at Beth Hatefutsoth, the Museum of the Jewish Diaspora in Tel Aviv, where several figurines hover around a sickbed in a small, simple house.

The second approach to healing that the Talmud sanctified in Jewish life was folk healing. The Talmud has pages of advice and information on matters of health and illness, nearly all magical and folkloric. One lengthy section (Gittin 67a-70b) is a virtual manual of home remedies on ailments from head to feet. Scattered throughout the Talmud are comments on disease prevention, the causes of illness, and speculations on the metaphysical significance of disease. Some of the Sages were said to be healers.

All this attention to health and disease is extraordinary in any spiritual text. The Talmud's rationale was best expressed later by Maimonides when he wrote that one "should set his heart upon making his body perfect and strong so that his soul should be upright to know the Lord. For it is impossible for him to understand and reflect upon wisdom when he is sick or when one of his limbs is in pain." The folk remedies found in the Talmud signify a shift from the Bible's nearly exclusive emphasis on prayer toward a view that prayer and natural modes of healing are complementary. In the Talmud, illness was considered a phenomenon of nature (albeit a nature rife with magic and evil spirits), which should be treated with the remedies at hand. It was not necessarily a result of sinfulness. Furthermore, since the Talmud was to be a sacred text for the instruction of future Sages, implicitly the Talmud intended its students to be knowledgeable in the ways of healing.

The model of the rabbi/healer would continue throughout the Middle Ages, until medicine had become a restricted profession. Maimonides, Abraham ibn Ezra, Nachmanides, and Judah ha-Levi were the most notable of a great number of rabbis who adopted the mission of healing as part of their calling. In areas where doctors have been scarce, throughout the centuries and even today, lay healers steeped in Talmud, Kabbalah, and magical lore continue this tradition.

In the twelfth century, Maimonides introduced into Jewish law another approach to illness—the science of prevention, known as hygiene. In the *Mishneh Torah* and in his *Commentary on the Mishneh,* Maimonides stressed the importance of living healthfully, and he detailed proper practices of diet, sexuality, bowel function, and bathing. He took these not from the Talmud, but from Greek and Arabic medical texts, which were precursors of western scientific medicine. Following Maimonides' example, the Shulḥan Arukh made hygienic practices obligatory in Jewish religious law.

Maimonides may have systematized and modernized attitudes toward hygiene that were already in place in Jewish culture. Many of the biblical commandments and talmudic practices had beneficial, if unintentional, hygienic consequences, notably rituals around preparation of food, sexual continence, Sabbath rest, bathing, and cleaning. Such customs are said to have saved Jews in the Middle Ages from the worst ravages of the bubonic plagues.

After talmudic times, Jews were increasingly attracted to scientific medicine and the healing professions. Jews achieved prominence as physicians first in Islamic countries and then later in medieval Christian Europe. These earliest Jewish physicians rejected talmudic folklore and substituted for it the book-learned medical heritage of Hippocrates and Galen. During an early medieval Islamic revival and the development of ancient Greco-Roman medical thought, some Jews became prominent medical scholars, practitioners, text writers, and translators. They adopted a system of thought whose premise was that health and illness were observable, knowable natural phenomena and not the effects of deities, devils, curses, or magic. Following the eclipse of Islam in Spain, Jewish physicians helped introduce key Arabic texts into Christian Europe, and during the Middle Ages they acquired a reputation for having exceptional technical skills. The earliest known Jewish medical writer, Asaph, wrote a Jewish oath patterned after the oath of Hippocrates, and so began a tradition of Jewish concern for professional ethics. Lasting contributions to medical ethics were made by a ninth-century Moroccan physician, Isaac Israeli, as well as Maimonides and a number of Renaissance physicians. By the sixteenth century, medicine was the second most popular profession among Jews in Europe (after money lending), and many Jews enjoyed illustrious careers as physicians to popes, kings, and other notables. The sixteenth-century book of Jewish law, the Shulḥan Arukh, endorses these developments. It includes a chapter of regulations for the Jewish physician, declaring that to engage in healing is a religious duty for the trained physician.

A later medieval Jewish response to illness drew from the tradition of mysticism. Following the dissemination of kabbalistic texts, Jewish mysticism influenced even scientifically trained physicians. In the same vein, the eighteenth-century Hasidic rabbi, Rebbe Nachman of Breslov, who suffered from tuberculosis, dismissed his doctors and argued that "the main thing is faith." He advocated ascetic practices and joyful encounters with God.

In summary, prayer, folk healing, visiting the sick, hygiene, medical science, and mysticism all figure prominently in the traditional Jewish approach to illness. Also, until modern times Jews have nearly universally had faith in a blissful afterlife, so that many may have been more inclined to accept the ravages of disease as a prelude to a sublime hereafter.

Finally, Jewish historical experience has inspired a literature of coping and survival, which serves as a model and inspiration. The basic Torah myth of redemption from slavery and spiritual transcendence, celebrated every Passover, has implications for individual suffering. Since biblical times, Jews have questioned whether suffering had some transcendent purpose. Many individuals have offered stories of personal resilience underscoring the healing value of relationships, study, prayer, work, creativity, optimism, will, and acceptance.

In our own time, Jews continue to examine, develop, and enrich their healing traditions. Jewish healing services with a multifaceted liturgy reflect the contemporary experience with disease. Clergy are re-examining their roles in the arena of illness and health. In books, periodicals, and conferences, Jewish ethicists examine the dilemmas of modern medicine through the prism of talmudic sensibilities. Virtually every modern Jewish fiction writer has authored some story on health and illness, and numerous autobiographical and narrative essays relate illness to Jewish life and teaching. The Jewish affinity for the healing professions persists to this day. In the last two centuries, Jews have made monumental contributions to medical research and continue to do so in the United States and in Israel. Ehrlich, Freud, Salk, and numerous Jewish Nobel Prize winners in medicine exemplify the extraordinary numbers of Jews who have made the modern world healthier.

All this Jewish activity in the realm of illness and health begs for some perspective, celebration, overview, and examination. Jewish life, culture, and religious teaching in this area tend to be thought of disjointedly, without any overarching concept of how Jewish thought, teachings, and living might affect physical healing. Can we pinpoint deep-rooted, common elements that underlie the creativity of the ancient Jewish psalmist and the thoughts and practices of the modern scientific researcher, the rabbi-healer, the modern mind-body therapist, the medieval philosopher, and the halakhist? Perhaps the most fundamental commonalities are a search for God, a reverence for life, a belief in the sacredness of health, and a life-defining conviction that illness is an evil to be banished.

—The Editors

To Cope, to Endure, to Sustain, to Transcend

Jacob was left alone. And a man wrestled with him until the break of dawn. When he saw that he had not prevailed against him, he wrenched Jacob's hip at its socket, so that the socket of his hip was strained as he wrestled with him. Then he said, "Let me go, for dawn is breaking." But he answered, "I will not let you go, unless you bless me." Said the other, "What is your name?" He replied, "Jacob." Said he, "Your name shall not be Jacob, but Israel, for you have striven with beings divine and human and have prevailed."

Genesis 32:25–29

Introduction

*W*hen we, or our loved ones, are seriously ill, we try to find the strength to live as fully as possible. While disillusionment and despair commonly accompany sickness, many people recover a sense of equilibrium, a sense of direction. Indeed, some people even experience a transformation, which gives them an enhanced sense of purposefulness and meaning in life.

How do we help ourselves and others cope with suffering and loss of function? It is our premise that we can learn from and be inspired by others who have lived through emotional and physical suffering similar to that which we, and our loved ones, are experiencing. These stories, some autobiographical, exemplify the inner resources that people draw on to cope and endure. The selections speak of prayer, companionship, helpfulness, determination, persistence, and patience. While some of these activities can be done alone, most require connection to family, friends, community, and the larger world.

The writers of the selections in this book affirm the support offered by Judaism—by Jewish belief, ritual, law, literature, history, lore, and plain Jewish living. The writers eschew bitterness and anger and embrace family and community. They tell us that they have lived through profoundly disturbing events and that they have spiritually rebounded. The act of telling is for the authors a creative and loving act of communion, of reaching out to us, and so it augments their own continued spiritual healing as well as giving us a model for our own.

1. David's Recovery

BIBLE

Through inner force or will, King David redirects himself
away from grief. Perpetual mourning, he realizes, wastes
God's gift of life.

Nathan went home, and the LORD afflicted the child that Uriah's wife had
borne to David, and it became critically ill. David entreated God for the boy;
David fasted, and he went in and spent the night lying on the ground. The
senior servants of his household tried to induce him to get up from the
ground; but he refused, nor would he partake of food with them. On the seventh day the child died. David's servants were afraid to tell David that the child
was dead; for they said, "We spoke to him when the child was alive and he
wouldn't listen to us; how can we tell him that the child is dead? He might do
something terrible." When David saw his servants talking in whispers, David
understood that the child was dead; David asked his servants, "Is the child
dead?" "Yes," they replied.

   Thereupon David rose from the ground; he bathed and anointed himself,
and he changed his clothes. He went into the House of the LORD and prostrated
himself. Then he went home and asked for food, which they set before him,
and he ate. His courtiers asked him, "Why have you acted in this manner? While
the child was alive, you fasted and wept; but now that the child is dead, you rise
and take food!" He replied, "While the child was still alive, I fasted and wept
because I thought: 'Who knows? The LORD may have pity on me, and the child
may live.' But now that he is dead, why should I fast? Can I bring him back
again? I shall go to him, but he will never come back to me."[1]

2. Empathy

BIBLE

Many of the psalms are prayers to God for a return to health,
e.g., Psalms 6, 38, 102, and 116. The beginning of Psalm 41
speaks of the spiritual solace in time of trouble that comes
from serving others.

For the leader. A psalm of David
Happy is he who is thoughtful of the wretched;
in bad times may the LORD keep him from harm.
May the LORD guard him and preserve him;
and may he be thought happy in the land.
Do not subject him to the will of his enemies.
The LORD will sustain him on his sickbed;
You shall wholly transform his bed of suffering.[2]

3. Study Torah

TALMUD

The study of Torah, said the Sages, has curative power. It inspires and guides through the power of its words and letters.

R. Joshua b. Levi stated: If a man is on a journey and has no company let him occupy himself with the study of the Torah, since it is said in Scripture, *For they shall be a chaplet of grace*. If he feels pains in his head, let him engage in the study of the Torah, since it is said, *For they shall be a chaplet of grace unto thy head*. If he feels pain in his throat let him engage in the study of the Torah, since it is said, *And chains about thy neck*. If he feels pains in his bowels, let him engage in the study of the Torah, since it is said, *It shall be a healing to thy navel*. If he feels pains in his bones, let him engage in the study of the Torah, since it is said, *And healing to all his flesh*.[3]

4. Piety and Faith

GLUCKEL OF HAMELN

In her memoir, which the Dutch Jewess Gluckel of Hameln wrote for her children in the seventeenth century, she gives us a glimpse of the simple piety, optimism, and faith that sustained her when the plague assailed her community.

While I lay in childbed with daughter Mata, whispers spread that the plague, God shield us! was abroad in Hamburg. Presently it reached a point that three or four Jewish houses, too, were stricken; nearly all the inmates died and the houses stood almost vacant. It was a time of bitter suffering and desolation, when God have pity on them, it went hard with the dead. And most of the Jews fled to Altona.

We had by us some thousands of Reichsthalers in pledges, covering among others small loans from twenty to thirty, and up to one hundred thalers; for in the money-lending business, small loans of ten Reichsthalers or even five shillings cannot be refused. Now the plague had swept through the city, and we were constantly beset by customers. Even if we knew they were already infected we must deal with them, at least to the extent of returning them their redeemed pledges; and had we fled to Altona, they would have followed on our heels. So we resolved to take our children and go to Hameln, where my father-in-law lived.

We left Hamburg the day after Yom Kippur, and the day before the Feast of Booths we arrived in Hanover, where we put up at the home of my brother-in-law Abraham Hameln. Since the feast was so near at hand, we decided to remain there for the week's holy days. I had by me my daughter Zipporah, now four years old, my two-year-old son Nathan, and my daughter Mata, a baby of close on eight weeks.

My brother-in-law Loeb Hannover prayed us to spend the first days of the festival in his house, where lay the synagogue. The second morning, while my husband was upstairs at services, I was still in my bedroom, dressing my daughter Zipporah. As I was drawing on her clothes, I saw that when I touched her she winced, and I asked her, "What be the matter, child?" "Mother dear," she said, "something hurts me under the arm." I looked and found that the child had a sore near her armpit. My husband, too, was bothered with a sore, which a barber in Hanover had covered with a bit of plaster. So I said to my maid whom I had with me, "Go to my husband—he is upstairs in the synagogue—and ask him who the barber was and where he lives. Then take the child to him, and have him lay on a plaster." In all this I dreamed of nothing wrong.

The maid went upstairs, sought out my husband, and spoke with him. You must know that to reach the men's synagogue, one had to pass through the women's section. As the maid left the men's section, my sisters-in-law Yenta, Sulka and Esther, who were sitting among the women, stopped her and asked, "What were you doing in the men's synagogue?" Whereupon the maid answered

5

in all innocence, "Our little girl has a sore under her arm, so I asked my master, who likewise had a sore, which barber had been tending him, and I will take the child there as well."

The women fell at once into a mad fright, not merely because they were natural weaklings in such matters, but coming from Hamburg we lay under grave suspicion. They quickly put their heads together, considering what to do.

It happened that a stranger, an old Polish woman who sat among them, overheard the talk and remarked their fright. So she said to them, "Be not alarmed, 'tis nothing, I'll warrant. I have had to do with such things a score of times, and if you wish, I'll go belowstairs and have a look at the girl, and I'll tell you if there is any danger and what's to be done." The women were satisfied and begged her look the child over forthwith, so that, God forbid! they run no risks.

I knew nothing of all this, and when the beldam came to me and said, "Where be the little child?" I replied, "Why do you ask?" "Why," she said, "I am a healer and I want to doctor the child, and she will be cured in a twinkle." I suspected nothing and led forth the child. She looked her over, and fled from her at once.

She darted up the stairs and cried at the top of her voice, "Away, away—run and flee who can—the pest is in your house, the girl is down with the plague!" You can well imagine the terror and screaming of the women, above all among such chicken-livers.

Men, women, and all, deep in their holy day prayers, fled wildly from the synagogue. They seized my child and the maid, thrust them out of the doors, and none dared shelter them. I need not tell you of our distress.

I wept and screamed in the same breath. I begged the people, for God's sake, "Think what you do," I said, "nothing is wrong with the child; surely you see, God be praised! the child is hale and well. She had a running pimple on her head; before I left Hamburg I treated it with salve, and now it has gone to a little sore under her arm. If anyone were really stricken, God forbid! there'd be a dozen signs to show for it. But look—the child plays in the grass and eats a buttered roll as nicely as you please."

But it was all of no avail. "If it is known," they said, "if His Highness the Duke hears that the like has fallen in his capital-seat, woe and woe unto us!" And the beldam thrust herself before me, and told me to my face that she'd give her neck if the child were not tainted.

What was to be done? I besought them, "In all mercy let me stay with my child. Where the child stays, there will I. Only let me go to her!" But they would not hear of it.

Presently my brothers-in-law Abraham, Leffman and Loeb took counsel with their wives and bethought themselves what to do: where to put the maid and child and how to keep the whole matter secret from the authorities, for we all would have lain in mortal danger had noise of it come to the Duke.

At length they settled on a plan. The maid and child, clothed in old rags, were to go to a neighbouring village, not a Sabbath day's journey from Hanover. The name of the village was Peinholz. There they were to betake themselves to a peasant's house, and say that the Jews of Hanover had refused to shelter them over the holy days, being already overrun with poor, and had even refused them entry to the city. They must ask to pass the holy days in the village and offer to pay for the trouble. We know (they were to add) that the Hanover folk will send us food and drink, for surely they would not leave us in want during the holy festival.

Then they began negotiating with an old man, a Polack, who was staying over in Hanover, as well as with the Polish beldam whom I mentioned, to accompany the maid and child and see how matters fared. But neither of them would stir unless they were paid thirty thalers on the spot, to run so dire a risk. Whereupon my brothers-in-law Abraham, Leffman and Loeb held another consultation, and summoned the *melamad* [school-teacher], who was likewise a great *Talmud* scholar, to judge whether it be lawful to break the holy day by the payment of money. In the end they all agreed the money might be paid, since human life lay at stake.

So in the midst of the holy festival we were forced to send away our beloved child and allowed the thought that, God forbid! she be tainted. I will let every father and mother judge what this required of us.

My blessed husband stood in a corner and wept and prayed to God, and I in another corner. And, of a surety, God hearkened to us for the sake of my husband's merits. I do not believe that a heavier sacrifice was required of our father Abraham when he made to offer up his son. For our father Abraham acted at the bidding and for the love of the Lord, and thereby tasted joy even in his grief. But the decree fell so upon us, hemmed in by strangers, that it nigh pierced our hearts. Yet what could be done? We must needs bear all in patience. "Man is bound to give thanks for the evil, just as he gives thanks for the good."

I turned the maid's clothes inside out, and wrapped my child's things in a little bundle. I slung the bundle on the back of the maid like a beggar, and the child, too, I dressed in tatters. And in this fashion my good maid and my beloved child, and the old man and the beldam, set out for the village. You may know how we loaded the child with farewell blessings, and the hundreds of tears we shed. The child herself was happy and merry as only a child can be. But we and those of our own in Hanover wept and prayed to God, and passed the holy feast-day steeped in woe.

The child and her companions meanwhile reached the village and were well received by a peasant, since they had money in purse—something one can always put to use. The peasant asked them, "Since this is your feast-day, why don't you abide with the Jews?" They answered, "Hanover is overrun with poor and we were not allowed to enter the city, but we know full well the Hanover Jews will send us food for over the festival."

As for us, we returned to synagogue, but the prayers were through. At that time Judah Berlin, who had already done business with us, lived still unmarried in Hanover. Living there, too, was a young Polish Jew named Michael, who taught the children and who was likewise a sort of half-servant in the house, according to the German custom when folks had in a *Talmud* student to teach their children. (Later he took a wife in Hildesheim where he is now *parnas* and lives in wealth and honour.)

Anyway, as people were leaving synagogue, my brother-in-law Loeb had us called to dinner, for, as I said, he had invited us to stay with him, the day before the festival. But my husband said, "Before we eat, I must fetch food to the child and her companions." "In truth," said the others, "you are right. We will not eat until they too have something." The village, I repeat, was nearby, as close as Altona to Hamburg.

So food was gathered together, everyone giving something from his own pot. The question now arose, who will take them the food? And everyone proved afraid. Then Judah Berlin spoke up, "I will take it," and Michael said, "I will go with you." My blessed husband, who loved the child dearly, accompanied them. But the Hanoverians would not trust him, for they thought, if my husband goes he will not restrain himself from approaching the child. So my brother-in-law Leffman went along too; and they all went together and took the food with them.

Meanwhile the maid and child, and their companions, for hunger and nothing else to do, were walking in a field. When the child saw my husband, she was filled with joy, and childlike, wanted to run at once to her father. Whereupon my brother-in-law Leffman cried out, they should hold in the child and let the old man come fetch the food. Of a fact, they must needs bind my husband with a rope, to keep him from running to his child, for he saw that she was hale and well and yet he could not go to her; whereat he and the child wept.

So they placed the food and drink on the grass, and the maid and her companions fetched it away; and my husband and his friends moved off together. This continued until the eighth day of the festival.

The old man and the beldam were provided with plaster and ointment and everything wherewith to heal the sore. Indeed, they healed it nicely, and the child was hale and well and pranced about the field like a young deer.

We now said to the Hanover folk, "How far will your folly lead you? The child, you can see, is healthy as can be and the danger is over and gone—let then the child return!" So they took counsel again, and decided not to let the child and her companions come back before Simhat Torah, the ninth day of the feast. There was naught for us to do but abide by it.

On Simhat Torah, Michael went out and brought the child and her companions back to Hanover. Who never saw the joy of my husband and myself and everyone present—we needs must weep for joy and everyone wanted to eat the child alive! For she was as lovely and irresistible a mite as ever you saw. And for a long while after she was commonly called the Virgin of Peinholz.[4]

5. The Remedy of Trusting God

HASIDIC LORE

In this Jewish folk tale, simple faith in God mitigates suffering. In our own time, we have relearned the providential effect on health of optimism and belief.

When God sends evil days upon us, we shall do well to remember the remedy contrived by the physician in the story told by Rabbi Abraham ben Sabbatai Levi. A great king, he tells us, once imprisoned his physician, and had him bound hand and foot with chains, and fed on a small dole of barley-bread and water. After months of this treatment, the king dispatched relatives of the physician to visit the prison and learn what the unhappy man had to say. To their astonishment he look as hale and hearty as the day he entered his cell. He told his relatives he owed his strength and well-being to a brew of seven herbs he had taken the precaution to prepare before he went to prison, and of which he drank a few drops every day. "What magic herbs are these?" they asked; and he answered: "The first is trust in God, the second is hope, and the others are patience, recognition of my sins, joy that in suffering now I shall not suffer in the world to come, contentment that my punishment is not worse, as well it could be, and lastly, knowledge that God who thrust me into prison can, if He will, at any moment set me free."[5]

6. Strengths in the Soul

ADIN STEINSALTZ

According to Jewish mystical belief, each and every human soul has innate strength and processes, which are reflections of like activities within God. Note the following descriptions of Netzah, Hod, *and* Yesod, *which are particularly relevant during times of illness. Rabbi Steinsaltz is a noted Israeli talmudist.*

Just as they do in the higher world, the ten *Sefirot* exist in the human soul; and from their mutual interrelations are derived and manifested all the broad span of thoughts, feelings, and experiences of man. Thus, the first three *Sefirot* assert the aspects of pure consciousness: *Hokhmah,* expressing the power of original light, is that which distinguishes and creates and is the basis of intuitive grasp; *Binah,* expressing the analytical and synthetic power of the mind, builds and comprehends forms and probes the meaning of that which comes from the *Sefirah* of *Hokhmah;* and *Daat,* expressing the crystallization of awareness in terms of conclusions and the abstract ascertaining of facts, is that which enables consciousness to make a transition from one form of existence to another, thereby ensuring its continuity. Then following these are the three *Sefirot* of the higher emotions: *Hesed, Gevurah,* and *Tiferet. Hesed* as grace and love is the inclination toward things, the desire for, or attraction to beings, the outgoing flow and opening up to the world, that which gives of itself, whether in terms of will or affection or relation and, in giving, opens up to the *Sefirah* of *Gevurah*, or strength. *Gevurah* is thus an inward withdrawal of forces, a concentration of power which provides an energy source for hate, fear, and terror as well as for justice, restraint, and control. *Tiferet* is harmony and compassion as well as beauty, being a synthesis or a balancing of the higher powers of attraction and repulsion, and leads to moral as well as to aesthetic acceptance of the world. From these we proceed to the three *Sefirot* that act directly on the actual world of experience: *Netzah, Hod,* and *Yesod*. *Netzah* is the will to overcome, the profound urge to get things done. *Hod,* in striving to achieve and attain that which is desired, is also the power to repudiate the obstacles that rise from reality, and to persevere. *Yesod* is the power of connection, the capacity and the will to build bridges, make contacts, and relate to others, especially in the way this is done with teacher, father, and other figures of meaning and authority. Finally, the *Sefirah* of *Malkhut* is the realization, or living through, of this potential in the essential being: it is the transition from soul to outer existence, to thought, and to deed. It also effects the transmutation of consciousness back to *Keter,* the first and the highest of the *Sefirot,* which is also the essence of will and contains in itself all the higher powers that activate the soul from above.[6]

7. Sustaining Work

HASIDIC LORE

A Hasidic folk tale teaches us that even in the last moments of our lives, we can find ways to be ourselves and to be of help to others.

Rabbi David Leikes lived more than a hundred years. He was esteemed as an authority on rabbinic civil law, and his decisions were admired by all the judges.

Once, when the aged rabbi was on his deathbed, a very complicated case arose. His demise was expected any moment. The judges hoped that the ancient rabbi's mind might still be sufficiently clear to aid them, perhaps for the last time. They visited his home and stated their request. The rabbi's children protested vigorously and argued against troubling him, lest thereby his end be hastened.

Suddenly the door opened, and the dying rabbi entered. "Did you know," he said, "that we are taught by the Talmud [B. *Shabbat* 10a] that one who judges a case correctly becomes thereby God's partner? Yet you wish to deprive me of this opportunity!"

He gave his decision in the difficult case in a manner so remarkable that it left no doubt as to its correctness. He returned to his bed with the help of his children, and a moment later he died.[7]

8. *And Yet*

KADYA MOLODOWSKY

Illness frequently compounded the many difficulties of our immigrant eastern European ancestors. This poem was written by a turn-of-the-century Yiddish poetess.

My skin is so thin
that a single bullet,
one small steel bee
can kill me,
can kill you,
can kill him,
my dears.

My heart is so small
that it won't hide all
of my tears,
and if even one drop spilled
it would choke me,
it would choke you,
it would choke him,
my dears.

My life is so hard
that no boats at sea

or trains on the land
can ever take me
where I want to go,
my dears.

And yet—
with death stalking me,
hiding my tears,
desperate—
I am an arrow set in the bow
and my will is the hand

that aims me
where I will go
and will arrive,
my dears.[8]

9. Praying Together

SHOLEM ASCH

Jewish communal ritual may lift the soul beyond earthly cares. In this passage from the novel East River *by Yiddish writer Sholem Asch, the elderly and ailing Moshe Wolf, after a long absence, revisits the Hasidic prayer house of his youth.*

In Moshe Wolf's voice was a new softness and contentment. "Deborah," he said, "before we move away from here for good, I'd like once more to spend the Sabbath at my old Hasidic prayer house downtown, with my old friends and kinsmen. Who knows if I'll ever see them again?"

"But with your sick heart—where will you stay over Friday night?"

"I'll stay at Shmuel Chaim's, where else—the same as before. He still has the dairy store on Norfolk Street, across the street from the prayer house. You'll take me there on Friday afternoon, and on Saturday night, when the Sabbath is over, you can come for me."

"But Moshe Wolf, God forbid, it's a risk for your health . . ."

"To pray on the Sabbath with the friends of my young days? No, Deborah, it's not a risk. Our holy writings declare that if one sets out on a journey to perform a good deed, no harm can come to him."

"And what will the doctor say? Will Dr. Chazanowitch allow it?"

"Foolish woman, who says he's got to know anything about it? Naturally, a stubborn unbeliever like him would say no."

Deborah yielded. Early on Friday, when Nat was away from the house, she packed some night clothes for Moshe Wolf, together with his prayer shawl, and took a taxi—"a fortune of Irving's hard-earned money," she complained—and took him down to Shmuel Chaim's flat on the floor above his kosher dairy store.

"Malke, my crown, my jewel," she said to Shmuel Chaim's wife, "I have brought you a guest for the Sabbath. He took it into his head that he had to come down once more, at least before we move uptown, near my son."

"You understand, Shmuel Chaim," Moshe Wolf said. "I had to come. I had to be with all of you once more before we move away. Who knows when . . . ? You understand me, Shmuel Chaim."

"Of course I understand you, Moshe Wolf. Why shouldn't I understand?" Shmuel Chaim was a small, thin man with a long graying beard. "It's been a wonder to me that you stayed away so long."

Moshe Wolf sighed. Yes, it had been a long time, but there had been reason enough. So many things had happened, so many things.

"Don't worry, Deborah. We'll take care of him," Malke said cheerfully. "We'll take care of him."

"If God wills," Deborah sighed devoutly. "I'll come for him tomorrow night, when the Sabbath is over."

The Hasidic prayer house on Norfolk Street was located on the upper floor of a two-story building across the street from Shmuel Chaim's store, in a long, low-ceilinged hall, with whitewashed walls. It was only on Friday evenings and Saturdays that the congregation had the use of the hall; during the weekdays and on Sundays it was rented out to lodges, societies, clubs, and the like for their regular meetings. Flags and banners and emblems were stacked in a corner of the room. Photographs of club functionaries hung on the walls. In the afternoons the hall served as the office of an East Side marriage broker, and in the mornings an old-world rabbi sat at a desk advising the clients who came to consult him on matters of ritual or domestic problems. On the few evenings when no lodge meetings were scheduled, the room was let out for various purposes—sometimes to a dancing teacher giving lessons to members of a young couple's club, or to a radical group for lectures on socialism given by a well-known lecturer.

But always on Friday evenings the hall became a sanctuary for the spirit. Shmuel Chaim, who was sexton and "treasurer" of the Hasidic group, would come up to the hall early in the afternoon. He would clear the hall of the reminders of its weekday uses and sweep the floor, sprinkling it with sawdust for cleanliness. From the corner behind a protecting curtain, where it had reposed all week, he would bring out the small Ark of the Law and place it against the east wall. The Scroll, which he kept at home between Sabbaths so that it might be safe from the contamination of the weekday goings-on in the room, he would bring over from his flat, carefully wrapped in a prayer shawl, and place it in the Ark. Malke, his wife, would polish the heavy brass candlesticks and Shmuel Chaim would set them on the alter.

As dusk began to descend, the devout assembled, as in the town of their younger days, gathered around their rabbi, breathing in the glow which shone forth from the saintly presence, the earthly symbol of the Messiah himself. Now, too, they stood in their shiny and worn caftans, skullcaps on their heads. They stood there, these remnants of a devouter Israel, in an East Side hall, yet transported to the rare spheres where the holy Sabbath reigned. The candles flickered at the altar. The Scroll reposed in its Ark. At the eastern wall stood Reb Leibush, messenger of their rabbi far away in the old world, and Shmuel Chaim chanted the ancient, familiar Sabbath eve greeting—"Come, my friend, to greet the Bride, to give welcome unto the Sabbath."

Outside in the street was the modern Babylonia, where store windows were bright with electric light. Raucous gramophones split the air with chants and popular tunes. Both sides of the street were lined with pushcarts, with flaring kerosene torches lighting up the piles of goods—shirts, dresses, corsets, shoes, remnants of woolens and silks, bankrupt stock and fire-damaged merchandise. There were pushcarts piled high with pots and pans, hardware, dishes, and glass. Old Jews stood about, strings of suspenders and belts and neckties over their shoulders. Women stood in front of barrels of herrings and pickled cucumbers, peppers, and tomatoes.

The noise and confusion mounted skyward—peddlers calling out their wares, altercations, shrieks of playing children. Over all rose the glare of the flaming torches and the red glow of burning crates, garbage, and sweepings, the bonfires built by the children in the middle of the gutters. The flames of sound flared and leaped up like the flames of the bonfires. "Women, women, hurry! Corsets, underwear!" And from an open window a woman's harried voice calling "Jimmie, Jimmie!"

In the prayer house, above the babel of noise, stood the small group of the devout, rocking back and forth in devotion, held together by the vision they saw behind their closed eyes. They were dancing on green fields, going forth with their rabbi to greet the Sabbath, bathing their souls in the fragrant scents of the trees and flowers. It was good to worship among the trees and wild grasses, to hear the song of adoration each blade of grass and each leaf sang to the Eternal, the Creator of all things. The blades of grass sang their songs of praise without any other thought; they sought no reward. They sang their song of praise out of serene joy.

So they too sang. They sought no reward. They asked for nothing from the Creator of all things; they sought only to unite in the joy that streamed out of the holy Sabbath. Sabbath was a Queen, the Queen Sabbath, the eternal spirit of peace. No, Sabbath was more than a Queen; Sabbath was the Bride, the eternal Bride, arrayed in her shining garments so that the saints and sages and virtuous might greet her. They beheld her with the eyes of the soul. A rain of mercy came floating from the clouds, and they saw her walking forth, her feet naked, her body clad in shimmering raiment, haloed by the stars, the Sabbath crown on her head, her face covered with a black veil, in mourning for Israel in exile. They saw her coming toward them, and they stretched out their arms to her in adoration. Their hearts melted in longing and their lips sang—"Come, my friend, to greet the Bride, to give welcome unto the Sabbath!"

When the services were over, the congregants gathered together for learning and discourse. They were waiting to hear from the lips of Reb Leibush words of saintliness and devotion to quicken their souls and hearten them through the week of toil in the cursed sweatshops of their exile. Reb Leibush was delicate and fragile-looking. An ethereal quality shone out from his long pale face; it seemed as though any moment he would be wafted on the wings of pure spirit to some higher sphere. He was tall and gaunt. His wise rabbinical forehead rose high on an enormous head entirely disproportionate to his fragile body. His pale yellow beard was so scanty that each particular hair seemed to have been set carefully into the flesh by a parsimonious hand. His watery blue eyes either gazed timidly to the side or were downcast. During his devotions he swayed with such unexpected dexterity that at one moment the upper part of his body would be parallel to the floor and at the next he would be bent down so that his head almost touched his toes. His words could almost be seen rising past the bones and sinews of his gaunt throat before they escaped from his lips.

Reb Leibush ordinarily was a silent man, hardly ever saying a word until, between the meals on the Sabbath, he would expound the Torah, or on these Friday nights when he would discourse on the mystic books of the Kabbala to quench the spiritual thirst of the devout followers of his rabbi.

How had this rare plant of the ecstatic East been transplanted to the cold shores of America? The truth was that Reb Leibush had come to the New World on a mission from the Hasidic Court in the old country to the rabbi's devout followers in America, so as to hold them fast to the rabbinical grace and at the same time raise enough money to publish the writings of the rabbi's grandfather, the founder of the Hasidic dynasty. The war that had broken out in Europe after he left had prevented his return. The wealthy Hasidim in the New World had fobbed him off with modest gifts of money; they had moved away from the East Side; now they lived in the elegant districts farther uptown. Only the poorest of the poor were left in the East Side prayer house, the artisans and laborers who spent their weeks in factories and shops. It was these who had taken the rabbi's representative to their souls; they squeezed enough pennies out of their meager wages to provide for him in the home of an orthodox kinsman.

All week Reb Leibush wandered about as though he were in a pagan wilderness. In the house where he lived, there were only women and children, with their constant noise and tumult and squabbling. Sewing machines rattled and creaked all day. During the day the bed on which he slept was folded up and kept behind a curtain in a corner; he had no place to sit in comfort and reflect. He spent most of his time in a small synagogue near by, where the sexton permitted him to sit at the table and pore over the holy volumes.

The week days were long and weary and lonely. But on Friday night his Sabbath of pure joy began. After the Friday evening prayer services he did not hurry to go home; there was no one for him to go home to. Some of the congregation, too, were alone and lonely; they had left wives and children behind them in the old country; they lived with strangers; they, too, were in no hurry to depart from the intimate and familiar atmosphere of the prayer house. Even those with families preferred to remain until late in the night. Shmuel Chaim had brought a carafe of Sabbath wine and two Sabbath loaves which his wife, Malke, had prepared; there were a few pieces of savory fish, too. Shmuel Chaim dragged out a table and set it before the altar, covered it with a white cloth, and put on the loaves and the fish. Reb Leibush sat at the head of the table and pronounced the benediction.

What does the devout man need to be joyous? A loaf of bread and words of wisdom from his rabbi. Reb Leibush had already recounted some of the rabbi's precious words—they would be remembered over and over and would bring solace to weary hearts during the long week in the shop. Now he was preparing to ascend to higher spheres. His eyes were closed behind his hands, and he was swaying like a blade of wheat in the fields. His body trembled with awe and terror at the majesty of the words he uttered. It was not on the Torah he was discoursing now; he was telling of the mysteries of the Zohar.

"It is written that God said unto Moses—Thou shalt cleave unto the Lord thy God. But how shall man, made of uncleanness and sunk in the sin of the world, laboring in the sweat of his brow—how shall he cleave unto God, may His name be blessed, whose majesty man cannot conceive? Therefore is it that God created the Zaddik, the saint. For the saint is he on whom the foundation of the world rests. He is God's vessel, who brings man close to Him and holds him embraced in His spirit. And therefore does the pious Hasid seek to unite with his Zaddik, become one with him, and purify himself of all other desires. Through the Hasid's love to the Zaddik he is one with him, and through the Zaddik's love to God, may His name be blessed, we may be united with Him in the highest holiness."

Reb Leibush paused. He closed his eyes and stood motionless. Even the hairs of his thin beard were still. About his pale face there was an otherworldly glow which smoothed out the aged folds and wrinkles, and made it younger and of an unearthly beauty. "Come, let us unite with the Zaddik!" The words came from his lips in a whisper of ecstasy.

An even deeper silence descended on the room. The worshipers around the table stopped their pious swaying and, like the speaker, sat motionless. Some of them covered their eyes with their hands. Others bent forward and sat with closed eyes, transported to distant worlds. The otherworldly glow that shone from the face of Reb Leibush seemed to radiate from their faces too, smoothing away all mundane cares and bathing them in a strange effulgence. The candles flickered in the holders; so tremulous was the silence that the soft spluttering of the melting wax could be heard. Shadows gathered in the corners of the room, as though the Sabbath candles had driven them there, like evil spirits, far from the worshipers who sat immobile in the Sabbath holiness, transported into limitless spheres. Gone were the shops, and factories, and all the alien world. Even the clamorous street disappeared, together with the glaring electric lights which gleamed through the windows, and all the hubbub and noise and confusion. They were in a world where there was only grace and beneficence, only joy and rejoicing. There they would find the Zaddik, the holy flame, like an angel of Heaven, who was compounded only of love for God. And they were one with him through the love which he had set aglow in their hearts, and they could feel it flaming up in them, filling them with unaccustomed strength. Now the flame flared higher; they were bound together in one unity; together they were united with the Zaddik to Holiness itself, to the spirit of grace and holiness of which they were now a part.

Moshe Wolf sat among them. He had lost all awareness of self. The threads that tied him to the world of sorrows were all severed. He was not Moshe Wolf the storekeeper, the troubled father, with a Christian daughter-in-law and a Christian grandchild. That was another Moshe Wolf, the man of yesterday and tomorrow, with whom he had nothing to do. This Moshe Wolf, sitting at the table among his fellow pietists and Hasidim, holding his hands over his eyes and projecting himself into worlds of purity and grace, was a free soul, a Sabbath soul, living only in the ecstasy of the Sabbath. He was pure ecstasy, for he was part of the Ineffable. He had discarded all cares; he was living in the world from which he once had come, in the world of eternal joy and goodness to which he longed to return.

"Great Zaddik on whose sanctity the foundations of the world are built!" Reb Leibush murmured. He shuddered as though a wind were passing over him.

"Zaddik of goodness!" the congregants around the table murmured, trembling and swaying.

Again there was a silence, a breathless stillness.

"Prayer and God, may His name be blessed are one. Through prayer man is bound to God. Open up your hearts and let the Blessed one enter into you through prayer."

The congregants moaned and swayed, moaned and swayed.

"And now," Reb Leibush intoned, "now we enter into the highest stage of ineffable bliss. Through union with the Zaddik we are united with the Holy One..."

Reb Leibush swayed like a lone tree in a field. A moan escaped his lips. "The pillar of the world, Zaddik is his name. He bears the sorrow of the world. The woes of the son of man penetrate into his heart; for he is the heart of the world. And just as the heart feels the pain of the flesh, so does the Zaddik feel the pain of the world. He is the true Zaddik, the great Zaddik, he is Messiah the King. He suffers with us and for us. Well has it been said, the souls of the lesser Zaddikim fly about the world and when they see the sons of men who are oppressed in suffering, and when they see how the wicked of the world lengthen the exile of the righteous, then they hasten to bear the news to the Messiah the King. And the Messiah goes into a palace in Paradise which is known as the Palace of the Sons of the Shepherds. And the Messiah enters and takes unto himself all the pain and suffering which oppresses Israel. For if he did not lighten the sufferings of Israel, then no man in the world would be able to bear the pain of the sins which have been committed against the Torah. For when the Jews were in their own land, the Zohar tells us, they lightened their sufferings and their misfortunes through the sacrifices which they brought into the Temple. But now the Messiah carries the burden of man's sufferings, as it is written—'he was wounded for our transgressions, he was bruised for our iniquities; the chastisement of our peace was upon him; and with his stripes we are healed.'"

Reb Leibush was again silent, as though he was brooding over his words.

"And there is a *midrash* which tells that the Messiah lies stretched out on a couch in Paradise and from his eyes pour rivers of tears over the sufferings of the world. And the prophet Elijah sits by him and wipes away his tears and comforts him and says to him—'Do not weep, my son, for soon God will open His heart of grace.'"

From here and there among the congregants came moans that seemed to be torn out of their hearts over the sufferings of the Messiah. The voice of Reb Leibush became joyous as though he were seeking to exorcise the sadness.

"Today is the Sabbath, and the Sabbath is pure joy, for it stems from the highest heights and the deepest springs of eternal truth. Sabbath is the substance and the achievement. For the Sabbath is rest and rest is joy. And joy can be achieved only through the highest virtue, which is love; in love is thé Sabbath, and the Messiah, and the Mantle of Grace. 'Let me be faint with love for God as man is faint with love for his beloved,' sang the sainted rabbi. 'I am faint with love,' sang Solomon the great king. And the Zohar declares that in one of the hidden corners of heaven there is a palace which is known as the Palace of Love. There gather the secret things, the most secret of the secret. There the pure souls gather and God is among them and they unite with him, through his kiss of love. And when man purifies himself of all uncleanness and unites with God, not for gain but because he is faint with love for God, then he is worthy to share the reward of Moses the Patriarch—to sit with God in the Palace of Love and to partake of the ecstasy of God's kiss."

All the night Moshe Wolf lay on the iron cot which Malke had prepared for him. His mind and heart were full with the words he had heard from Reb Leibush's lips. If only he could earn the grace to be with God in the Palace of Love which Reb Leibush had described. If only he could earn the grace—if but for the moment of the winking of an eye—to be there, with all of the holy Zaddikim, and to expire with love for God. He could see the Palace before his very eyes. There were no walls, no ceiling. There was only an expanse of space, roofed over with blue clouds. And all around were green pastures, the same fields he remembered from his old home, the green pastures near the stream and the forest in Lenschiz, where the peat fields began. And above them were tall birch trees, and lambs pastured on the field—as David the shepherd had sung: He maketh me to lie down in green pastures. And there, among the green fields, was the Palace of the Shepherds, and the children of Abraham, Isaac, and Jacob, who were shepherds, and Moses, and David; and the Messiah, King of Messiahs, lay on a golden couch. He was sick, sick with love for the world, sick with the desire to save it, sick because of the sufferings which he had taken unto himself. And the prophet Elijah sat beside him and wiped his tears away and comforted him. And around the Messiah were gathered all of the Zaddikim, and they were faint with love for God and with yearning for him. They stretched out their arms and cried, "My soul yearns unto God," just as he himself was faint with love for God and yearning to bring his soul under the wings of the divine grace and hide under it, like a dove that hides its head between its sheltering wings . . .

But how could he aspire to taste that divine joy and ecstasy! Even the very thought was a sin, a pride and a haughtiness of the spirit. What had he done in his life? How had he spent his days?

Moshe Wolf summoned the book of his life before his memory. He had labored all day in a store, devoting his days to trade and vanity of spirit. "Ah, the black days," he moaned. "Never time to pray to God in dignity and peace!" True, here and there he had done a slight service for others, given a poor man food on credit, overlooked a debt, forgotten a reckoning, helped where he could, made no difference between Jew and Gentile . . . But what grace, what virtue was there in all of this? After all, a man has not a heart of stone . . . He had a son, a cripple, on his hands; and, yes, he had tried to be good to him. Should he seek reward for that? Was it not his debt? "Like as a father pitieth his children." Had not the Psalmist sung the words? He had not wanted to profit from another's toil; even now he did not want to profit. God knew how heavy it was for him to accept his son's charity. But was this a virtue because of which his portion should be Paradise? And had he not taken a Gentile daughter-in-law into his house, befriended her, eaten the food she prepared? What, did he think that this too would be overlooked and forgotten?

He felt a surge of strength. He would not let himself be drawn into the pit of Gehenna from whose depths the destroying angels were stretching forth their arms to draw him in. No, dear God, You are the father of all mercifulness! You know that there was nothing else I could do. You Yourself commanded that we be merciful to all Your creation. No, it will not be counted against me for a sin. God will show His compassion. . . . But surely I have not earned Paradise.

The tortured thoughts haunted him through the night. Several times it came to him that he was defiling the Sabbath, Sabbath was joy, and melancholy on the Sabbath was a great sin; he must not tarnish the ecstasy of the Sabbath. But his heart was heavy, as though a mountain of sorrows had piled on him. He tried to crawl out from under it, but he stumbled and fell, then found his footing, and stumbled and found himself again. "God, have mercy on me. I have no one but You."

His heart felt lighter. He saw now that everything was right. So was it destined to be; so should it be. Nathan, too, would find his way. He had Heimowitz now; Heimowitz would watch out for him, like a father. And, who knew, if he, Moshe Wolf, were no longer here, Deborah would open her heart to him. After all, a mother—and who can love a child more than a mother? And there would be Irving, too. Whatever had happened, Irving had always been a good son and a good brother. They would see to him, they would watch over him . . .

"And who presumes to say that Moshe Wolf, a poor grocer, must be in the Palace of Righteousness with the Zaddikim? What deeds of virtue have I performed to earn so great a portion? And why should I not be content in the humblest palace among the humble people, or even outside, at the window, and listen to the pleasant songs of yearning which the Zaddikim within sing to the Lord of all things? Let them only permit me to stand at the window and listen to the songs of longing and desire."

He remembered the words of the Sabbath song—"Prepare the Sabbath feast for the worshipers." See! The Zaddikim were expiring with longing for the effulgence of God, for the love of God . . .

And, in his sleep, Moshe Wolf joined them, to expire with them, in longing . . . and in love . . .'

10. Love, Work, and Compassion

HIRSHEL JAFFE

The struggle with illness may not have a clearly marked "finish line." A young congregational rabbi, stricken with leukemia, continues on as husband, father, pastor, and counselor; and the fulfillment of these activities diminishes his fear for himself.

August 3, 1982

The hospital food is lousy, but I ate dinner anyway. I won't be able to snack after midnight like I do at home because of the early-morning surgery.

Judi and Rachel and Nina went out to eat with Jim and Marcia and their girls. All my visitors have left. For the first time I am all alone in here.

Everything has happened so fast, I haven't had time to sort out my thoughts and feelings. So I have decided to get my experiences and thoughts down on tape. Like a diary. I've never done anything like this before—never had the time or patience to be very introspective. But now I want to record what's happening to me because I think that will help me deal with it.

This is such a totally strange experience for me. There are moments when I can't believe I am really seriously ill. I've never even had the flu. For twenty years I've been the rabbi calling on hospital patients. I've witnessed everybody else's illnesses. Over the years I've learned just what to say to patients and how long to stay with them. I know when to listen and when to recite the appropriate psalm. But not for a single day in my entire life have I ever been hospitalized. I could always leave the hospital room, walk to an elevator, and go out and jog.

But now it's a whole new ball game. I'm on the other side of the bed. Even if I never have to worry about my illness again, I sense this is going to change me, because now I'll know what it is to be sick in a hospital. I know from now on I won't be so rushed when I visit people, like I'm checking them off a list. And I won't wait so long to get there.

I can already see this experience will make a big difference in my work. Last week after I knew my diagnosis, I had to conduct a funeral for a lovely woman in my congregation, a Holocaust survivor. I got through the ceremony, but I was dwelling on my own mortality. At the cemetery when her daughter threw dirt onto her grave I thought, "That could be Rachel or Nina doing that for me."

And I wonder how my congregants will react. What happens to a congregation when its rabbi is afflicted with a dreaded disease? They think a rabbi is like a representative of God; they might have trouble seeing me as less than perfect. I hope they will realize I'm not perfect and they'll accept me now as just another human being like themselves with troubles of his own.

When Talmudic scholars asked, "Who is eligible to lead the Jewish people?" they answered it must be someone who is like everyone else—fully involved in life, married, raising children, struggling, and suffering. A rabbi is not priestly or above it all. Our Jewish spiritual leaders have always lived and worked like other people, never isolating themselves from the routine, everyday aspects— both good and bad—of life. Rabbi Hillel said, "Do not separate yourself from the community."

My illness is certainly affecting my daughters' lives. I could see that Rachel and Nina were anxious to leave my room today when they were visiting me. They've never seen their daddy sick before. They were trying to act nonchalant and cheer me up, but this must be so frightening to them. They looked so beautiful in their summer dresses. Nina has an absolutely radiant face when she smiles, and Rachel is going to be a very pretty teenager.

They know something is wrong with Daddy's blood and that it's serious. Nina empathizes so much and lets you know how she feels. She sat with Judi and me in the hospital when they put my blood through the Coulter Counter. She saw the surprised look on the technicians' faces when my blood count registered so low, and she blurted out, "Is my daddy going to die?" We all just looked at each other. It was heartbreaking.

Rachel is more laid-back, but I'm sure she is just as anxious as Nina is. She just doesn't express it. It will be good for them to stay at the Rudins' in the Poconos while I have the surgery. They'll be distracted there and have a good time, and they won't have to see me right away after the operation. That might be pretty scary for them.

Judi is so cool in tough situations. That's why she was such a good nurse in the trauma unit when we lived in Dallas. She's joking now as always. I know she's trying to keep my spirits up. But I can read the expression in her big dark eyes, and I can tell she's shaken. She can't hide it from me.

She's so unaffected and refreshing. Everything is either black or white with Judi. There are very few grays. She keeps me thinking straight. I've always known I could never bullshit Judi, even when we were dating. That's why I was drawn to her—she doesn't give in to others, she has her own strong values, she's her own person. I know if things ever got rough I could depend on her because she's so strong. I hope I can draw on some of her strength now.

I'll need it . . .

October 4, 1982

Flew out to Chicago yesterday to see the leading expert in hairy-cell leukemia. When I had my splenectomy, Judi kept asking the physicians, "Who knows the most about Hirshel's disease?" She kept after them until they gave her the name of this man. I'm lucky she was so persistent. She wants to make sure I have the best care possible.

I was surprised to see how young this specialist is. Only in his early forties and already head of his department. He's obviously brilliant. He's ebullient too, good at lifting a patient's spirits.

When he looked at my records and saw I'm a rabbi, he said, "My son is becoming a Bar Mitzvah soon." He asked me a lot of questions about my running. He told me he wants to lose some weight and asked me how to start jogging.

He is wonderfully supportive. He was confident after the painful bone marrow examination that I'll have a long remission. I returned home elated, but somehow Judi seems to be shielding herself. She's not as optimistic as I am . . .

October 11, 1982

Last week I was resting at home when suddenly I heard a van pull into our driveway. I looked out the window and saw Myron and some other friends from the congregation unload something from the van. I ran outside. They were starting to build a sukkah right in our backyard to help us celebrate Sukkot. It was a complete surprise. I couldn't believe it.

Myron works in the carpet business, and he used those big, empty carpet tubes as the framework for the little hut. Then they put leaves and cornstalks on the tubes to make the shelter. It was very clever.

Then the next night my orthodox rabbi friend brought over a lulav and etrog for me to hold and wave in praise of God's goodness for keeping me alive. It was a wonderful symbol of friendship to me . . .

October 18, 1982

I'm slowly but surely getting back to work. It's hard. I realize now I may never have the energy I did before. My stomach is giving me trouble. I have to watch what I eat. And I have to stop taking all these damned pills the doctor prescribed. But I push myself and work as much as I can. My physicians told me it's good therapy to get back to work as soon as possible.

I guess I'm trying to prove to myself that I can function. I think if I'm working well, I must feel well. And working does help me feel better, as the doctors said it would. It takes me out of myself. It lifts my spirits, and I think I am almost conquering the disease.

It's interesting—the Hebrew word for "sick" comes from the word chalah, which means emptiness. But a healthy person is a bah-ree, from the word bahrah, which means "to create." A healthy person is one that can create or work; the unhealthy person's life is empty because he's not productive.

It's amazing how much insight the *Bible* has about human nature. The writers obviously realized how valuable work is for a person's self-esteem. The work ethic has always been important in Judaism. Work was given as a convenant by God, just as the *Torah* was. Even God worked when He created the World! Work is so important in Judaism that we shouldn't look down on any type of labor. You should work not only to support yourself but to keep out of trouble. I remember one Talmudic scholar warned us that idleness causes bad things.

Working really does help you keep your mind off your illness. A couple of years ago I preached a sermon on Norman Cousin's book about his illness. He writes about how he felt so much better when he brought his work to the hospital, even though at first the hospital staff didn't like it. He believes creativity helps cure illness. Cousins tells this incredible story about a time he visited Pablo Casals when the great musician was in his late eighties. Casal's body was all stooped, and his hands curled up, and he was in unbearable pain. But when he sat down at his cello or at the piano, his spine and fingers mysteriously straightened and he was able to play magnificently and overcome his pain. When he was immersed in his work, his great art, the pain disappeared.

Of course I have to pace myself. So I choose my priorities more carefully now. My congregation doesn't let me overdo it. Somebody has taken over my confirmation class, and there is even talk about getting me an assistant rabbi. I know this leukemia has shaken my people. I can tell some of them are ambivalent about my illness. It's been hard for them because now they realize I have serious problems to cope with like everybody else. They can see that the leader of the flock can't always lead and now sometimes needs a shepherd of his own to guide him.

Sometimes my congregants make me feel I'm failing them because they expect me to be a cheerleader for everybody like I always was. Before I came back to work, one man said, "Oh, Rabbi, its not the same when you're not here to conduct services. We feel rudderless." Of course he was only trying to compliment me, but that made me feel bad because I wasn't up to it.

I feel I have to muster up my energy and put on an act—hide my illness and make my voice sound lively—so I can give them hope. My congregants would be dismayed if they knew they were making it difficult for me because they want to help me so much, but it's becoming a problem that I can't escape.

I feel I have to live up to their expectations of me. I don't express my true feelings because I don't want them to know how scared and worried I really am.

Some of my congregants have been almost apologetic because of my illness. They hate to burden me with their problems, and they're anxious about me and over solicitous. It's funny—they tell me conflicting things. One person will say, "Gee you look great," and on the same day another person will tell me, "You look tired, Rabbi—go home and get some rest."

It's tough to answer people honestly when they send me such mixed messages. Sometimes I'll say something like, "Don't worry, I know. Believe me, I'm being careful with my health."

But other times I either ignore the comment or answer vaguely because I've just heard the opposite thing five minutes before. Yet when I do that, I feel bad because I know they are trying to look out for me and they are genuinely concerned. This confusion only compounds my feelings of inadequacy. I'm haunted as a rabbi by having to be all things to all people.

It's painful now to carry out some of my rabbinic duties because I am so close to the situations I used to deal with in a more detached way. A few days ago I went to the hospital to see a congregant who has cancer. He's only forty-five years old. Well, I saw him and I kept my composure, but while I was driving home I thought, "We have the same disease, we're nearly the same age, just a few short weeks ago I was lying in the hospital!" It was like a mirror, a reverse image of what I've just gone through—lying there all day, all alone, waiting for someone to telephone me or come to see me, and terrified by all the cold, impersonal hospital procedures. It was very difficult for me to make that visit, but I knew I had to do it. I have to return to real life.

And on Yom Kippur, even though Herb Drooz was there to take over for me, I felt I had to read the list of the congregation's deceased at the memorial service. Drooz is a lovely man, but he didn't know the people who had died. I said to myself, "Hirshel, get up there and read the names." I wanted to do it because I had been part of their lives, I had consoled their families, and they are all doing so much for me now. So I got up and read the names.

I knew I had done the right thing. But reading the names of people who have died since last year's High Holidays was a very emotional experience for me because I know next year I might be on that Yahrzeit list. Another rabbi might be reading my name next year and the years after that, and I won't be here. Every week at the end of the Sabbath service when I read the names of the dead I confront the fact that my name could soon be on that list . . . nothing left of me except my name and fading images in my family's and friends' memories . . .

January 16, 1983

My prisoners at Greenhaven seem so concerned about me. Like that big get-well card with all their signatures they sent when I was in the hospital last summer. Here are these guys—very hardened criminals, some of them. Murderers, rapists, the whole bit, not the world's nicest people. But they must have a little soft spot because when I visit them they always ask me how I feel, and I know they really mean it.

I guess my work with these prisoners has had some effect, though I'm so often filled with doubt. It makes me realize why I've kept this prison chaplaincy. Sometimes I've asked myself, "Is this worthwhile? What am I doing here?" Some congregants want me to give it up now that I'm ill. They're worried about the extra strain it puts on me.

It's very tough duty, emotionally draining. Not too many chaplains want to serve here. It's not a pleasant place, and almost impossible to avoid conflict. The inmates take out all their frustrations on me because I'm the chaplain, and they get angry when I can't perform miracles for them. It can be dangerous here too. One disturbed guy did scare me—the other prisoners had to calm him down. An inmate brutally murdered a woman guard right next door to the Jewish chapel.

There's so much to do here, and the prison bureaucracy doesn't make things easy. Greenhaven has the largest concentration of Jewish prisoners— about forty—in the United States. The name of the group is Congregation Hatikvah, which means "hope." On the wall of the small chapel there is a painting of hands breaking chains. An inscription on the picture, a quotation from the prayer book, reads, "He frees those who are bound."

The prisoners besiege me with requests. I perform all the Jewish rites, conduct services, counsel the inmates, make phone calls for them, write letters asking for clemency, organize volunteer groups to visit the prison, and get them kosher food.

But I can see now I've touched them, after all. Has it taken my illness for me to know that? Did I have to get sick for the inmates to discover they can care about someone? Maybe those who say there is meaning in suffering because you learn from it and because it brings out the best in you and in others are right. I'd feel better knowing there is some good reason for this leukemia ...

January 21, 1983

We flew up to Martha's Vineyard yesterday!

Judi took the initiative, as usual. Leave it to her to do something crazy like that. Yesterday was a beautiful day, in the fifties with bright sunshine. Judi drove to Marine Air Terminal next to LaGuardia, and she said, "Hirshel, we're going to Martha's Vineyard. I want you to know that you can make it up there." It seemed so crazy, but it meant so much to me to get there. So we flew up. I got really emotional when we landed. Judi thought I was overdoing it, but she understood. All the time I kept thinking, "I've made it back to the Vineyard."

Everything was just as I remembered it. There were the dunes and the bike paths, the boats and our house at South Beach. The house is closed up for the winter, so we spent the night at the Charlotte Inn in Edgartown. The fire was marvelous.

It was a beautiful twenty-four hours. A time for love ...

November 5, 1983

This illness has taught me the real meaning of the rabbinate. The most important thing is not who can be the best scholar. I remember in rabbinical school I was always winning contests for Hebrew proficiency or grammar. The other guys were married, but all I ever did was study. I always put so much value on intellectual achievement. My whole family does. But now I've moved away from the cerebral. It's who can best minister to people's needs that really matters. It's who can touch people, who can comfort people.

We weren't properly prepared for pastoral work in rabbinical school. Our professors lived in an ivory tower. They had a cynical view of congregational life. They wanted us to be scholars. We got emotional about the tradition and what the rabbis said twenty centuries ago, and there were some very moving stories, but there was nothing about today. We didn't intern at hospitals or consult with psychiatrists or train with senior rabbis in the field. This is changing in seminaries now.

Some of this you just can't learn in school—it has to come from long experience. I've learned in my twenty years as a rabbi and especially since this illness that God wants heart. There's a Hebrew expression, *Rachmana liba baey*—"God wants heart." I think the word *rachmanis* is the key word in Judaism. More important than any theology or system of thought is the caring, the compassion, the loving, the *rachmanis*. Judi always nags me about this. She'll say, "Hirschel, you didn't really touch that boy in the Bar Mitzvah today. You didn't really mean it."

I'm thinking about this tonight because this afternoon I had a fight with an older rabbi in a nearby community. He had castigated a woman for not following Jewish law, and he hurt her feelings. She came to me and related her story. So today I went back to this rabbi who is rooted so rigidly in the tradition and I said to him, "Don't you know the teaching in our Talmud, *Rachmana liba baey?* That over and above what is theologically accurate or what is proper according to the law, what is just, God wants compassion, He wants feeling, He wants heart?"

I've tried to make my congregants aware of *rachmanis* too. When I first came back from the hospital last year, I challenged everyone in the congregation. That was my first message to the board of trustees when I went back to work. I made them promise they would give the same comfort to everyone else that they gave to me. We formed a caring committee and we have pins with little people holding hands on them. The committee organizes minyans and visits people in nursing homes and hospitals, and they visit the handicapped. They take the retarded to services at our temple . . .

April 6, 1984

Where is my remission? I guess it's coming to an end. Only a temporary stay.

Why did this have to happen now, one week before Rachel's Bat Mitzvah? We've been looking forward to it so much. Couldn't this damned leukemia have waited just a little while longer? Why does fate—or is it God—have to be so cruel? What a blow!

My children used to play the board game "Chutes and Ladders" when they were younger. One minute you're at the finish line nearly winning and the next second you're sliding back on a big chute to the beginning of the board and you've lost. I've decided that life is just like that. One minute you're at the top and the next minute you're sliding down to the bottom.

Today while Judi was driving us back to Newburgh from our appointment with the specialist in Albany, she started to cry. Her mascara was running all over. The tears were just gushing out. I was afraid we'd have an automobile accident. I reached over and put my arm around her to comfort her. I guess reality hit her. It was like a backlash of all she has gone through. We were both sharing the same feeling—is this it?

Judi has never cried like that before, at least not in front of me. Her eyes mist over when someone does something nice for us and she realizes they really care. But she's never totally broke down before. The tough exterior is cracking. She said to me "Hirshel, I'm crying because I feel bad because you can't do anything about it. I feel helpless."

"I can do something, Judi," I told her. "I can fight it with this drug treatment."

Then it hit me again how devastating all this has been for Judi. She is under enormous pressure. I think it's harder for her than for me because she's just a spectator and she feels helpless. Everyone has said they could never endure what she has.

Our love has grown since my illness hit us. In this stark situation, stripped of our usual defenses, Judi and I have seen even more deeply into each other. Our marriage has really been put to a test, and our relationship has held fast and been strengthened. The marriage vows say, "in good fortune and in adversity." Well, we sure have hit the adversity part of the bargain, and Judi has really lived up to her vows.

Sometimes we think that famous biblical proverb, "A woman of valor, who can find?" is trite. But this illness has shown me it's not. How many wives could cope with this? Most people would run away if they could. I know often marriages break up in situations like ours because couples can't deal with the tensions and guilts and uncertainties that surface in a crisis like this.

A couple really has to be strongly committed to each other to pull through something like this together. Thank God I have somebody to share this with. The Song of Songs says, "Set me as a seal upon my heart, for love is stronger than death."

Judaism holds marriage in such high regard that it compares the love between God and His people, Israel, to the relationship between husband and wife. The Jewish tradition insists that marriage is the best way to fulfill the human sexual drive and need for love. In a passage in the *Babylonian Talmud* a sage counsels, "A man who does not have a wife lives without joy, without blessing, and without goodness." A later scholar added, "And without peace."

Of course the rabbis, always realists, recognized that marriage and family life are full of complexities and pitfalls. They offer lots of advice—some of it very humorous—about how to settle conflicts between husband and wife, spouses and in-laws, and parents and children.

I couldn't cope with all this tumult in my life without Judi's endurance and love. Judi has held our family together during this crisis—all the while working at a full-time job! She has kept the girls going, trying to make their lives as normal as possible and still deal with their feelings too, and that hasn't been easy.

I can really see the rabbis were right when they said the wife sets the tone for the whole household, that "All depends on the woman." According to the Wisdom of Ben Sira, "A good wife makes a happy husband; she doubles the length of his life. A staunch wife is her husband's joy; he will live out his days in peace."

I know this puts a big burden on the wife, especially today, when most women work outside the home ...

April 12, 1984

The septic tank gave out today. The sewage is backed up in our basement and our garage. Two days before Rachel's Bat Mitzvah! Is this unbelievable!? Everyone is coming in for the Bat Mitzvah tomorrow, and the house is a mess.

We'll have to recarpet the basement at least. And install a new septic tank in the backyard. That's going to cost a fortune. Right now, on top of all the Bat Mitzvah expenses. And we sure didn't need this aggravation now. There's enough on our minds with the last-minute Bat Mitzvah arrangements. This really is the last straw!

I know I shouldn't be so upset. I thought since my illness I had learned to put little things like this in the right perspective! Money isn't important, especially in light of my latest jolting medical setback. The only thing that really matters is that I lick this disease. Things like the septic tank will take care of themselves ...

April 14, 1984

Well, it's all over—the ceremony, the reception, the luncheon. Nearly everybody has gone home. After so much planning it's hard to believe it went by so quickly.

After such a horrible start everything turned out beautifully. It's amazing—it all worked out!

At first it seemed like everything was conspiring to go wrong: the septic tank, this gigantic gaping hole in the backyard. I could easily have said, "That's my life, one gaping hole." I started to shave and suddenly the guy is yelling, "No water, don't use the water." I thought, "Here I am trying to get ready for one of the biggest days in my life and I can't even shave!"

Then when we got over to the synagogue, I discovered the tables weren't in the social hall for the luncheon as they were supposed to be. I had to get them from the religious school, where the custodian had set them up for the kids' model seder tomorrow morning. It's right before Passover, and the temple isn't functioning. The custodian is half asleep in the youth lounge, where he is secretly harboring a three-legged cat, and I have to fight to get tables for my own daughter's Bat Mitzvah luncheon. I had to set up the tables and chairs myself.

About half an hour before the service was supposed to start my parents telephoned the temple from a nearby gas station to say their car stalled in the middle of an intersection. My neighbor went to pick them up and found my dad almost not wanting to leave the gas station because he's worrying about what's going to happen to his car. Then we got another telephone call at the temple from Judi's brother, Steve. He was at a mall trying to buy a new pair of slacks because his girlfriend decided the pair he brought along didn't fit quite right.

But the moment the service started everything somehow fell into place. All the tensions disappeared and everybody was relaxed. I could relax too because Jim was officiating, so I could sit with the congregation and really be just myself, a person, a Jew, a proud daddy.

During the Bat Mitzvah service this morning I tried not to think about my leukemia. I didn't want anything to spoil this day for me. But how can you avoid dwelling on it? You can't program yourself. I'm living life and having very happy moments like this, but the balloon pops every once in a while and I worry what my next blood test will show.

I was wondering if Jim would mention my illness. He didn't. It wasn't necessary—I think it was uppermost in everybody's mind. He did say one thing, though, something like, "We all know the struggles the Jaffes have gone through to reach this day." Then Jim said something so beautiful. He said, "But after a troubled time you burst through to the blue skies."

His words "blue skies" evoked so many images for me. I remembered lying in the hospital after my spleenectomy and seeing little airplanes through my window and longing to be free of my hospital prison. And I remembered dropping down onto the beach on Martha's Vineyard in a beautiful multicolored parachute pulled by a tow rope attached to a speeding jeep. When they let go of the tow rope at two thousand feet, I felt really free as I floated back to earth. So Jim used a very meaningful and apt image.

When he said those things, Judi and I were up on the pulpit. We could look out to about six rows in the congregation, and I whispered, "Judi, the entire fifth row is breaking up." All the women were crying. So were some of the men.

And of course, all through the service the "Shehecheyanu" kept running through my mind. For months I've been thinking, "I have to make it to Rachel's Bat Mitzvah." I didn't think, "Let me live," but I said, "Dammit, I'm going to make it, because I want to hear that line, say that line, feel that line: 'Thank you, God, for keeping me alive and sustaining me and letting me reach this day.'"

This morning when the day had finally come it wasn't even necessary to utter the prayer. Just being there was a "shehecheyanu." I was there, and so was everybody else. I saw the doctor who discovered my leukemia when he looked through his microscope. And my surgeon friend who pushed me to get a checkup when I told him I didn't feel well. I saw all my friends who have been so wonderful. The whole cast of characters was there, but in a much different situation. It was staggering.

But, really, I didn't let my thoughts dwell on my illness this morning. I was too elated.

I think the best part of the day was seeing how proud and happy Judi was. Judi was more a mother and more real today than I have ever seen her. She just beamed when Rachel, looking so beautiful and radiant, recited her Torah portion and gave her little speech. It was her child, her scene, and she was totally caught up in it.

During the ceremony this morning I also remembered the Rosh Hashana prayer that asks, "Who shall live and who shall die?" I thought, "I shall live in spite of what happens." I'm not saying I'm physically going to live. Who knows? But for whatever time I have left I won't live as if I were haunted. No, I'll live fully and completely.

My physical life is diminished, my bone marrow is overrun with diseased cells, and my immune system is vulnerable. But I feel spiritually I'm more of a person now, finally, that I am in the blue skies. I'm holding up my family. I feel more in command of things. I've yielded something to eternity, which is my medical fate. You can't change that.

But, strangely, somehow I feel more alive.

By facing death I am learning how to live.[10]

11. The Will to Live

MAX LERNER

In the penultimate years of a long, productive life in scholar-ship and journalism, Max Lerner meditates on mortality and his love of living.

At the start of this narrative I quote from Jacob's wrestling with the angel of God, and his emergence from that fateful night, scathed but triumphant: "For I have seen God face to face, and my life is preserved."

It is the theme of this memoir that all illness and healing, all aging, all living and dying, are a wrestling with the angel. We get wounded and are preserved—or not. But always the frame is a double one, of life and death as adversaries, but also as polar phases of each other.

Jacob's unique night and his emergence at daybreak define both frames. There have been many interpretations of the passage in the literature of Biblical criticism. My own emphasis is on Jacob's death/life testing by God in the guise of his messenger, after Jacob's own self-testing in his reconciliation with his brother Esau. But in a larger sense the shrinking from a full encounter with the angel, whether of death or life, becomes a form of death-in-life, while the recurring and pervasive denial of death becomes in the end a denial of life itself. In life-threatening crises the task is to fight death without denying its reality and the preciousness it lends to life, while at the same time asserting life.

In the cosmic drama of our lives, Death plays the heavy and dominates the stage. The curtain is never in doubt: the question is not whether it will in the end come down, with Death in the possession of the stage, but how late or soon, and in what fashion. Yet we cannot, when young, make death credible to ourselves: death is real, but it is others, not we, who die.

There is an intellectual part of me which was obsessed for years with the death literature of the Greek and Elizabethan playwrights and the seventeenth-century English divines, a part which was startled by my illness into a recognition that it applied to me, too. There is another part—the sheer animal faith—which asserts that I am not subject to these sickly cerebrations.

A September 1986 journal entry suggests the tenacity of this animal faith:

> Conversation at table about reaching 2000. I was of course the vulnerable one. Yet I declared that when I am feeling pretty well, like now, I find it unimaginable that I will die. Cognitively I know I will, with my logical-rational brain center, but organismically I cherish the unexamined faith that I am here forever.

A little more than a year later, after my eighty-fifth birthday celebration, my daughter Joanna Townsend, in an amused, affectionate way, hit on what animated my struggle against death: "R. asked Joany how come my continuing high spirits at my doddering age. I like Joany's answer: 'My father can't imagine a world without him.'" Many, if less cockily, will share this equating of the world's existence with their individual consciousness.

But whatever the rhetoric of bravado we may thrust at death, there is a reality of death that each of us meets in a characteristic way. We are in general a long-lived family. My grandmother in Russia, Gita Raisse, lived to be 100 and died of shock (as the family tradition goes) when Hitler's troops invaded her little village. My father's death and my mother's, two years apart, occurred in my mid-fifties, but they seemed part of the natural order of things. Both were in their late eighties, had lived lives of struggle and work in Russia and America, and seemed ready for death. Coming out of a coma, my father's last words to me were, "They are calling me from Zion." My oldest sister, Ida Borish, clung to life with a worn-out heart until ninety-two. Sylvia Williams, two years her junior, and just as tenacious of life, died two years later at the same age.

It was different with the death of my brother Hyman. The reality of death came hard to me as a nine year old in a wintry Catskill house, watching as my brother, three years older, gasped out his life on the sick bed next to the only stove, with the sobbing family clustered around. Hyman had developed a rheumatic heart as a boy of eight or nine, working overhard as part of an immigrant family, delivering milk at night in Bayonne. He caught pneumonia in a punishing farm winter, and his heart wasn't sturdy enough to tide him over it.

It was my primal death scene, marking the clear start of the death-line that runs through every life, consciously or not. "After the first death there is no other." As we huddled forlornly the next day around Hyman's grave, I thought I could never again have an experience to compare with it, and it has all but remained true.

The exception was my daughter Pamela, who died at twenty-nine, a young wife and mother. Like Hyman she had not learned to die. She was a sensitive, aesthetically talented girl. At college she developed a cancer of the thyroid. After intensive radiation it appeared to be contained. She married, had two children, looked forward to a promising life. But the cancer returned and spread to her lungs.

What I felt most about Pamela's death—as about Hyman's a half-century earlier—was the enormity of the blow, which matched my powerlessness to prevent it. I raged, raged, against the dying of their light. The two deaths established the pattern of my basic case against death. The injustice of these young deaths in the cutting off of potentials seemed more poignant than the snuffing out of the skills and insights accumulated by those who live longer.

That was the death-line which has stayed with me. The ways in which we experience the death of others defines, of course, how we face our own. True, I was neither nine nor twenty-nine but just short of seventy-eight when my first cancer struck and my own death loomed. "Just when I had begun to understand the wind instruments," said Franz Joseph Haydn, wistfully. I too felt I had just found my stride. By a stark displacement I saw in my own death not the death of my parents but what I had felt in the deaths of my brother and daughter.

I now see how much I had fixed on early and unjust deaths as the very paradigm of mortality. Unlike Hamlet, death was not for me the "undiscovered country." I felt instead that it limited further discoveries in our lives, cutting them short. Historically it was the young deaths that struck my imagination— Mozart, Keats, Emily Dickinson, Randolph Bourne, John Reed, William Bolitho, Franz Kafka, John and Robert Kennedy, Martin Luther King.

They haunt me, I think, because I mourn any portion of life unreasonably and unjustly denied, which subtracts from the life as dreamt. For what we strain for in our lives is what we long for as we face death. The poet wants to write the great poem he has envisioned, the lover to make the final romantic conquest, the researcher to complete his grand research, the composer to write the ultimate symphony, the architect to build the structure of his dreams.

James Joyce tells us that "history is a nightmare from which I am trying to awake." The history of a life-menacing illness has a similar nightmare quality. For me it came with the wild contingency of the tumor, the harrowing search for its source, the torment of choices, and always the hard immediacy of Death as the Adversary to be placated, outwitted, forever to be fought—the master of the scene, preparing a reception for me. As this retrospective journal entry suggests, I was determined at least for some time to disappoint him:

> I am amused at what I was supposed to feel as I faced death. The thanatolo-gists I read tell me my first phase had to be total terror, followed by denial and despair, followed by bargaining (with doctors, fate, God), followed by some kind of resolution, whether in internal rage, or surrender, or what my head nurse in intensive care at Southampton called the "Dying Swan" syn-drome.... It is suggestive but not really a good fit for what actually happened in one mind. Yes, I had a few flashes of rage, Dylan Thomas-style, but I didn't sustain them. Rage can be cleansing, but it gets boring after a while when it turns into self-pity. I tried not to bargain or surrender, nor yet to go for that acceptance-with-dignity stuff and play the Dying Swan.... I tried to summon what inner resources I had in fighting not only the tumors but doubt and despair and statistical defeatism. I found an ally—when the time came—in the mind-body healing process. During the worst stretches I fought mostly by continuing to write and teach and rejoice in the gift of life.... To Hell with the thanatologists and their schemas! It was the only way I knew to face and outface the Adversary, Death, with whom I had to come to terms—but not (if I could help it) on his terms alone.

I add contrasting case histories of how two writers I value faced their deaths. One was Gregory Bateson, student of Balinese culture, of the behavior of dolphins and otters, of the "double-bind" in family systems—a generalist's generalist.

In an interview with Daniel Goleman, Bateson talked about his then im-pending death. He had rejected both chemotherapy and radiation for his can-cer, because he wanted to keep his mind clear to finish a last book he was writing. Besides, on principle he was ready to die.

When his interviewer probed the reasons for his readiness, Bateson was very sure of his ground:

> In the end we live by the self-limiting nature of individuals. It's very impor-
> tant that I shall die; you need me to. . . . If I stick around I'd go on writing
> books and putting words on blackboards, and, in the end, there'd be no room
> left for you or anyone else to put words on blackboards. . . . As they say in New
> Guinea, "The shit would come up to the floor." This is the moral to their myth
> about the origin of death. You see, the people I studied in New Guinea live on
> platform houses that are built eight feet off the ground. If you want to go in
> the middle of the night, especially if it is raining, you move a floorboard, squat
> over the gap, go, and go back to bed. According to the myth, people were im-
> mortal until, finally, the shit came up to the level of the floor. At this point they
> decided that death was necessary.

I am unpersuaded by Bateson's argument from the evolutionary necessity of self-limitation. The crowding comes from too many births, rather than from too late deaths. There is room in this society for me and for you. I don't have to stop putting words on blackboards so that you can put up a blackboard of your own. In fact, the longer we both manage to live, the greater the chance that we can learn from each other's blackboards.

There is a moving footnote to Bateson's last days. Goleman tells how two friends of Bateson met in the corridor outside his hospital room. Ram Dass believed in easing death as a spiritual passage for the terminally ill, while Kenneth Pelletier believed in the art of healing by visualizing the tumor. Bateson's wife, Lois, told Goleman that "Ram was there to help Gregory die, Ken to help him live . . . and Ken is winning."

He didn't win, nor did Ram Dass. Death won. Yet despite his vivid New Guinea myth, I am happy that Bateson made the choice, after all, of claiming life in the face of death.

I do not equate Death with a Satanic principle of evil. I see him rather as something sacral, part of the veil of the cosmos I cannot pierce, a stern judge administering inexorable laws. Nor is he an abstraction separable from life. He is part of life's experience, the final experience.

One of the strangest greetings ever offered to death I attributed to my second writer Henry James. I quote from the account of his biographer, Leon Edel:

Early in the morning of Thursday, 2 December 1915, James' maid ... heard
the Master calling. She entered his bedroom. He was lying on the floor, his left
leg had given way under him ... Edith Wharton reported he told (a friend) ...
that in the very act of falling he heard in the room a voice which was distinctly ... not his own, saying "So here it is at last, the Distinguished Thing."

Who but a novelist, with a haunting sense of tradition, would have used
that particular phrase after emerging from a major stroke? Yet the phrase has
meaning in describing an attitude toward death that many have felt: that it is
the distinctive working out of the life experience, when the quality of the life
will be reflected in the style of the death. An antithesis of the Dylan Thomas
"rage" against death, it is a serene acceptance of this unique finality.

There are few, seriously ill, watching for Death's possible approach, who
have not at some point prepared themselves to say, "So here it is at last!" Where I
differ from James is in his noun. Far from regarding Death as a "thing," I person-
alize him, as so many have done in dwelling on Death's meaning. Emily Dickinson left a somber portrait of Death coming for her in a horse-drawn carriage:

Because I could not stop for Death—
He kindly stopped for me—
The Carriage held but just Ourselves—
And Immortality ...

Others have seen death arriving as a phantom rider on a phantom horse. I
like the immediacy of Thomas Wolfe's "I have seen the Dark Man very close."

During my illness Death became almost a familiar; he and I drew closer
together as I came to terms with my mortality. In keeping with the Jewish tradition, I veered between I-Thou talks with him and a feeling of awe for the Angel
of Death, who is at times one with the Angel of God. The rabbinical legends
about the Old Testament heroes recount God's vow that Moses will die in the
wilderness without seeing the Promised Land, and the efforts of Moses to dis-
suade God from carrying it out. The argument between them was long and
labyrinthine. Moses used every possible trick to persuade God to repeal the
sentence of his appointed death, but God was wily, and besides He had the
power. Moses called on every force of Nature to intercede for him, but the
intercessions were in vain. Fighting to the end, he accepted his doom only

when his powers of discourse and his wisdom had been passed on to his successor, Joshua.

In a similar vein King David, seeking to learn the day of his death, was told only that he would die at seventy, on a Sabbath. Determined to outwit the Angel of Death, he postponed it week after week by busying himself every Sabbath in the study of the Torah, which gave him at least a temporary immunity from the Angel. But the Angel, insistent and cunning, contrived in the end to distract David from his studies by a noise in the garden. As David descended the palace staircase, it collapsed and he was killed.

In both instances the response to the command of the Angel of Death was, in effect, "Don't you see how involved I am with the work of God, and how many depend on me? Go away! I'm not ready." That was, I confess, my own response when the angel came knocking. He found me, despite my illness, in the midst of life. I was neither prophet nor king, nor was I involved with the work of God, yet I was nonetheless unready to be summoned from my worldly joys and plans.

For me it was a question of incompletions. Of the books half-written: I felt their structure and shape in my very bone and wanted to see them whole. Of my children and their children in turn: I wanted to see how the drama of life would unfold for them. Of the great world events I was watching: I wanted to see how the plot would turn out. Of the essential meaning of existence: if life is a suspense story, I wanted to read further and uncover the critical clue.

Even Moses and David, with all their worldly power and their pipeline to God, couldn't stonewall His angel indefinitely. In the end each had to open the doors wide. Immanuel Kant spoke jokingly of the "regime of reprieves" he had received from his doctors. Like Moses and David, I got several reprieves from the Angel. Like them I can't count on his continuing them indefinitely.

My father used to tell me some of these stories of the Malech h'amovits, the Angel of Death. In his opinion it was a question of being fully engaged in life. "If you run fast enough," he said, "the Angel won't be able to catch up with you." I loved my father, but I feared he was wrong.

Yet on second thought, was he? The Biblical commentators, sitting in their Yeshivas, arguing over ancient texts, were wise men. They wouldn't have composed the stories about their heroes and the Angel of Death for fun. Granted, they were saying that even lawgivers and kings, with all their power, can't bargain with Death forever. But could they have been saying more? That it is exactly when you are running fast, immersed in life, that you dare ask for a reprieve from death, to live fully a bit longer?

If the answer is even a tentative yes, it may offer a clue to the elusive mystery of the mind-body connection and its impact on the healing process. What heals us, granting us reprieves, postponing Death for a time, may be after all—as with Moses and King David—our fierce will to live.[11]

12. Learning and Helping

WILLIAM CUTTER

Illness, for hospital chaplain William Cutter, can be a great educator. It can improve our ability to help others.

Pulitzer Prize-winner Annie Dillard (1989) once charged all would-be writers with a curious demand: "What would you begin writing if you knew you would die soon? What could you say to a dying person that would not enrage by its triviality?" If writing and reading about anything can be spoken of in such ultimate terms, how much more important must writing be when the very subject of the writing is death and illness itself!

There is a lot of writing about this subject, and many people buy books about illness. Each generation in America produces more literature about the subject: more stories, more hope of miraculous cure, more criticism of current medical practice, and more new language to do all that work. Metaphors abound to help us in the work of writing and reading, and the words used to describe our sickness and our health are especially rich and plentiful. The most interesting example of this linguistic excitement may be Jonathan Miller's *The Body in Question* (1978), in which the British physician-dramatist explains the very function of our organs in terms of machinery from the industrial revolution. But the point is that language helps as we struggle to explain why being sick is so important.

Even universities tell young scholars that they will either publish or they will perish, which is really figurative language for announcing the importance of putting things into writing. The universities are right in another figurative way, and so I often suggest that patients keep a diary, some kind of record, of their experiences with serious illness.

Patients who write about their illnesses or who at least find the proper figures of speech to describe them have a way of gaining control, and a way of giving some concrete figuration to the potential emptiness that lies behind every illness. One either finds a way to deal with the emptiness, or one perishes to some extent.

My essay will have a lot to do with the metaphors of illness; and it will take advantage of some of that great abundance of writing that has been done over these past twenty years. Annie Dillard's words are appropriate for me in a surprising way: it was my own experience of illness and my own interest in writing about that illness that changed my thoughts about the meaning of illness and death. On the one hand, I learned that I had more spiritual layers—higher levels of consciousness, if you will; and on the other hand, I learned to pay more attention to my immediate and very physical surroundings, so I learned also to touch "lower" more everyday realities. I learned to keep my inner eye on thoughts about God's purposes, while (in Milton Steinberg's words), embracing the physical world with open arms. And I learned about some often neglected issues in medical care.

The drama of illness made me more interested in living, in general. My interest began with my first moments in the hospital when I recalled Paddy Chayevsky's movie "Hospital" and worried that my urine test was going to be confused with someone else's; and it continues eleven years later, when I hear the stories that sick people tell me as I visit with them and their families. Although I felt quite ill, I was able to pay close attention to all kinds of things within the hospital: pictures on the wall, the way elevators felt as I was being wheeled around, the atmosphere of x-ray rooms, the sounds of people's voices and the reassurances of kind doctors. I have not lost my acuity for detail. Even my fantasies seem to have been permanently nourished, from my early experience with semi-consciousness. I once figured out, for example, that the monitors which were hooked up to record my heartbeat were actually keeping me alive. And in the intensive care unit I dreamed about a desert island and idyllic tropical settings during a brief episode of shock from a potassium deficiency. At the time I wondered why the name of that island was "Ischemia," and only later did I realize that ischemia is the name of lack of blood and oxygen in the coronary arteries. I still remember the sounds in the darkening life I was to inherit; and although the acoustics of memory have distorted some, they have provided a link between what I experienced and what I now believe.

Perhaps a rabbi should talk about what he believes. On my last day in the hospital, after seven months of admissions and releases, Rabbi Meier, the hospital chaplain, asked me how all of this experience had affected my belief in God. No one had ever asked that question of this rabbi before. The question was the first step in insinuating a religious frame of reference into my life, and a commitment to activity in and around health and disease: working with sick people, and helping my own students think more about the place of illness and wellness in their own training to minister to people's needs. To my surprise, the experience has helped me combine my more purely academic work with the real lived experience of people. I teach literature, and living life a little closer to the edge made me a better reader.

All those little things I had begun to notice during my first hours in the hospital were suddenly a composite of a much bigger and more meaningful universe. God is, indeed, in the details.

It is, then, a gift for some of us to have been sick. In the perfect world toward which Jewish tradition points, but which no tradition really believes has come, perhaps no one would be ill. But in the imperfect world we inhabit, it is sometimes necessary to experience wellness and illness as part of one continuum. If for me as a rabbi, the notion of having to die before one can live is incomprehensible, at least I can say that one may have to be sick in order to appreciate being well. I am, in general, grateful for the experience, if not always for the inconveniences I now live with. And I may qualify, by pure accident, for something that Professor Lewis Thomas would like to expect from his medical students: urging that all future doctors be made to undergo one serious viral illness in their early professional careers so that they would know what it is like to be sick.

Thomas has been worried over the years that doctors are increasingly estranged from their patients' feelings. Tracing this tendency to the time when the stethoscope replaced the doctor's ear against the patient's chest, Thomas (1983) has been able to accept the realties of technology while warning of its spiritual costs. I learned that all professions have their versions of being far away from their clients' heartbeats. And that has religious meaning as well.

I have hesitated to write about my medical experiences for public purposes. There is no false humility here, just a wondering if a healthy person ought to go around announcing his good fortune. I do not usually exhibit my cardiac scars around the hospital, for example, but when it seems appropriate, I do tell patients that I have been through serious cardiac surgery in order to encourage them to be optimistic. Now I can enjoy the twist of phrase that I sometimes publicize because I did not perish. So perhaps this is another legitimate instance of sharing my scars. How was my experience like that of everyone else? What might they learn from what happened to me?

What happened to me is similar to what happens to anyone who becomes sick suddenly. One day you are well, and the next day you are sick, and you cannot even be certain where the dividing line between the two conditions was laid down. Fortunately most of us who become sick develop a kind of amnesia which eradicates fear about being sick again or about re-experiencing the initial dark panic. But, of course, I do remember the moment when my illness became apparent. And I remember the awkward choreography between my wife, who was on the phone at the time, and me as I was trying to gain access to the line. (We have since put in other lines.) It was a deeply personal and maritally telling moment in our lives, but probably no different from the story of any other person who seems to get sick all of a sudden. As the great *Village Voice* writer, Paul Cowan, said of his own illness (1988): "We are all going to enter the land of the sick at one time in our lives. The question is only when."

On that evening over ten years ago, in order to determine which land of the sick I was entering, the young doctor at Cedars-Sinai Medical Center greeted me at the door to the emergency room. "What are you feeling?" he asked. "Is it like an elephant sitting on your chest?" And before slipping off into my ischemic fantasies, I found enough sarcastic energy to tell him that I had never had an elephant sitting on my chest. Although this question was innocent enough, it has always served as a reminder to me of two important truths about the sensitivity of patients. First, I learned that the people who are devoted to patients' health really must communicate carefully, since the patients are especially sensitive. Second, I learned that because patients are so sensitive, it is nearly impossible to avoid saying something that might offend them. This realization has given me the strength to go into hospital rooms, to serve as a chaplain and return to a kind of religious life to which I had originally intended to devote myself. In order to be able to help people you have to intuit their emotions, and thus reduce the risk of damaging their faith in you; but in order to begin the process, you have to be willing to take risks. I suspect that some rabbis do not visit patients enough because they are afraid of doing something ineffectual.

I learned something else from having started my journey in the emergency room. I call it the paradox of self-help. One of the most important things patients can do for themselves is to take responsibility for understanding their illnesses and for their own medical management. The "mode" of relationship with a physician has to be one of mutual respect and interdependence.

But those who enter the hospital in a state of emergency begin in just the contrary mode: one of total dependence, weakness and gratitude for the strength of doctors and nurses. Most acutely ill patients have little capability of worrying about the development of mutual relationships with those who are helping.

Because I was lying on my back for the first several days in cardiac care units, I felt especially helpless. Every paternal or maternal reassurance by others and every kind and supportive word was encoded in my memory bank. It was some trick learning that this would not be an appropriate attitude for taking care of myself over the long haul. It took many years to move towards autonomy, but it is a move we all must make.

So if you ask me what I have learned from my illness, the answer would have to do with understanding the very particularity of life, its concreteness and actuality. I learned about the loss of power and about gaining it back; I learned some subtleties of interpretation; and I learned how to use memory for creative purposes. In my awareness of that sense of the real and the immediate, and the very tangible aspects of living, I have moved away from what had been a latent interest in traditional medical ethics questions and into a greater concentration on the day-to-day needs of patients. Along with Rabbi Levi Meier, I have come to call this area "soft ethics." This division of ethical studies has some parallels in the Jewish tradition's distinction between legal behavior (known as *halacha*), and more nuanced spiritual values (known as *musar* or *aggadah*).

The aspects of medical ethics which fascinate me now concern how patients experience their illnesses in the day-to-day business of being ill. While the more dramatic questions of life and death, medical experiments, transplants, euthanasia and abortion continue to be the stuff of which conferences are composed, for most patients and for most doctors there is a long agenda of items that fill the ill patient's day.

For every medical question about when life ends, and whether a patient is entitled to die at will, there are a hundred questions with ambiguous answers in which doctor and patient have to negotiate the daily terrain. How, for example, can a very sick patient be made to feel better about the cost of services? How might a nurse or front office manager create a hospitable frame within which the patient is treated? How much time can a doctor legitimately afford to spend with a patient, given the realities of overhead, reluctant insurance companies, and the pressure on the doctor from family and community? What can a patient's friends and associates do to ensure that the patient does not feel abandoned by the community? What are the things one might say to make a person feel stronger and more in charge of the future? How can a doctor relieve a patient of the burden of a nagging spouse? Where do nurses fit into a doctor's plan? And, finally, how can all of us help to get our language clear so that we more or less know what the other person is saying? Are there metaphors more suitable to ethical relationships?

For the most part, I find Jewish bioethics "out of sync" with the real and desperate needs of people, and not related to the most pressing areas in which Jewish life impinges on the medical situation: doctors' fees; the personal suffering of the families of ill people, and the abrasive interaction between family members; the dignity of patients who are suffering the indignity of illness; the chaotic way in which families of ill people have to make decisions; and the loneliness of all the people going through the tunnel of illness. For my students who will lead communities some day, there are problems on a larger scale which will involve them in building facilities: what can we do about hospital architecture to make patients and their families feel more human? Are there places to sit down when talking with a doctor? Do the walls of testing rooms look like prison cells or do they look like helping environments? What does it feel like to spend your illness looking up at people's nostrils? How, in general, can communities come to understand that the care of people in trouble is an ethical priority, inspiring us to make it possible to be ill and to feel human at the same time? ...[12]

13. Choosing

VIKTOR FRANKL

How did some outlive the death camps? It was not just a matter of luck, but also of will, we are told by survivor Viktor

Frankl in his seminal work Man's Search for Meaning. *He turned his own agony into empathy and his observations into a form of psychotherapy.*

We can answer these questions from experience as well as on principle. The experiences of camp life show that man does have a choice of action. There were enough examples, often of a heroic nature, which proved that apathy could be overcome, irritability suppressed. Man *can* preserve a vestige of spiritual freedom, of independence of mind, even in such terrible conditions of psychic and physical stress. We who lived in concentration camps can remember the men who walked through the huts comforting others, giving away their last piece of bread. They may have been few in number, but they offer sufficient proof that everything can be taken from a man but one thing: the last of the human freedoms—to choose one's own attitude in any given set of circumstances, to choose one's own way.

And there were always choices to make. Every day, every hour, offered the opportunity to make a decision, a decision which determined whether you would or would not submit to those powers which threatened to rob you of your very self, your inner freedom; which determined whether or not you would become the plaything of circumstance, renouncing freedom and dignity to become molded into the form of the typical inmate.

Seen from this point of view, the mental reactions of the inmates of a concentration camp must seem more to us than the mere expression of certain physical and sociological conditions. Even though conditions such as lack of sleep, insufficient food and various mental stresses may suggest that the inmates were bound to react in certain ways, in the final analysis, it becomes clear that the sort of person the prisoner became was the result of an inner decision, and not the result of camp influences alone. Fundamentally, therefore, any man can, even under such circumstances, decide what shall become of him—mentally and spiritually. He may retain his human dignity even in a concentration camp. Dostoevski said once, "There is only one thing that I dread: not to be worthy of my sufferings." These words frequently came to my mind after I became acquainted with those martyrs whose behavior in camp, whose suffering and death, bore witness to the fact that the last inner freedom cannot be lost. It can be said that they were worthy of their sufferings; the way they bore their suffering was a genuine inner achievement. It is this spiritual freedom—which cannot be taken away—that makes life meaningful and purposeful.

An active life serves the purpose of giving man the opportunity to realize values in creative work, while a passive life of enjoyment affords him the opportunity to obtain fulfillment in experiencing beauty, art or nature. But there is also purpose in that life which is almost barren of both creation and enjoyment and which admits of but one possibility of high moral behavior: namely, in man's attitude to his existence, an existence restricted by external forces. A creative life and a life of enjoyment are meaningful. If there is a meaning in life at all, then there must be a meaning in suffering. Suffering is an ineradicable part of life, even as fate and death. Without suffering and death human life cannot be complete.

The way in which a man accepts his fate and all the suffering it entails, the way in which he takes up his cross, gives him ample opportunity—even under the most difficult circumstances—to add a deeper meaning to his life. It may remain brave, dignified and unselfish. Or in the bitter fight for self-preservation he may forget his human dignity and become no more than an animal. Here lies the chance for a man either to make use of or to forgo the opportunities of attaining the moral values that a difficult situation may afford him. And this decides whether he is worthy of his suffering or not.

Do not think that these considerations are unworldly and too far removed from real life. It is true that only a few people are capable of reaching such high moral standards. Of the prisoners only a few kept their full inner liberty and obtained those values which their suffering afforded, but even one such example is sufficient proof that man's inner strength may raise him above his outward fate. Such men are not only in concentration camps. Everywhere man is confronted with fate, with the chance of achieving something through his own suffering.

Take the fate of the sick—especially those who are incurable. I once read a letter written by a young invalid, in which he told a friend that he had just found out he would not live for long, that even an operation would be of no help. He wrote further that he remembered a film he had seen in which a man was portrayed who waited for death in a courageous and dignified way. The boy had thought it a great accomplishment to meet death so well. Now—he wrote—fate was offering him a similar chance.

Those of us who saw the film called *Resurrection*—taken from a book by Tolstoy—years ago, may have had similar thoughts. Here were great destinies and great men. For us, at that time, there was no great fate; there was no chance to achieve such greatness. After the picture we went to the nearest café, and over a cup of coffee and a sandwich we forgot the strange metaphysical thought which for one moment had crossed our minds. But when we ourselves were confronted with a great destiny and faced with the decision of meeting it with equal spiritual greatness, by then we had forgotten our youthful resolutions of long ago, and we failed.

Perhaps there came a day for some of us when we saw the same film again, or a similar one. But by then other pictures may have simultaneously unrolled before one's inner eye; pictures of people who attained much more in their lives than a sentimental film could show. Some details of a particular man's inner greatness may have come to one's mind, like the story of a young woman whose death I witnessed in a concentration camp. It is a simple story. There is little to tell and it may sound as if I had invented it; but to me it seems like a poem.

This young woman knew that she would die in the next few days. But when I talked to her she was cheerful in spite of this knowledge. "I am grateful that fate has hit me so hard," she told me. "In my former life I was spoiled and did not take spiritual accomplishment seriously." Pointing through the window of the hut, she said, "This tree here is the only friend I have in my loneliness." Through that window she could see just one branch of a chestnut tree, and on the branch were two blossoms. "I often talk to this tree," she said to me. I was startled and didn't quite know how to take her words. Was she delirious? Did she have occasional hallucinations? Anxiously I asked her if the tree replied. "Yes." What did it say to her? She answered, "It said to me, 'I am here—I am here—I am life, eternal life.'"

Any attempt at fighting the camp's psychopathological influence on the prisoner by psychotherapeutic or psychohygienic methods had to aim at giving him inner strength by pointing out to him a future goal to which he could look forward. Instinctively some of the prisoners attempted to find one on their own. It is a peculiarity of man that he can only live by looking into the future—*sub specie aeternitatis*. And this is his salvation in the most difficult moments of his existence, although he sometimes has to force his mind to the task.

I remember a personal experience. Almost in tears from pain (I had terrible sores on my feet from wearing torn shoes), I limped a few kilometers with our long column of men from the camp to our work site. Very cold, bitter winds struck us. I kept thinking of the endless little problems of our miserable life. What would there be to eat tonight? If a piece of sausage came as extra ration, should I exchange it for a piece of bread? Should I trade my last cigarette which was left from a bonus I received a fortnight ago, for a bowl of soup? How could I get a piece of wire to replace the fragment which served as one of my shoelaces? Would I get to our work site in time to join my usual working party or would I have to join another, which might have a brutal foreman? What could I do to get on good terms with the Capo, who could help me to obtain work in camp instead of undertaking this horribly long daily march?

I became disgusted with the state of affairs which compelled me, daily and hourly, to think of only such trivial things. I forced my thoughts to turn to another subject. Suddenly I saw myself standing on the platform of a well-lit, warm and pleasant lecture room. In front of me sat an attentive audience, on comfortable upholstered seats. I was giving a lecture on the psychology of the concentration camp! All that oppressed me at that moment became the objective, seen and described from the remote viewpoint of science. By this method I succeeded somehow in rising above the situation, above the sufferings of the moment, and I observed them as if they were already of the past. Both I and my troubles became the object of an interesting psychoscientific study undertaken by myself. What does Spinoza say in his *Ethics?* — *"Affectus, qui passio est, desinit esse passio simulatque eius claram et distinctam formanus ideam."* Emotion, which is suffering, ceases to be suffering as soon as we form a clear and precise picture of it.

The prisoner who had lost faith in the future—his future—was doomed. With his loss of belief in the future, he also lost his spiritual hold; he let himself decline and became subject to mental and physical decay. Usually this happened quite suddenly, in the form of a crisis, the symptoms of which were familiar to the experienced camp inmate. We all feared this moment—not for ourselves, which would have been pointless, but for our friends. Usually it began with the prisoner refusing one morning to get dressed and wash or to go out on the parade grounds. No entreaties, no blows, no threats had any effect. He just lay there, hardly moving. If this crisis was brought about by an illness, he refused to be taken to the sick-bay or to do anything to help himself. He simply gave up. There he remained, lying in his own excreta, and nothing bothered him anymore.

I once had a dramatic demonstration of the close link between the loss of faith in the future and this dangerous giving up. F—, my senior block warden, a fairly well-known composer and librettist, confided in me one day: "I would like to tell you something, Doctor. I have had a strange dream. A voice told me that I could wish for something, that I should only say what I wanted to know, and all my questions would be answered. What do you think I asked? That I would like to know when the war would be over for me. You know what I mean Doctor— for me! I wanted to know when we, when our camp, would be liberated and our sufferings come to an end."

"And when did you have this dream?" I asked.

"In February, 1945," he answered. It was then the beginning of March.

"What did your dream voice answer?"

Furtively he whispered to me, "March thirtieth."

When F — told me about this dream, he was still full of hope and convinced that the voice of his dream would be right. But as the promised day drew nearer, the war news which reached our camp made it appear very unlikely that we would be free on the promised date. On March twenty-ninth, F— suddenly became ill and ran a high temperature. On March thirtieth, the day his prophecy had told him that the war and suffering would be over for him, he became delirious and lost consciousness. On March thirty-first, he was dead. To all outward appearances, he had died of typhus.

Those who know how close the connection is between the state of mind of a man—his courage and hope, or lack of them—and the state of immunity of his body will understand that the sudden loss of hope and courage can have a deadly effect. The ultimate cause of my friend's death was that the expected liberation did not come and he was severely disappointed. This suddenly lowered his body's resistance against the latent typhus infection. His faith in the future and his will to live had become paralyzed and his body fell victim to illness—and thus the voice of his dream was right after all.

As we said before, any attempt to restore a man's inner strength in the camp had first to succeed in showing him some future goal. Nietzsche's words, "He who has a *why* to live for can bear with almost any *how*," could be the guiding motto for all psychotherapeutic and psychohygienic efforts regarding prisoners.

Whenever there was an opportunity for it, one had to give them a *why*—an aim—for their lives, in order to strengthen them to bear the terrible *how* of their existence. Woe to him who saw no more sense in his life, no aim, no purpose, and therefore no point in carrying on. He was soon lost. The typical reply with which such a man rejected all encouraging arguments was, "I have nothing to expect from life any more." What sort of answers can one give to that?

What was really needed was a fundamental change in our attitude toward life. We had to learn ourselves and furthermore, we had to teach the despairing men, that *it did not really matter what we expected from life, but rather what life expected from us.* We needed to stop asking about the meaning of life, and instead to think of ourselves as those who were being questioned by life—daily and hourly. Our answer must consist, not in talk and meditation, but in right action and in right conduct. Life ultimately means taking the responsibility to find the right answer to its problems and to fulfill the tasks which it constantly sets for each individual.

These tasks, and therefore the meaning of life, differ from man to man, and from moment to moment. Thus it is impossible to define the meaning of life in a general way. Questions about the meaning of life can never be answered by sweeping statements. "Life" does not mean something vague, but something very real and concrete. They form man's destiny, which is different and unique for each individual. No man and no destiny can be compared with any other man or any other destiny. No situation repeats itself, and each situation calls for a different response. Sometimes the situation in which a man finds himself may require him to shape his own fate by action. At other times it is more advantageous for him to make use of an opportunity for contemplation and to realize assets in this way. Sometimes man may be required simply to accept fate, to bear his cross. Every situation is distinguished by its uniqueness, and there is always only one right answer to the problem posed by the situation at hand.

When a man finds that it is his destiny to suffer, he will have to accept his suffering as his task; his single and unique task. He will have to acknowledge the fact that even in suffering he is unique and alone in the universe. No one can relieve him of his suffering or suffer in his place. His unique opportunity lies in the way in which he bears his burden.[13]

Seeking Meaning in Suffering

But Joseph said to them, "Have no fear. Am I a substitute for God? Besides, although you intended me harm, God intended it for good, so as to bring about the present result—the survival of many people."

Genesis 50:19–20

Introduction

*J*n the midst of illness and suffering the heart cries out, "Why?" We address the Creator of the Universe and with that one word ask, "Did I do something to make this happen to me? Can I repent and undo it and take away this suffering?" With that one word we say, "I don't want this to be happening to me. It's unexpected and unfair." Jews have asked these questions and expressed these feelings throughout the centuries as they have faced pain and illness. Sometimes, according to our texts, there appears to be a concrete answer to the question, "Why?" Sometimes, there is no discernible answer at all.

Our holiest sources retain the ambiguity of reality. Sometimes they insist that pain is a consequence of sin. Sometimes they affirm that pain is not a consequence of sin and that it seems meaningless and mean. The Tanakh contains within it the views expressed in the Book of Deuteronomy, which clearly and repeatedly links suffering to sin, as well as the views expressed in the books of Wisdom Literature, such as Ecclesiastes and Job, which explicitly admit that the righteous suffer and that some pain has no cause and no cure. The wisdom of Judaism is that it redacted these opposite views together into the same holy book, thus affirming the vast range of human experience.

Judaism also allows us to reject suffering. One is not only encouraged, but commanded, to seek a cure. When suffering is unavoidable, our sources recognize that we can work with God to give suffering meaning. When we experience pain and use that experience to make ourselves more empathetic to others who suffer and to perform increased acts of lovingkindness, we act as God's partner, giving meaning to the inherently meaningless. Then the *answer to the question, "Why?" can become "To give me the motivation and insight to be more understanding and generous to those in pain. This experience may allow me to ennoble my own life by acting as God's partner in bringing healing not just to myself, but to others as well. I would not have known how much suffering hurts if not for this experience."*

14. Following God's Intentions

BIBLE

Judaism embodies the belief, in every generation, that God is one and that all reality is interconnected and forms one logical whole, even though we humans cannot grasp all of it. Health and illness, therefore, both stem from the ultimate Source. The Torah offers guidance on how to give our lives meaning and how to understand our illnesses in the context of God's will for the world. These concepts of meaning, reward, and punishment may be difficult for us to work with yet they have comforted centuries of sufferers by giving their suffering meaning and context.

See, then, that I, I am He;
There is no god beside Me.
I deal death and give life;
I wounded and I will heal:
None can deliver from My hand.[1]

There He made for them a fixed rule, and there He put them to the test. He said, "If you will heed the LORD your God diligently, doing what is upright in His sight, giving ear to His commandments and keeping all His laws, then I will not bring upon you any of the diseases that I brought upon the Egyptians, for I the LORD am your healer."[2]

Now, if you obey the LORD your God, to observe faithfully all His commandments which I enjoin upon you this day, the LORD your God will set you high above all the nations of the earth. All these blessings shall come upon you and take effect, if you will but heed the word of the LORD your God:

Blessed shall you be in the city and blessed shall you be in the country.

Blessed shall be the issue of your womb, the produce of your soil, and the offspring of your cattle, the calving of your herd and the lambing of your flock.

Blessed shall be your basket and your kneading bowl.

Blessed shall you be in your comings and blessed shall you be in your goings.[3]

But if you do not obey the LORD your God to observe faithfully all His commandments and laws which I enjoin upon you this day, all these curses shall come upon you and take effect:

Cursed shall you be in the city and cursed shall you be in the country.

Cursed shall be your basket and your kneading bowl.

Cursed shall be the issue of your womb and the produce of your soil, the calving of your herd and the lambing of your flock.

Cursed shall you be in your comings and cursed shall you be in your goings.

The LORD will let loose against you calamity, panic, and frustration in all the enterprises you undertake, so that you shall soon be utterly wiped out because of your evildoing in forsaking Me. The LORD will make pestilence cling to you, until He has put an end to you in the land that you are entering to possess. The LORD will strike you with consumption, fever, and inflammation, with scorching heat and drought, with blight and mildew; they shall hound you until you perish. The skies above your head shall be copper and the earth under you iron. The LORD will make the rain of your land dust, and sand shall drop on you from the sky, until you are wiped out.[4]

But if you do not obey Me and do not observe all these commandments, if you reject My laws and spurn My rules, so that you do not observe all My commandments and you break My covenant, I in turn will do this to you: I will wreak misery upon you—consumption and fever, which cause the eyes to pine and the body to languish; you shall sow your seed to no purpose, for your enemies shall eat it. I will set My face against you: you shall be routed by your enemies, and your foes shall dominate you. You shall flee though none pursues.[5]

15. Sarah Is Rewarded

Sickness is rarely expected. It blindsides most people and disrupts their lives. Blessing, too, can come unexpectedly, yet, since we have often hoped and prayed for it so fervently and thought of it so fondly, we are able to incorporate good fortune into our lives more easily. In this story, which is read on the Jewish new year, the prayers of Abraham and Sarah, who have entered into a covenant with God, are answered: they are blessed with a child.

The LORD appeared to him by the terebinths of Mamre; he was sitting at the entrance of the tent as the day grew hot. Looking up, he saw three men standing near him. As soon as he saw them, he ran from the entrance of the tent to greet them and, bowing to the ground, he said, "My lords, if it please you, do not go on past your servant. Let a little water be brought; bathe your feet and recline under the tree. And let me fetch a morsel of bread that you may refresh yourselves; then go on—seeing that you have come your servant's way." They replied, "Do as you have said."

Abraham hastened into the tent to Sarah, and said, "Quick, three seahs of choice flour! Knead and make cakes!" Then Abraham ran to the herd, took a calf, tender and choice, and gave it to a servant-boy, who hastened to prepare it. He took curds and milk and the calf that had been prepared and set these before them; and he waited on them under the tree as they ate.

They said to him, "Where is your wife Sarah?" And he replied, "There, in the tent." Then one said, "I will return to you next year, and your wife Sarah shall have a son!" Sarah was listening at the entrance of the tent, which was behind him. Now Abraham and Sarah were old, advanced in years; Sarah had stopped having the periods of women. And Sarah laughed to herself, saying, "Now that I am withered, am I to have enjoyment—with my husband so old?" Then the LORD said to Abraham, "Why did Sarah laugh, saying, 'Shall I in truth bear a child, old as I am?' Is anything too wondrous for the LORD? I will return to you at the same season next year, and Sarah shall have a son." Sarah lied, saying, "I did not laugh," for she was frightened. But He replied, "You did laugh . . ."

The LORD took note of Sarah as He had promised, and the LORD did for Sarah as He had spoken. Sarah conceived and bore a son to Abraham in his old age, at the set time of which God had spoken.[6]

16. God Makes Israel Sick and Then Well Again

BIBLE

When sufferers ask, "Why?" they are often expressing the sentiment, "I don't want this to be happening! Help me out of this!" In this passage, the Israelites wonder why they have left Egypt to wander in the desert. In response, God sends them both a sickness and a cure. In this Torah tale, there is no explicit answer to the Israelites' question. There is only wondering and wandering.

They set out from Mount Hor by way of the Sea of Reeds to skirt the land of Edom. But the people grew restive on the journey, and the people spoke against God and against Moses, "Why did you make us leave Egypt to die in the wilderness? There is no bread and no water, and we have come to loathe this miserable food." The LORD sent *seraph* serpents against the people. They bit the people and many of the Israelites died. The people came to Moses and said, "We sinned by speaking against the LORD and against you. Intercede with the LORD to take away the serpents from us!" And Moses interceded for the people. Then the LORD said to Moses, "Make a *seraph* figure and mount it on a standard. And if anyone who is bitten looks at it, he shall recover. Moses made a copper serpent and mounted it on a standard; and when anyone was bitten by a serpent, he would look at the copper serpent and recover.[7]

17. Elisha Revives a Child

BIBLE

This story is one of the best known in Jewish Scripture. In it, a boy who has done no wrong, and whose parents are righteous, is stricken horribly but then saved. The reason for the child's illness is never given. His recovery is an example of the mirac-

ulous cure we often fear to hope for when we are ill. Some
things, this tale suggests, are never revealed to us.

One day Elisha visited Shunem. A wealthy woman lived there, and she urged
him to have a meal; and whenever he passed by, he would stop there for a meal.
Once she said to her husband, "I am sure it is a holy man of God who comes
this way regularly. Let us make a small enclosed upper chamber and place a
bed, a table, a chair, and a lampstand there for him, so that he can stop there
whenever he comes to us." One day he came there; he retired to the upper
chamber and lay down there. He said to his servant Gehazi, "Call that Shunammite woman." He called her, and she stood before him. He said to him, "Tell her,
'You have gone to all this trouble for us. What can we do for you? Can we speak
in your behalf to the king or to the army commander?'" She replied, "I live
among my own people." "What then can be done for her?" he asked. "The fact
is," said Gehazi, "she has no son, and her husband is old." "Call her," he said. He
called her, and she stood in the doorway. And Elisha said, "At this season next
year, you will be embracing a son." She replied, "Please my lord, man of God, do
not delude your maidservant."

The woman conceived and bore a son at the same season the following
year, as Elisha had assured her. The child grew up. One day, he went out to his
father among the reapers. [Suddenly] he cried to his father, "Oh, my head, my
head!" He said to a servant, "Carry him to his mother." He picked him up and
brought him to his mother. And the child sat on her lap until noon; and he died.
She took him up and laid him on the bed of the man of God, and left him and
closed the door. Then she called to her husband: "Please, send me one of the
servants and one of the she-asses, so I can hurry to the man of God and back."
But he said, "Why are you going to him today? It is neither new moon nor sabbath." She answered, "It's all right."

She had the ass saddled, and said to her servant, "Urge [the beast] on; see
that I don't slow down unless I tell you." She went on until she came to the man
of God on Mount Carmel. When the man of God saw her from afar, he said to
his servant Gehazi, "There is that Shunammite woman. Go, hurry toward her
and ask her, 'How are you? How is your husband? How is the child?'" "We are
well," she replied. But when she came up to the man of God on the mountain,
she clasped his feet. Gehazi stepped forward to push her away; but the man of

God said, "Let her alone, for she is in bitter distress; and the LORD has hidden it from me and has not told me." Then she said, "Did I ask my lord for a son? Didn't I say: 'Don't mislead me'?"

He said to Gehazi, "Tie up your skirts, take my staff in your hand, and go. If you meet anyone, do not greet him; and if anyone greets you, do not answer him. And place my staff on the face of the boy." But the boy's mother said, "As the LORD lives and as you live, I will not leave you!" So he arose and followed her.

Gehazi had gone on before them and had placed the staff on the boy's face; but there was no sound or response. He turned back to meet him and told him, "The boy has not awakened." Elisha came into the house, and there was the boy, laid out dead on his couch. He went in, shut the door behind the two of them, and prayed to the LORD. Then he mounted [the bed] and placed himself over the child. He put his mouth on its mouth, his eyes on its eyes, and his hands on its hands, as he bent over it. And the body of the child became warm. He stepped down, walked once up and down the room, then mounted and bent over him. Thereupon, the boy sneezed seven times, and the boy opened his eyes. [Elisha] called Gehazi and said, "Call the Shunammite woman," and he called her. When she came to him, he said, "Pick up your son." She came and fell at his feet and bowed low to the ground; then she picked up her son and left.[8]

18. We Suffer for Others

BIBLE

The "Suffering Servant" portrayed in this famous passage from the prophet Isaiah can be an inspiration when we are ill. He feels great pain but he is not defeated. Not only that, his suffering has meaning for himself and those around him.

"Who can believe what we have heard?
Upon whom has the arm of the LORD been revealed?
For he has grown, by His favor, like a tree crown,
Like a tree trunk out of arid ground.
He had no form or beauty, that we should look at him:

No charm, that we should find him pleasing.
He was despised, shunned by men,
A man of suffering, familiar with disease.
As one who hid his face from us,
He was despised, we held him of no account.
Yet it was our sickness that he was bearing,
Our suffering that he endured.
We accounted him plagued,
Smitten and afflicted by God;
But he was wounded because of our sins,
Crushed because of our iniquities.
He bore the chastisement that made us whole,
And by his bruises we were healed.
We all went astray like sheep,
Each going his own way;
And the LORD visited upon him
The guilt of all of us."

He was maltreated, yet he was submissive,
He did not open his mouth;
Like a sheep being led to slaughter,
Like an ewe, dumb before those who shear her,
He did not open his mouth.
By oppressive judgment he was taken away,
Who could describe his abode?
For he was cut off from the land of the living
Through the sin of my people, who deserved the punishment.
And his grave was set among the wicked,
And with the rich, in his death
Though he had done no injustice
And had spoken no falsehood.
But the LORD chose to crush him by disease,
That, if he made himself an offering for guilt,
he might see offspring and have long life,
And that through him the LORD's purpose might prosper.

Out of his anguish he shall see it;
He shall enjoy it to the full through his devotion.

"My righteous servant makes the many righteous,
It is their punishment that he bears;
Assuredly, I will give him the many as his portion,
He shall receive the multitude as his spoil.
For he exposed himself to death
And was numbered among the sinners,
Whereas he bore the guilt of the many
And made intercession for sinners."[9]

19. God, This Is More Than I Can Bear

BIBLE

This lament beautifully outlines the experience of illness—the physical pain, emotional turmoil, and social isolation—and points to their amelioration through a relationship with God.

A PSALM OF DAVID. *LEHAZKIR.*
O LORD, do not punish me in wrath;
do not chastise me in fury.
For Your arrows have struck me;
Your blows have fallen upon me.
There is no soundness in my flesh because of Your rage,
no wholeness in my bones because of my sin.
For my iniquities have overwhelmed me;
they are like a heavy burden, more than I can bear.
My wounds stink and fester
because of my folly.
I am all bent and bowed;
I walk about in gloom all day long.
For my sinews are full of fever;
there is no soundness in my flesh.

I am all benumbed and crushed;
I roar because of the turmoil in my mind.

O Lord, You are aware of all my entreaties;
my groaning is not hidden from You.
My mind reels;
my strength fails me;
my eyes too have lost their luster.
My friends and companions stand back from my affliction;
my kinsmen stand far off.
Those who seek my life lay traps;
those who wish me harm speak malice;
they utter deceit all the time.
But I am like a deaf man, unhearing,
like a dumb man who cannot speak up;
I am like one who does not hear,
who has no retort on his lips.
But I wait for You, O LORD;
You will answer, O Lord, my God.
For I fear they will rejoice over me;
when my foot gives way they will vaunt themselves against me.
For I am on the verge of collapse;
my pain is always with me.
I acknowledge my iniquity;
I am fearful over my sin;
for my mortal enemies are numerous;
my treacherous foes are many.
Those who repay evil for good
harass me for pursuing good.

Do not abandon me, O LORD;
my God, be not far from me;
hasten to my aid,
O Lord, my deliverance.[10]

20. Is It Fair?

BIBLE

Job has become synonymous with suffering we cannot under-stand. In this passage, Job refuses to lose faith even as he ex-presses his pain and anguish.

One day the divine beings presented themselves before the LORD. The Adversary came along with them to present himself before the LORD. The LORD said to the Adversary, "Where have you been?" The Adversary answered the LORD, "I have been roaming all over the earth." The LORD said to the Adversary, "Have you noticed My servant Job? There is no one like him on earth, a blameless and upright man who fears God and shuns evil. He still keeps his integrity; so you have incited Me against him to destroy him for no good reason." The Adversary answered the LORD, "Skin for skin—all that a man has he will give up for his life. But lay a hand on his bones and his flesh, and he will surely blaspheme You to Your face." So the LORD said to the Adversary, "See, he is in your power; only spare his life." The Adversary departed from the presence of the LORD and inflicted a severe inflammation on Job from the sole of his foot to the crown of his head. He took a potsherd to scratch himself as he sat in ashes. His wife said to him, "You still keep your integrity! Blaspheme God and die!" But he said to her, "You talk as any shameless woman might talk! Should we accept only good from God and not accept evil? For all that, Job said nothing sinful. . . .

Job said in reply: . . .
If I speak, my pain will not be relieved,
And if I do not—what have I lost?
Now He has truly worn me out;
You have destroyed my whole community.
you have shriveled me;
My gauntness serves as a witness,
And testifies against me.
In His anger He tears and persecutes me;
He gnashes His teeth at me;
My foe stabs me with his eyes.

They open wide their mouths at me;
Reviling me, they strike my cheeks;
They inflame themselves against me.
God hands me over to an evil man,
Thrusts me into the clutches of the wicked.
I had been untroubled, and He broke me in pieces;
He took me by the scruff and shattered me;
He set me up as His target;
His bowmen surrounded me;
He pierced my kidneys; He showed no mercy;
He spilled my bile onto the ground. . . .

Terror tumbles upon me;
It sweeps away my honor like the wind;
My dignity vanishes like a cloud.
So now my life runs out;
Days of misery have taken hold of me.
By night my bones feel gnawed;
My sinews never rest.
With great effort I change clothing;
The neck of my tunic fits my waist.
He regarded me as clay,
I have become like dust and ashes.

I cry out to You, but You do not answer me;
I wait, but You do [not] consider me.
You have become cruel to me;
With Your powerful hand you harass me.
You lift me up and mount me on the wind;
You make my courage melt.
I know You will bring me to death,
The house assigned for all the living.
Surely He would not strike at a ruin
If, in calamity, one cried out to Him.
Did I not weep for the unfortunate?

Did I not grieve for the needy?
I looked forward to good fortune, but evil came;
I hoped for light, but darkness came.
My bowels are in turmoil without respite;
Days of misery confront me.
I walk about in sunless gloom;
I rise in the assembly and cry out.
I have become a brother to jackals,
A companion to ostriches.
My skin, blackened, is peeling off me. . . .

The LORD said in reply to Job.

Shall one who should be disciplined complain against
    Shaddai?
He who arraigns God must respond.

Job said in reply to the LORD:

See, I am of small worth; what can I answer You?
I clap my hand to my mouth.
I have spoken once, and will not reply;
Twice, and will do so no more.

Then the LORD replied to Job out of the tempest and said:

Gird your loins like a man;
I will ask, and you will inform Me.
Would you impugn My justice?
Would you condemn Me that you may be right?
Have you an arm like God's?
Can you thunder with a voice like His? . . .

Job said in reply to the LORD:

I know that You can do everything,
That nothing you propose is impossible for You.
Who is this who obscures counsel without knowledge?
Indeed, I spoke without understanding
Of things beyond me, which I did not know.
Hear now, and I will speak;
I will ask, and You will inform me.
I had heard You with my ears,
But now I see You with my eyes;
Therefore, I recant and relent,
Being but dust and ashes.[11]

21. Suffering and Compassion

TALMUD

While we may not know why pain has come to us we can give it meaning and put it to use. The great sage Rabbi Judah ha-Nasi brought sufferings upon himself. His house steward was rich from selling the manure of Rabbi's many horses, yet even their neighing could not drown out his cries of anguish. Rabbi's suffering came to him when he refused to show mercy to a calf and only left him when he showed kindness to a much lowlier animal.

Rabbi observed: Suffering is precious. Thereupon he undertook [to suffer likewise] for thirteen years, six through stones in the kidneys, and seven through scurvy: others reverse it. Rabbi's house-steward was wealthier than King Shapur. When he placed fodder for the beasts, their cries could be heard for three miles, and he aimed at casting it [before them] just then when Rabbi entered his privy closet, yet even so, his voice [lifted in pain] was louder than theirs, and was heard [even] by sea-farers. Nevertheless, the sufferings of R. Eleazar son of R. Simeon were superior [in virtue] to those of Rabbi. For whereas those of R. Eleazar son of R. Simeon came to him through love, and departed in love those of Rabbi came to him through a certain incident, and departed likewise.

"They came to him through a certain incident." What is it?—A calf was being taken to the slaughter, when it broke away, hid his head under Rabbi's skirts, and lowed [in terror]. "Go," said he, "for this was thou created." Thereupon they said [in Heaven], "Since he has no pity, let us bring suffering upon him."

"And departed likewise." How so?—One day Rabbi's maid servant was sweeping the house; [seeing] some young weasels lying there, she made to sweep them away. "Let them be," said he to her; "It is written, and his tender mercies are over all his works." Said they [in Heaven], "Since he is compassionate, let us be compassionate to him."[12]

22. Was It from Sin?

TALMUD

The view that death comes from sin, as well as that righteous persons die, is one held unapologetically by the Sages.

Mishnah: For three sins women die in childbirth: because they are not observant of [the laws of] *niddah, hallah,* and the kindling of the [Sabbath] lights.[13]

R. Oshaiah said: He who devotes himself to sin, wounds and bruises break out over him, as it is said, *Snipes and wounds are for him that devoteth himself to evil* (Proverbs 20:30). Moreover, he is punished by dropsy, for it is said, *and strokes reach the innermost parts of the belly* (Proverbs 20:30). R. Nahman b. Isaac said: Dropsy is a sign of sin.

Our Rabbis taught: There are three kinds of dropsy: that which is punishment of sin is thick; that caused by hunger is swollen and what is caused by magic is thin.[14]

23. The Reward in the Hereafter

MIDRASH

Why must we grow old, suffer, and die? The following midrash suggests that our three founding patriarchs, Abraham, Isaac, and Jacob, brought these attributes to us, and to humanity, in order that we might more easily make the transition from earthbound being to pure soul and memory.

R. Judah b. R. Simon said: Abraham requested [the appearance of] old age, pleading before him: "Sovereign of the Universe! When a man and his son enter a town, none know whom to honour." Said the Holy One, blessed be He, to him: "As thou livest, thou has asked a good thing, and I will commence with thee." Thus from the beginning of the Book until here old age is not mentioned, but when Abraham arose [the appearance of] old age was granted to him: *And Abraham was old, well stricken in age* (Genesis 24:1). Isaac demanded suffering, pleading thus: "Sovereign of the Universe! When a man dies without previous suffering, Judgment threatens him; but if Thou didst cause him to suffer, Judgment would not threaten him." Said God to him: "By thy life! thou has asked well, and it will commence with thee." Thus suffering is not mentioned from the beginning of the Book until here, but when Isaac arose, suffering was granted to him: *And it came to pass, that when Isaac was old, and his eyes were dim* (Genesis 27:1). Jacob demanded illness, saying to Him "Sovereign of the Universe! A man dies without previous illness and does not settle his affairs with his children; but if he were two or three days ill, he would settle his affairs with his children." "By thy life," replied God, "thou has asked well, and it will commence with thee": *and one said to Joseph: Behold, thy father is sick* (Genesis 48:1). R. Levi said: Thus Abraham introduced old age, Isaac suffering, and Jacob illness. Hezekiah brought in a new thing— repeated sickness. "Sovereign of the Universe," he pleaded. "Thou has kept man in good health until the day of his death! But if a man fell sick and recovered, fell sick and recovered, he would fully repent." Said God to him: "By thy life! thou hast asked well, and with thee it will commence." Thus it is written *The writing of Hezekiah king of Judah, when he had been sick, and was recovered of his sickness* (Isaiah 38:9). R. Samuel b. Nahman observed: This intimates that between one sickness and another he had an illness more severe than both.[15]

24. Reviewing Life

ZOHAR

> *According to the mystical system outlined by the Zohar, our*
> *beings have three sorts of life or souls and each plays a part*
> *in our life, in our response to illness, and in our way of dying.*

Rabbi Hezekiah began by quoting "And it came to pass that when the sun was going down, a deep sleep fell upon Abram, and a dread, a great darkness fell upon him" (Genesis 15:12). This verse has already been explained. This day indeed is the day of strict Judgment when they take man away from this world. For it has been taught: That moment when the day arrives for man to leave this world is the time of the great Judgment-day, when the sun is hidden from the moon, as it is written "before the sun is darkened" (Ecclesiastes 12:2). This is the holy soul *(neshamah)* that is withheld from man thirty days before he leaves the world, and it is the image that disappears from him and is not to be seen. Why does it disappear from him? Because the holy *neshamah* ascends and passes from him and is not to be seen. For do not say that when man has died and is powerless the *neshamah* passes from him. But while he is still alive and has strength the *neshamah* passes from him, and it no longer illumines the *ruah,* and the *ruah* no longer illumines the *nefesh,* and then the image passes from him and no longer sheds light upon him. From that moment on they all proclaim [his dying day], even the birds of heaven. Why is this? Because the *neshamah* will already have ascended from him, and the *ruah* no longer illumines the *nefesh,* and the *nefesh* is weakened, and eating and all the bodily desires will have departed from him and passed away.

Rabbi Judah said: Even when a man is confined to his sickbed and cannot pray, the *neshamah* passes from him and ascends, and the *ruah* does not then illumine the *nefesh* until judgment has been passed on the man. If the judgment is favorable the *neshamah* returns to its place and sheds light on all. This is when judgment is still in the balance. But when it is no longer in the balance, then thirty days [before death] the *neshamah* leaves first of all, and the image passes away from him.

It has been taught: When they judge a man in the world above they bring the *neshamah* up before the court and judge according to its evidence, and it testifies about everything. It testifies about all the man's thoughts, but it does not testify about his deeds, because these are all written in a book. And man is judged on the basis of them all. When they judge a man in the world above he has far more physical suffering than at other times. If they judge him favorably, then he recovers and sweat breaks out all over his body, and the *neshamah* returns to its place and illumines everything. A man never rises from his sickbed until they have judged him in the world above.

You might object and say that there are many guilty and wicked men in the world who survive. Yes, but the Holy One, blessed be He, examines every man's case. And if He sees that, even though he has no merit now, he will have merit in the future, He judges him favorably. Or sometimes it happens that he is destined to have a righteous son, and decisions of the Holy One, blessed be He, are for the good, and He sees everything, as it is written "As I live, says the Lord [God], I have no pleasure in the death of the wicked but that the wicked turn from his way [and live]" (Ezekiel 33:11). Consequently, all the guilty men in the world who survive are being judged favorably by the Holy One, blessed be He.

Sometimes the time allotted to these illnesses is fulfilled, as it is written "Evil and faithful illnesses" (Deuteronomy 28:59). They do [their work] with fidelity, for after they have descended upon a man they leave him once they have fulfilled their allotted time, whether he is righteous or wicked, and everything is done justly, as we have said.[16]

25. *Illness and Guilt*

SHOLOM ALEICHEM

Sholom Aleichem's short story, "At the Doctor's", is a monologue of a patient with persistent stomach pain. It presents a study in bio-psycho-social pathology. Here pain is an expression of frustration, anger, and disconnectedness, which in turn have resulted from envy, greed, and exploitation. The man's very soul is sick; his personality has become an expression of his illness. Though the physician is a good listener, he is powerless to help.

Just do me a favor, doctor. Listen to me until I finish. I don't mean listen to my heart or anything like that. About my sickness, we'll talk later. In fact, I myself will tell you what's wrong with me. I just want you to listen to what I have to say, for not every doctor likes to listen to his patients. Not every doctor lets his patients talk. That's a bad habit of theirs—they don't let their patients open their mouths. All they know is how to write prescriptions, look at their watches and take your pulse, your temperature, and your money. But I've been told you're not that sort of doctor. They say you're still young and you're not yet as passionate for the ruble as the rest of them. That's why I came to consult you about my stomach and get your advice. Look at me now and you're looking at a man with a stomach. But when? On condition that the stomach is a stomach. But when your stomach just isn't a stomach, your life's not worth a damn. I know what you'll say next: man must keep living! But I don't need your help for that. That got me the taste of the strap when I was a boy in Hebrew school.

My point is that so long as a man lives, he doesn't want to die. To tell you the truth, I'm not afraid of death at all. First of all, I'm over sixty. And second of all, I'm the sort of fellow to whom life and death are the same. That is, sure, living is better than dying, for who wants to die? Especially a Jew? Especially a father of eleven children, may they live and be well, and a wife—despite the fact that she's my third—but a wife for all that. To make a long story short, I come from Kamenitz, that is, not really from Kamenitz proper, but from a little place not far from Kamenitz. I'm a miller—unfortunately—I own a mill. That is, the mill owns me, for you know what they say. Once you're dragged into it, you're finished. You've got no choice. It's a vicious circle and it just keeps on going. Figure it out for yourself. To buy wheat, I have to put up cash. To sell the flour, I have to give credit. I get a note here, a note there and I have to deal with low-down characters and women. Do you like women, doctor? Go give them an account of things! Why this, why that? Why didn't their Sabbath loaf come out well? Well, what fault is it of mine? Not enough heat in your stove, I say. Rotten yeast, perhaps. Wet wood. So what do they do? They step all over you, make mud of you, and swear that the next time their loaves are going to come flying straight at your head. Do you like having breads aimed at your skull? Those are the retail customers for you. But you think the wholesale buyers are any better? Not on your life!

When a wholesale customer first comes into the mill and wants me to give him credit, he flatters and compliments and sweet-talks me to beat the band. He's so butter-soft you can apply him to a third-degree burn. But when it comes to paying, he rattles off a list of complaints. The shipment came late, the flour-sacks were torn, the flour was bitter, moldy, and stale, and a dozen other phony excuses.

But money?

"Money?" he says. "Send me a bill."

In other words, it's as good as half-paid. Send him a bill and he'll say—tomorrow. . . . Send one the next day and he'll say—the day after tomorrow. There's no end to it. The next thing you do is threaten him with a lawsuit and finally you take him to court. You think that settles it? The court gives you a lien on his house. So what? When you get there, the whole place, lock, stock, and barrel is in his wife's name anyway. What can you do? Call him a crook? Well, let me ask you, how can you not have stomach trouble with a business like this? It's not for nothing that my wife says to me: "Give up the mill, Noah, give it up." She's not my first wife, you know, but my third. And a third wife, they say, is like the December sun. But you can't do away with her, she's still your wife. "Give it up," she says, "let it and the wheat business burn to a crisp and then I'll know you're alive and around."

"Ha," I say, "if it only *would* burn. It's insured for plenty."

"I don't mean it that way," she says. "I mean you're always running here and there. For you there's no Sabbath, no holiday, no wife, no children. Why? Why all the tumult?"

For the life of me, doctor, I myself don't know what I'm dashing around for. But what can I do? That's my nature, the deuce take it. I like to panic and rush. What do I get out of it? Headaches, that's all. But I'll take on any business deal you offer. For me there's no bad deal. Bags, wood, auctions. Anything.

You think the mill is my only business? You're mistaken if you do. For you're looking at a man who's a partner in a timber firm, supplies food for the local jail, and has a share in the meat-tax concession—on which I lose money every year. Doctor, I wish you'd make in a month what I lose in a year. Then you'd say I was a friend of yours. So, why bother with it? To spite them all. Me? I'm a man who likes to win out. I don't care if I ruin the whole town and myself included so long as I win out in the end. I'm not such a bad guy at heart, but I have my little whims. I'm a hot-head. When you step on my honor, I'm dangerous. To top it off, I'm a stubborn mule, as well. In the old days, I took my little synagogue to court just for an "Amen" that didn't please me. I was ready to give my all just to see them lose out. And they did. I can't help it. That's the way I am. The doctors tell me it's nerves and it's got to do, they say, with the stomach. Despite the fact that it makes no sense, logically. What connection is there between nerves and the stomach? Strange bedfellows! After all, where are the nerves and where is the stomach? Doesn't medical science say that the nerves are mostly in the brain? And the stomach ... the devil knows how far away it is! Wait a minute, doc ... hear me out ... I'll be through in a minute. I want to tell you the whole story so that you'll be able to tell me why this plague had to come upon me, my stomach, I mean.

Maybe it's because I'm always scurrying about and am never at home. Even when I am at home, I'm not at home. It's a joke and I'm ashamed to say it—but I swear I don't even know how many children I have and what their names are. A home's no good without a master and without a father. You ought to take a look at my house—knock wood and see what a mess it's in. It's like a boat without a rudder. The place is in an uproar and a tumult day and night. It's frightening! Eleven kids from three wives, may no harm come to them, is nothing to sneeze at! While one has tea, another has a snack. When I'm saying my morning prayers, the other one decides to go to sleep. That one filches a potato, the next one wants some herring. This one wants a dairy meal, that one yells his lungs out for meat! After you're washed and sitting at the table ready to say the blessing over the bread—well, there's no knife in sight to cut the bread with. And in the midst of it the little ones are making a racket, fighting with each other, raising all hell—it's enough to make you run away. Why does all this happen? Because I'm never at home and never have any time for them, and my old lady, God bless her, is too good. Well, that is to say, she's not good. She's more of a softie. She can't handle the children. You have to know how to handle them. So they step all over her. She curses, pinches, rips chunks of flesh out of them, but what good is it? She's a mother, after all. A mother's no father, you know. A father grabs hold of a kid and beats hell out of him. That's what my father did to me. Perhaps your father did the same to you doctor? What do you say? Well, good for you! I don't know ... maybe you would have been better off without the beatings. What are you squirming about for? I'm going to finish in a moment.

I'm not just barking at the moon, doctor. I want you to know what sort of life I lead. You think I know how much I'm worth? Possibly I'm rich, quite rich. Then again, chances are that—just between you and me—I don't have much at all. I don't know! All day long it's repairs. Like they say: one window pane goes, another comes in its place. You can't help it. Another thing—whether you can afford it or not, you got to give your child a dowry. Especially if God has been kind and you've got grown daughters. All right, doctor, you just try and have three grown daughters—God bless them—and marry them off all in one day and then we'll see if you'll be able to sit home and relax even for a day. Now you know the reason for all my running around from pillar to post. And when you rush about like that you catch cold in the rain, or gulp down a quick meal in a flea-bitten inn which gives you heartburn and indigestion. And what about all the odors and stale air in the car—isn't that enough to give you a stomach? My only bit of luck is that nature has protected me and I'm not the sickly sort. I've been immune to sickness since I was a boy. Don't mind me being a scarecrow, all skin and bones. That's what my business did for me. Height like mine runs in the family, by the way. We're all tall and thin. I had a few brothers and they were all like me, may they rest in peace. Nevertheless, I was always healthy, never had any stomach trouble, had nothing to do with doctors or illwinds—may it continue that way! But recently they started stuffing medicines and pills and herbs down my throat. Each one comes with a different remedy. This one says: diet, starve yourself. That one says: don't eat at all. You think that's the end of it? Another quack comes along and tells me to eat, but really pack it in. It looks like doctors prescribe what they themselves enjoy doing. I'm surprised they haven't told me to start swallowing rubles yet. They can drive you crazy. One doctor told me to walk a lot. Just get on my feet and head for God-knows-where. Then the other doctor tells me to lie flat on my back and not budge a muscle. Now try and guess which one of them is the bigger ass! You want more proof? One of them kept me on a fifty-two week silver-chloride diet. Pure silver-chloride. When I went to a second doctor, that one told me: "Silver-chloride? God forbid! Silver-chloride will be the death of you." So he prescribed a yellow powder, you probably know which one I mean. Then I went to a third doctor and don't you think he took the yellow powder and ripped up the prescription and prescribed an herb? And some herb it was! You can take my word for it that before I got used to that grass I was spitting gall. I used to curse that doctor three times a day, once before each meal when I took the herb. I hope that only half of what I wished him comes true. While taking that herb I used to see the Angel of Death face to face. But what won't a man do for his health's sake? The upshot was that I came back to the first doctor, the one who gave me silver-chloride, and told him the story about the bitter herbs which made my life miserable. He was mad as hell and bawled me out as if I'd stepped on his hat.

"I prescribed silver-chloride," he said. "Silver-chloride! So why are you skipping around like an idiot from one doctor to another?"

"Shh! Tone it down," I said. "You're not alone here. I didn't sign any contracts with you. The next fellow has to make a living too. He's got a wife and family, same as you."

Well, you should have seen him! He blew his stack as if I'd told him God knows what! The long and the short of it was that he asked me to go back to the other doctor.

"I don't need your advice," I told him. "If I want to go, I'll go on my own."

Then I pulled out a ruble and put it on his desk. You think he threw it back at my face? Not at all. They like those little rubles. Boy do they like those rubles! More so than us plain folk. To sit down and examine a patient properly—that they'll never do. They don't let you say an extra word. Recently, I visited a colleague of yours. You know him, so I won't mention his name. I came into his office and before I could say boo he told me to—begging your pardon—strip and lie down on the sofa. Why? He wanted to examine me. Fine and dandy. Examine me! But why can't I say a word? What good does his finger-tapping and pinching do me? But no, he was in a rush. Had no time. He said that there were other people there, on the other side of the door, each waiting for his "next." You doctors have taken up the latest fashions. You have your "nexts" just like the ticket windows at the depot or the stamp lines at the post office. What's that you say? You don't have time either? Oho, now tell me that you too have "nexts" waiting out there! You're just a young doctor! Where do you come off having a waiting line? If you continue this way, you hear, you're going to have troubles, not a practice. And you don't have to get hot under the collar about it either. I didn't expect to come here without paying. I'm not the sort of person who'll ask you to do anything for him for nothing. And though you didn't want to hear me out—one thing has nothing to do with the other. I'll pay you for the visit. What's that? You don't want anything for it? Well, I'm not going to force you. You probably have your own source of income. Perhaps you clip bond coupons? Your kitty's swelling, eh? Well, in any case, may God be with you and may the kitty grow and grow. Goodbye! Pardon me if I've taken too much of your time. But that's what a doctor's for.[17]

26. Reaching Out for Healing

RACHEL COWAN

Psalm 41 is one of ten that are recommended for meditation when one is in need of healing (along with Psalms 16, 32, 42, 59, 77, 90, 105, 137, and 150). In this commentary, Rabbi Rachel Cowan suggests that the question "Why me?" is not so much a request for information, but an expression of hurt and despair.

1. **To the Chief Musician: A Song of David**
2. Happy is one who attends to the needy;
   On an evil day, Adonai will rescue her
3. Adonai will guard her, Adonai will give her life;
   She will be considered fortunate on this earth,
   not subject to the whims of enemies;
4. Adonai will nurture her on her sickbed;
   Even when her illness advances, and her rest is
   Disturbed.
5. As for me, I said,
   "Adonai, have pity;
   Heal my soul, for I have sinned against You."
6. My enemies speak evil against me:
   "When will she die and her name be obliterated?"
7. Even when my enemy comes to visit me,
   her concern is empty and false;
   her heart gathers malicious thoughts,
   which she then goes out and spreads.

As we struggle to come to terms with illness, we hear our own voices in this meditation on suffering. The soul-wrestling of the psalmist speaks powerfully to us. Overwhelmed by the rush of fear, anger, and grief, she wonders whether she will find the strength and courage to face her situation. Empathizing with her anguish, we nonetheless see that she has only begun the long journey to comprehend her situation and to transcend it. Right now, the faith she asserts so bravely at the end is hollow. She is alone. Many of us know that pain.

Lying in bed after the diagnosis, confused by the bewildering choices of treatments, weak and exhausted, she asks herself the inevitable question, "Why *me?*" She was one who always (v. 2) "attends to the needy," and, in general, she was (v. 3) "considered fortunate on this earth."

She is her own first target (v. 5) "Adonai, have pity/Heal my soul, for I have sinned against you!" She must deserve this illness, for why else would she be punished? Reviewing her life over these past few years, she finds so many flaws. She did not visit her father enough when he was ill, she screams at her children too often, she got the job her colleague had desperately wanted. She is often stressed, she is too fat, she eats the wrong foods, she doesn't exercise. Maybe she had wanted this. Her psyche colluded with her biology to transform some cell, or to fail to fight some cell, and now she is ill. Somehow, she feels, she deserves this.

There is even some comfort in blaming herself, for it helps her feel she has some control over the situation —the power to change her behavior. If, however, she can be gentle with herself, she may find in illness an opportunity for *t'shuvah,* for turning her life in a direction that is more clearly aligned with her true values.

Illness does not cause her faith to break. She has not yet begun, though, to reshape it in face of her experience. She has not wrestled with God. Rather, she casts God as avenger, not as healer. She prays that God will become an ally to destroy her enemies, who, alas, include her friends. "Punish them, and I will know You are just, that there is fairness in the world." *They* should be suffering, not her—they who speak falsely when they visit, who gossip afterward, who predict a poor prognosis. Even her best friend has been disloyal. Nobody really understands her, nobody really cares. She is alone, weak, hurting. They are well. They live in a different place from the one to which she has been unwillingly transported. They live in the land of the well. She in the land of the sick.

She is in a place many of us can recognize. But it is not a place we can afford to stay for long, once we have vented our anger, plumbed the depths of betrayal and isolation. For she has cut herself off from her most important source of strength—her community—and she is seeking from God a false solace.

To begin to find healing, she will need to reach out to others, and to let others reach out to her. Starting with one or two friends, she can begin to let people see her when she is ill and wan and not at her best. They can help her reestablish a relationship with her best friend. Perhaps for now she is not strong enough for honest discussion, but if she asks for help—a phone call, a meal, a visit—the two of them could realize their importance to each other.

Through connections with family and friends, she can begin to emerge from her depression. She can begin to reaffirm her own worthiness. She knows she has been well thought of, and that she has a gift for empathy. Now, knowing pain and despair, she will be able to reach out with empathy to others.[18]

27. The Empowering Force

MORDECAI M. KAPLAN

Mordecai Kaplan, founder of Reconstructionist Judaism, offers a somewhat radical answer to the perpetual question of why the righteous suffer.

Could you simplify the answer you gave to the question, "How would you answer the question of a child who asked, 'Why did God make polio?'" After reading your answer, I still don't know how to answer the child.

Children often ask questions which philosophers have asked from time immemorial, and to which they give answers in accordance with their general outlook on life. With every change in the intellectual climate, the answers change, but the questions remain. In my answer to the question, I did not so much endeavor to reply directly to the child, as to point out the need for more earnest intellectual consideration of the problem which is too often evaded.

Nevertheless, since it must be a painful and shocking experience to a child to be told that the God whom he is expected to love and worship is responsible for his tragic affliction, I shall endeavor to answer the question in a way that might mitigate the evil effects of his suffering on his faith in God's goodness and help. Such an answer would be the following:

God did *not* make polio. God is always helping us humans to make this a better world, but the world cannot at once become the kind of world He would like it to be. When men make use of the intelligence God gave them, they learn more and more of the laws of health, by which all kinds of illness can be prevented or cured. When the doctor relieves your pain, when he helps you to get back more strength and better control over your muscles, it is with the intelligence that God gives him. When you use braces and other devices that help you get around and do some of the things you want to do, their manufacture is due to the intelligence and the concern for your welfare, that God puts into the minds of those who make these devices. Do not feel that God does not care for you. He is helping you now in many ways, and He will continue to help you. Maybe some day you will be restored by His help to perfect health. But if that does not happen, it is not because God does not love you. If He does not grant you all that you pray for, He will find other ways of enabling you to enjoy life. Be thankful to God for all the love and care that people show toward you, since all of that is part of God's love, and do not hesitate to ask God for further help. If the people around you are intelligent and loving, that help will come to you.[19]

28. God Is in Caring

HAROLD S. KUSHNER

Rabbi Harold Kushner's best-seller, When Bad Things Happen to Good People, *reaffirms his faith after it was tested by the prolonged illness and death of his son Aaron.*

I believe in God. But I do not believe the same things about Him that I did years ago, when I was growing up or when I was a theological student. I recognize His limitations. He is limited in what he can do by laws of nature and by the evolution of human nature and human moral freedom. I no longer hold God responsible for illnesses, accidents, and natural disasters because I realize that I gain little and I lose so much when I blame God for those things. I can worship a God who hates suffering but cannot eliminate it, more easily than I can worship a God who chooses to make children suffer and die, for whatever exalted reason. . . .

God does not cause our misfortunes. Some are caused by bad luck, some are caused by bad people, and some are simply an inevitable consequence of our being human and being mortal, living in a world of inflexible natural laws. The painful things that happen to us are not punishments for our misbehavior, nor are they in any way part of some grand design on God's part. Because the tragedy is not God's will, we need not feel hurt or betrayed by God when tragedy strikes. We can turn to Him for help in overcoming it, precisely because we can tell ourselves that God is as outraged as we are. . . .

Bad things that happen to us in our lives do not have a meaning when they happen to us. They do not happen for any good reason which would cause us to accept them willingly. But we can give them a meaning. We can redeem these tragedies from senselessness by imposing meaning on them. The question we should be asking is not, "Why did this happen to me? What did I do to deserve this?" That is really an unanswerable, pointless question. A better question would be "Now that this has happened to me what am I going to do about it? . . ."

We, by our responses, give either a positive or a negative meaning. Illnesses, accidents, human tragedies kill people. But they do not necessarily kill life or faith. If the death and suffering of someone we love makes us bitter, jealous, against all religion, and incapable of happiness, we turn the person who died into one of the "devil's martyrs." If suffering and death in someone close to us bring us to explore the limits of our capacity for strength and love and cheerfulness, if it leads us to discover sources of consolation we never knew before, then we make the person into a witness for the affirmation of life rather than its rejection. . . .

How does God make a difference in our lives if He neither kills nor cures? God inspires people to help other people who have been hurt by life, and by helping them, they protect them from the danger of feeling alone, abandoned, or judged. God makes some people want to become doctors and nurses, to spend days and nights of self-sacrificing concern with an intensity for which no money can compensate, in the effort to sustain life and alleviate pain. God moves people to want to be medical researchers, to focus their intelligence and energy on the causes and possible cures for some of life's tragedies. . . .

We were sustained in Aaron's illness by people who made a point of show-ing that they cared and understood: the man who made Aaron a scaled-down tennis racquet suitable to his size, and the woman who gave him a small hand-made violin that was a family heirloom; the friend who got him a baseball au-tographed by the Red Sox, and the children who overlooked his appearance and physical limitations to play stickball with him in the backyard, and who wouldn't let him get away with anything special. People like that were "God's language," His way of telling our family that we were not alone, not cast off.

In the same way, I firmly believe that Aaron served God's purpose, not by being sick or strange-looking (there was no reason why God should have wanted that), but by facing up so bravely to his illness and to the problems caused by his appearance. I know that his friends and schoolmates were affected by his courage and by the way he managed to live a full life despite his limitations. And I know that people who knew our family were moved to handle the difficult times of their own lives with more hope and courage when they saw our example. I take these as instances of God moving people here on earth to help other people in need.

When a person is dying of cancer, I do not hold God responsible for the cancer or for the pain he feels. They have other causes. But I have seen God give such people the strength to take each day as it comes, to be grateful for a day full of sunshine or one in which they are relatively free of pain.[20]

29. To Meet the Test

ESTHER GOSHEN-GOTTSTEIN

We might imagine that the most pious and observant among us are immune from the agonized, and often frustrating and fruitless, search for meaning in which most of us engage. We would be in error. This search is engaged in by all, and the questions asked along the way are universal. Esther Goshen-Gottstein's husband, Moshe, suffered sudden catastrophic brain damage during what should have been routine surgery.

"Out of the depths have I cried unto thee, oh Lord." The words of the psalmist turning to God for help are still relevant in any seemingly hopeless situation. Even the physicians had spoken of the need for God's intervention in order to restore Moshe to us.

Alon, throughout these difficult weeks, implored me to believe in the Almighty, who could be trusted to return Moshe to us in good health. If only one could will one's faith!

I was determined not to bargain with God; there was going to be no "If Thou wilt give Moshe back to me safe and sound I will . . ." Such a bargain reminded me of Jeptha, who promised to sacrifice the first living creature he encountered on his way home if God enabled him to win a battle. The creature turned out to be his own daughter, who welcomed him on his return! Such bargains are too risky; one can never tell in advance where they will lead.

Traditional Jews recite psalms whenever anyone's life is in danger. Many of Moshe's friends and relatives all over the world read psalms daily on his behalf once the news was out that he had not awakened from his operation.

There is also a special blessing, a *Mee She'berach,* uttered in synagogue on behalf of a critically ill person. The patient is identified by name as the son of his mother rather than the son of his father. (This is because theoretically, paternity is always doubtful.) I received dozens of phone calls from friends requesting the name of Moshe's mother. All of them wanted to make a *Mee She'berach* for Moshe ben Devora.

I frequently heard the comment: "Moshe *must* recover—so many people are praying for him." It was as if the more people implored God on his behalf, the more likely God was to answer their prayers.

When matters get really desperate, observant Jews sometimes use a special method to counteract the death sentence that is presumed to have been passed on the ill person by God's Court of Law. This method involves changing the person's name. By receiving a new name, he or she becomes a new person, one who has not been sentenced to die. Changing the patient's name also changes the divine decree from illness to health. A name such as Chaim ("life") or Raphael ("let God cure") or Hezekiah (a king of Judah who recovered from serious illness) is usually chosen.

About two weeks after Moshe's surgery, Jonathan called upon roughly thirty relatives, friends, and colleagues to meet at the Western Wall—for Jews the holiest place in the world since the destruction of the Temple. They recited psalms in unison; then Jonathan announced that Moshe's name had been changed to Hezekiah—Chizkiyahu in Hebrew. Many people sighed in relief once the renaming ceremony had taken place. For them it was if Moshe had been born again as Chizkiyahu.

In times of uncertainty one clutches at straws. Where science throws up its hands in ignorance and omnipotence, the mystical takes over. It was reported to me that an employee of the Hebrew University had consulted a kabbalist (mystic) about Moshe's condition. The kabbalist was said to be able to discover the future through studying certain texts. He predicted that if Moshe survived week two, with all its medical emergencies, he would recover. I eagerly lapped up this prophecy.

Why did this terrible catastrophe befall Moshe? The question haunted me day and night. Of course I knew rationally that any number of complications could result from major surgery. But how many patients (if you exclude those who have brain surgery) remain in a deep coma? Certainly only a tiny fraction. Why did Moshe have to be among these exceptional few? I knew that this question is asked by everyone afflicted by life-threatening calamities: "Why my child; why my marriage partner; why me?"

There are no ready answers. But in times of deep crisis, those who believe in God have a definite advantage. It seemed to me that Alon perceived this dreadful disaster as a trial by God. Here was a neat reversal: an awful tribulation turned into the privilege of the chosen few. But surely this way of understanding what had befallen Moshe raised more questions than it answered. Why was Moshe considered especially worthy of God's love and therefore in need of being tested by Him? And was it really Moshe, the unconscious patient, undergoing the ordeal, or was it those nearest to him, who were fully aware of what was happening? Suppose we were the objects of God's trial. Why then were we being tested in this way? What was our special merit or fault that we deserved such exceptional treatment? To me it smacked of hubris to imagine that God had singled out Moshe and our family for such terrible and extraordinary trials.

If God was to be implicated at all it looked to me as if He were laughing at all of us by reversing everything. We were faced with the irony that a man who was all mind had been transformed into a man who was seemingly mindless. Was God demonstrating to us that there is no certainty in this life? Suddenly, in less than no time, anything can happen: presence can turn into absence.

But it seemed even more plausible to me that, if there is a God, He has nothing to do with the fate of individual people. In other words, I saw no meaning in Moshe's appalling condition. It had merely occurred, without any reason or purpose.

However, I feel that this was my greatest test. Irrespective of a divinity, I had to prove myself to myself in the face of terrible adversity. I was both the agent and the judge of my own behavior. I set myself certain aims which I tried to fulfill. I had to remain strong to be a support and model for my children. I had to keep coping with life, even when the temptation was to surrender entirely to pain and grief.[21]

30. Act of Sacrifice

LESLIE WHAT

The mother of an infant about to undergo brit milah *recounts the story of her own recent mastectomy. Witnessing the brit milah affirms her faith that acts of sacrifice, even when not the direct commandments of God, can elevate the human spirit and bring us closer to the Divine.*

It is your eighth day of life and the day of your *brit milah,* the covenant between every Jewish boy and his Creator. I lean against the wall like a broken fixture, propped up on either side by my best friends, Miriam and Judith.

Your father holds you in a football grip and gazes into your sleepy eyes. If I look at you I'll cry. Instead I look at Judith, who squeezes my hand.

On the dining-room table are two unlit candles, a prayer book, a silver goblet. A small steel tray holds surgical instruments, covered under a sterile drape.

There was no equivalent tradition for your sister Leah. Now it has become fashionable to hold naming ceremonies for girls, but we didn't think of it ten years ago, and I'm sorry. Leah, across the room, seems hurt; she's jealous of the gifts and attention you're receiving. You fuss, perhaps because the men are conversing so close to you. I ache at the sound of your voice, and bring my arms up to hug across my chest.

I remember those first few weeks after Leah's birth when I was a reservoir for the waters of life. Leah squalled and my body rained milk. Leah squalled and I gave myself to her until her suckling brought physical release for us both. I can't give you that, my son, because of the mastectomy. I do have feeling in my chest: of fullness, of tension, of something pent up inside. Perhaps a kind of essence of mother's milk flows through my veins, if not my breasts. Perhaps it is nothing of the sort, only the phantom pain of an amputee who seeks to give a greater meaning to her suffering.

"What name have you given this child?" the mohel asks formally.

"Israel," your father answers—meaning, 'he who struggles with God.'

"That should be your name," my friend Miriam whispers and I smile. She and Judith, like me, are also in their late 30s. Judith has recently started to darken her hair, while Miriam thinks the gray has given her status that she lacked before. I've avoided looking in the mirror since my surgery, and have forgotten whether my hair has grayed or not.

Judith married young and has three daughters. Miriam waited long after graduate school and now wants desperately to have a child, but she hasn't been able to conceive. She looks to me, as if to reassure herself that I am strong enough to go through with this.

Watching Miriam, I see how we women feel tension in our upper bodies. We hug and press our shoulders to each other, we heave our chests, we sigh. Miriam moves away and hunches over her torso, diminishing the size of her breasts. Though she knows that one has nothing to do with the other, Miriam has said to me that she would sacrifice this part of herself if that would help her become a mother.

The men, even your father, hold themselves much lower while they contemplate the inevitable. They stand with their arms at their sides, hands brushing thighs as if poised to cup their groins the moment the first cut is made.

"Circumcision is an irrational act," the mohel tells us, "performed because the Holy One has asked it of us."

My husband nods in agreement, but he is trembling and I know his mind is elsewhere. As for me, I am not sure that I agree circumcision is irrational. Perhaps it is, but no more so than the fact that I had both breasts removed when only one was infected with a marble-sized clump of cells. I allowed it because I was deemed a "high risk," since my mother and a maternal aunt died young of breast cancer. There was no guarantee that a mastectomy would cure me, yet I listened to my doctor, a mere man whose only leap of faith may have been on his eighth day when he was circumcised.

"This new life is a miracle," the mohel says, and I agree with him.

If you were planned, dear son, it was not by me. I expected to die after the surgery. The radiation and chemotherapy treatments stunted my will along with my cancer. But then I became pregnant, and once again I found strength to go on. I can't explain where that strength came from—God? love? a universal consciousness? Whatever name you call this thing that exists beyond the physical self.

"Barbaric, isn't it?" Judith, the mother of three girls, whispers, interrupting my thoughts.

"Why do you say that?" I argue, though I have often voiced Judith's line myself.

"What gives us the right?" she adds, and I hear her words as if they were an accusation, as if this ceremony were all my idea.

But you must know, little son, that *brit milah* is not a choice *we* made for you. That decision was made long ago. You will bear a scar to show the promise made to God in your name. You will be bound by this covenant to follow God's law.

Maimonides said that circumcision was prescribed to weaken man's sex drive: Nachmanides said the covenant was a reminder—not for us—but for God, to remember us. I'm only your mother, but I say this: You will give a small piece of yourself back to God and that gift will help us all remember there is more in life than one individual's desire. There are leaps of faith.

"Abraham received the first covenant of circumcision at age 99," says the mohel. "God rewarded Abraham for his great faith, promising that Sarah would conceive their child."

When God commanded Abraham to sacrifice his son Isaac, how is it that his faith never faltered? Didn't he wonder why God was making him go through such pain? I try to have faith, but I can't stop worrying. I'm terrified, lamb, not knowing how badly my chemotherapy has harmed you.

"Baruch atah . . . ," the mohel says. He lights the candles, then dips a cotton ball into the wine and touches it to your lips.

You begin to suck lazily. It is customary to give the baby boy wine, in the hope of sweetening at least some of the pain. There is so much truth in this I tremble. I know so well how we can swallow bitterness when the promise of sweetness is offered at the same time.

"We are ready to begin." The mohel watches your father, who coughs.

I have seen this before and I know, without looking, what happens next. Soon you scream.

Moments later, the mohel wraps you tightly in a blanket, then hands you to your father, who brings you to me to calm. I hurry from the room, passing Leah, who smiles anxiously. You have suffered so much that even your own sister now has sympathy for you.

I cradle you as I carry you to the bedroom. I sit upon the bed, cooing to you, nursing you with formula until your eyelids flutter and you intermittently suckle in sleep. I must nurse you with this bottle, for I too have given something to God.

After a while, I will allow myself tears, but now I sit holding you, stroking the incredibly soft and wrinkled skin at the base of your head. You are so warm, so alive, so precious that I feel tremendous joy and release in being near you.

I drape a clean diaper on my shoulder, and hold you so your chin rests on that shoulder, so your tummy presses against my chest. I stroke your back with my fingertips, and gently kiss the side of your head.

"It's all over now," I tell you. I want so much for that to be true. I close my eyes and speak in a whisper. "Dear God," I pray, wishing I had some concrete assurance that I was being heard.

"Please, God," I say. "Please. Let this little piece you've taken today be all that you ever ask this child to give."[22]

31. That I May Do Great Things

ANONYMOUS

Asking for specific things from God opens up the possibility that God may answer, "No." This prayer shows us that what we want for ourselves may differ from what God wants for us.

I asked God for health that I might do great things,
I was given infirmity that I might do better things.
I asked for strength that I might lead,
I was given weakness that I might learn humbly to obey.
I asked for riches that I might be happy,
I was given poverty that I might be wise.
I asked for power that I might have the praise of people,
I was given weakness that I might feel the need of God.
I asked for all things that I might enjoy life,
I was given life that I might enjoy all things.
I got nothing that I asked for, but everything that I hoped for.

Almost despite myself, my unspoken prayers were answered.
I am among all people most richly blessed.[23]

32. The Meaning of Transcendence

ERIC J. CASSELL

Transcendence, writes Dr. Cassell, involves the ability to change perspective and direction after suffering a loss. Cassell has written extensively about the physician-patient relationship and the psycho-social ramifications of illness.

Persons are able to enlarge themselves in response to damage, so that rather than being reduced by injury, they may indeed grow. This response to suffering has led to the belief that suffering is good for people. We would not have such a belief, however, were it not equally common knowledge that persons can also be destroyed by suffering. If the leg is injured so that the athlete can never run again, the athlete may compensate by learning another sport, or skill, or mode of expression. And so it is with the loss of relationships, loves, roles, physical strength, dreams, and power. The human body may not have the capacity to grow another part when one is lost, but the person has.

The ability to recover from loss without succumbing to suffering is sometimes called resiliency, as though merely elastic rebound is involved. But it seems more as if an inner force is withdrawn from one manifestation of person and redirected to another. If a child dies and the parent makes a successful recovery, the person is said to have "rebuilt" his or her life. The verb suggests, correctly, I think, that the parts of the person are assembled in a new manner allowing renewed expression in different dimensions. If a previously active person is confined to a wheelchair, intellectual or artistic pursuits may occupy more time and energy. Total involvement in some political or social goal may use the energy previously given to physical activity. We see an aged scholar, for whom all activity is restricted by disease and infirmity, continue to pursue the goals of a lifetime of study and we marvel at the strength of "the life of the mind."

Recovery from suffering often involves borrowing the strength of others as though persons who have lost parts of themselves can be sustained by the personhood of others until their own recovers. This is one of the latent functions of physicians: lending strength. A group, too, may lend strength: Consider the success of groups of the similarly afflicted in easing the burden of illness (e.g., women who have had a mastectomy, people with ostomies, fellow sufferers from a rare sickness, or even the parents or family members of the diseased).

Meaning and transcendence offer two additional ways by which the destruction of a part of personhood or threat to its integrity are meliorated. The search for the meaning of human suffering has occupied humanity on an individual and cultural level throughout history. Assigning meaning to the injurious condition often reduces or even resolves the suffering associated with it. Most often a cause for the injury is sought within past behaviors or beliefs. Thus, the pain or threat that causes suffering is seen as not destroying a part of the person because *it is* part of the person by virtue of its origin within the self. The concept of Karma, in Eastern theologies, is a complex form of that defense against suffering, because suffering is seen to result from behaviors of the individual in previous incarnations. In our culture, taking the blame for harm that comes to oneself because of the unconscious mind reduces suffering by locating it within a coherent set of meanings. Physicians are familiar with the question: "did I do something to make this happen?" A striking example of this mechanism is when a woman takes the blame for rape, as though she had done something to invite it. It is more tolerable for a terrible thing to happen because of something one has done—and even suffer the guilt—than that it be simply a stroke of fate; a random, chance event. Like Job's friends warding off the possibility of an unjust God, others around the victim often encourage self-blame.

Transcendence is probably the most powerful way in which one is restored to wholeness after an injury to personhood. When experienced, transcendence locates the person in a far larger landscape. The sufferer is not isolated by pain but is brought closer to a personal source of meaning and to the human community that shares that meaning. Such an experience need not involve religion in any formal sense; however, in its transpersonal dimension is deeply spiritual.

In Judaism, as in virtually all theologies, the issue of suffering is central. The book of Job presents the perplexing puzzle of humankind; not only do the righteous suffer, but the best may suffer the worst fate. Other biblical passages suggest that personal suffering offers a means for self-transcendence and a concern for the suffering of others. Acting virtuously necessarily entails suffering. As Rabbi Jack Bemporad has said, "In standing for justice and righteousness the righteous and the Godly suffer, as did God's obedient servants, the prophets. . . . This is the dilemma of the prophet—obedience brings suffering instead of joy." But transcendence brings relief to the pain and deprivation—to the suffering itself—by giving it a meaning larger than the person.[24]

From Where Will My
Help Come?

*My soul peered through the lattices
within the void-and-emptiness
of my illness.
From its captivity, it called
to Was-Is-Will Be.
In the dark, it whispered:
In Your hands, I place
my spirit, my pain
my honor, my life, my death.*

Zelda[1]

Introduction

*H*ow does a conversation with God, in general, proceed? In Judaism, a conversational rhythm is established, through ritual, for the entire day, every day. A person addresses God through prayer, thanking God for the specific functions of the body each morning and for food and other blessings during prayer and at meals. How can we hear God's response? There are two main avenues: (1) through our experiences and (2) through studying Jewish holy texts each day.

When we, or people we care about, need healing, Judaism provides these conventional avenues of prayer as well as other prayers and practices that are "vessels," which may contain the deepest wishes of our hearts. These "vessels" include the practice of giving charity in honor of a loved one's recovery. Praying, and especially the recitation of psalms, is believed to aid in healing. Indeed, one book, the Tikkun *of Rebbe Nachman, is devoted to outlining the ways in which ten psalms in particular (16, 32, 41, 42, 59, 77, 90, 105, 137, and 150) can aid in healing. Rebbe Nachman also recommends reciting the names of one's teachers and experiencing, as one does so, all the enlightenment they imparted as a path toward healing.*

Prayers, in a form popularly known as a mi shebeirakh *(the first word of that prayer meaning "may the One who is blessed"), can also be offered in the synagogue on behalf of those who are sick. One might also check the* mezuzzot *on one's home and examine the scrolls inside them to ascertain their condition. According to Jewish belief, if the text inside the* mezuzzah *is damaged or written incorrectly, the occupants of the domicile are more vulnerable to illness and tragedy than if the* mezuzzot *are whole and well-written. Likewise, in the not so distant past, amulets and potions were used to heal illness and provide comfort.*

A conversation begun by saying "Please!" is generally concluded with an expression of thanks. Prayer, charity, and study are all potent ways of giving thanks to God. Another way to thank God for health is to appreciate every moment rather than taking life for granted. We occupy our bodies for a truly short time on this earth. Appreciating what we have while we have it may be one of the best tools we possess for enhancing our own health and our relationship with our Creator.

33. Oh God, Pray Heal Her

BIBLE

How do we ask for help? In the following passage, one of the most important healing stories in Judaism, we learn that we need pray only with fervor and few words. When the intent is so clear, even as few as five words can transmit the essence of prayer clearly.

The prayer at the end of this story becomes the basis for many healing prayers and mystical practices in Judaism. It is simple enough that it can be learned, and used, by almost anyone.

When they were in Hazeroth, Miriam and Aaron spoke against Moses because of the Cushite woman he had married: "He married a Cushite woman!"

They said, "Has the LORD spoken only through Moses? Has He not spoken through us as well?" The LORD heard it. Now Moses was a very humble man, more so than any other man on earth. Suddenly the LORD called to Moses, Aaron, and Miriam, "Come out, you three, to the Tent of Meeting." So the three of them went out. The LORD came down in a pillar of cloud, stopped at the entrance of the Tent, and called out, "Aaron and Miriam!" The two of them came forward; and He said, "Hear these My words: When a prophet of the LORD arises among you, I make Myself known to him in a vision, I speak with him in a dream. Not so with My servant Moses; he is trusted throughout My household. With him I speak mouth to mouth, plainly and not in riddles, and he beholds the likeness of the LORD. How then did you not shrink from speaking against My servant Moses!" Still incensed with them, the LORD departed.

As the cloud withdrew from the Tent, there was Miriam stricken with snow-white scales! When Aaron turned toward Miriam, he saw that she was stricken with scales. And Aaron said to Moses, "O my lord, account not to us the sin which we committed in our folly. Let her not be as one dead, who emerges from his mother's womb with half his flesh eaten away." So Moses cried out to the LORD, saying, "O God, pray heal her!" (*"Eil na r'fah na lah!"*)

But the LORD said to Moses, "If her father spat in her face, would she not bear her shame for seven days? Let her be shut out of camp for seven days, and then let her be readmitted." So Miriam was shut out of camp seven days; and the people did not march on until Miriam was readmitted.[2]

34. Bless the Lord, O My Soul

BIBLE

> *When we are ill, we can feel defeated and disconnected from life and loved ones. This psalm gives us the words to acknowledge our finitude while establishing a relationship with the Infinite One.*

Bless the LORD, O my soul,
all my being, His holy name.
Bless the LORD, O my soul
and do not forget all His bounties.
He forgives all your sins,
heals all your diseases.
He redeems your life from the Pit,
surrounds you with steadfast love and mercy.
He satisfies you with good things in the prime of life,
so that your youth is renewed like the eagle's.

The LORD executes righteous acts
and judgments for all who are wronged.
He made known His ways to Moses,

His deeds to the children of Israel.
The LORD is compassionate and gracious,
slow to anger, abounding in steadfast love.
He will not contend forever,
or nurse His anger for all time.
He has not dealt with us according to our sins,
nor has He requited us according to our iniquities.
For as the heavens are high above the earth,
so great is His steadfast love toward those who fear Him.
As east is far from west,
so far has He removed our sins from us.
As a father has compassion for his children,
so the LORD has compassion for those who fear Him.
For He knows how we are formed;
He is mindful that we are dust.

Man, his days are like those of grass;
he blooms like a flower of the field;
a wind passes by and it is no more,
its own place no longer knows it.
But the LORD's steadfast love is for all eternity
toward those who fear Him,
and His beneficence is for the children's children
of those who keep His covenant
and remember to observe His precepts.
The LORD has established His throne in heaven,
and His sovereign rule is over all.

Bless the LORD, O His angels,
mighty creatures who do His bidding,
ever obedient to His bidding;
bless the LORD, all His hosts,
His servants who do His will;
bless the LORD, all His works,
through the length and breadth of His realm;
bless the LORD, O my soul.[3]

99

35. The Lord Is My Shepherd

BIBLE

This prayer gives us an extended metaphor through which to consider our relationship with God. God is a shepherd and we are the sheep, following our leader as best we can. This framework is humbling, since human beings are depicted as followers, not masters of our destinies. For this very reason, since it reflects reality, this psalm comforts: we do not control our lives or our deaths to the extent we thought we did.

This psalm is often associated with death since it is frequently recited at funerals. However, it is truly a psalm of life, of healing and a return to health, guided by God.

The Lord is my Shepherd; I shall not want.
He maketh me to lie down in green pastures;
He leadeth me beside the still waters;
He restoreth my soul;
He guideth me in straight paths
  for His name's sake.
Yea, though I walk through
  the valley of the shadow of death,
I will fear no evil,
For Thou are with me;
Thy rod and Thy staff, they comfort me.
Thou preparest a table before me
  in the presence of mine enemies;
Thou has anointed my head with
  oil; my cup runneth over.
Surely goodness and mercy shall
  follow me all the days of my life;
And I shall dwell in the house
  of the Lord forever.[4]

36. O Lord, Do Not Punish Me

BIBLE

This psalm captures, in a very few words, the terror and agony of being ill. There is no polite glossing over the experiences and emotions we go through during sickness. What a relief!

It doesn't take a large stretch of the imagination to see the "enemies" here as disease and pain.

For the leader; with instrumental music on the *sheminith*. A psalm of David.

O LORD, do not punish me in anger
do not chastise me in fury.

Have mercy on me, O LORD, for I languish;
heal me, O LORD, for my bones shake with terror.
My whole being is stricken with terror,
while You, LORD—O, how long!
O LORD, turn! Rescue me!
Deliver me as befits Your faithfulness.
For there is no praise of You among the dead;
in Sheol, who can acclaim You?

I am weary with groaning;
every night I drench my bed,
I melt my couch in tears.
My eyes are wasted by vexation,
worn out because of all my foes.
Away from me, all you evildoers,
for the LORD heeds the sound of my weeping.
The LORD heeds my plea,
the LORD accepts my prayer.
All my enemies will be frustrated and stricken with terror;
they will turn back in an instant, frustrated.[5]

37. *Mi Shebeirakh: May the One Who Blessed*

PRAYER BOOK

Today, when we want to transform the most fervent wishes of our hearts for healing into prayer, we offer this blessing in synagogue, during the Torah service. There are private prayers one can offer as well, but this one not only has the potency of being offered during the recreation of the giving of Torah on Mount Sinai (i. e., the Torah service on Monday and Thursday mornings and Saturday morning and afternoon) but also gives the comfort of being said in a community of worshippers who can echo the prayer's intention and comfort the pray-er, as well.

May the One who blessed our ancestors, Sarah and Abraham, Rebecca and Isaac, Rachel and Jacob bless all the ill among us. Grant insight to those who bring healing, courage, and faith to those who are sick, and love and strength to all of us.

God, let Your spirit rest upon all who are ill and comfort us. May we soon know a time of complete healing, a healing of body and a healing of the spirit, and let us say, Amen.[6]

38. *You Saved My Life*

BIBLE

King Hezekiah fell into a state of hopeless illness, but then he was miraculously saved. (Isaiah 38:1–8) It is interesting that Hezekiah is praised in the sources for hiding away not only the copper serpent (Numbers 21: 4–9), but something called A Book of Healing. *Hezekiah hid this book away, according to Rashi, so that people might pray for mercy instead of relying on "miraculous" cures from the copper serpent and the cures in this* Book of Healing. *Hezekiah knew the value of prayer, which he offered in thanksgiving.*

A poem by King Hezekiah of Judah when he recovered from the illness he had
suffered:

I had thought:
I must depart in the middle of my days;
I have been consigned to the gates of Sheol
For the rest of my years.
I thought, I shall never see Yah,
Yah in the land of the living,
Or ever behold men again
Among those who inhabit the earth.
My dwelling is pulled up and removed from me
Like a tent of shepherds;
My life is rolled up like a web
And cut from the thrum.

Only from daybreak to nightfall
Was I kept whole,
Then it was as though a lion
Were breaking all my bones;
I cried out until morning.
(Only from daybreak to nightfall
Was I kept whole.)
I piped like a swift or a swallow,
I moaned like a dove,
As my eyes, all worn, looked to heaven:
"My Lord, I am in straits;
By my surety!"

What can I say? He promised me,
And He it is who has wrought it.
All my sleep had fled
Because of the bitterness of my soul
My Lord, for all that and despite it
My life-breath is revived;

You have restored me to health and revived me.
Truly, it was for my own good
That I had such great bitterness:

You saved my life
From the pit of destruction,
For you have cast behind Your back
All my offenses.
For it is not Sheol that praises You,
Not [the Land of] Death that extols You;
Nor do they who descend into the Pit
Hope for Your grace.
The living, only the living
Can give thanks to You
As I do this day;
Fathers relate to children your acts of grace:
"[It has pleased] the LORD to deliver us,
That is why we offer up music
All the days of our lives
At the House of the LORD."[7]

39. Hannah's Prayer

BIBLE

*According to the Sages (B. Berakhot 31a-b) Hannah is the
most perfect exemplar of prayer, and her desire is for physical
and spiritual wholeness and healing. These most basic wishes
of our hearts are where prayer most naturally begins.*

My heart exults in the LORD;
I have triumphed through the LORD.
I gloat over my enemies;
I rejoice in Your deliverance.
There is no holy one like the LORD,
Truly, there is none beside You;

There is no rock like our God.
Talk no more with lofty pride,
Let no arrogance cross your lips!
For the LORD is an all-knowing God;
By Him actions are measured.

The bows of the mighty are broken,
And the faltering are girded with strength.
Men once sated must hire out for bread;
Men once hungry hunger no more.
While the barren woman bears seven,
The mother of many is forlorn.
The LORD deals death and gives life,
Casts down into Sheol and raises up.
The LORD makes poor and makes rich;
He casts down, He also lifts high.
He raises the poor from the dust,
Lifts up the needy from the dunghill,
Setting them with nobles,
Granting them seats of honor.
For the pillars of the earth are the LORD's;
He has set the world upon them.
He guards the steps of His faithful,
But the wicked perish in darkness—
For not by strength shall man prevail.
The foes of the LORD shall be shattered;
He will thunder against them in the heavens.
The LORD will judge the ends of the earth.[8]

40. My Soul Meditates

DEAD SEA SCROLLS

In every age, Jews have turned to God as the ultimate healer.
This prayer is from the Second Temple period.

[For] the throes of death [encompass me]
    and Hell is upon my bed;
my couch utters a lamentation
    [and my pallet] the sound of a complaint.
My eyes are like fire in the furnace
    and my tears like rivers of water;
my eyes grow dim with waiting,
    [for my salvation] is far from me
    and my life is apart from me.

But behold,
    from desolation to ruin,
    and from the pain to the sore,
    and from the travail to the throes,
my soul meditates on Thy marvelous works.
In Thy mercies Thou has cast me aside;
season by season, my soul shall delight
    in the abundance of mercy.
I will reply to him who slanders me
    and I will rebuke my oppressor;
I will declare his sentence unjust
    and declare Thy judgment righteous.

For I know by Thy truth,
    and I choose Thy judgment upon me:
I delight in my scourges
    for I hope for Thy loving-kindness.
Thou has put a supplication
    in the mouth of Thy servant
and Thou has not threatened my life
    nor rejected my peace.
Thou has not failed my expectation,
    but hast upheld my spirit in face of the scourge.

For it is Thou who has founded my spirit
    and Thou knowest my intent;

in my distress Thou has comforted me.
I delight in forgiveness,
    and am consoled for the former transgression;
for I know there is hope in Thy grace
    and expectation in Thy great power.
For no man can be just in Thy judgment
    or [righteous in] Thy trial.[9]

41. To Give Thanks

TALMUD

What are some of the ways we can think of illness? We may
liken it to a dangerous journey or captivity.

Rab Judah said in the name of Rab: There are four [classes of people] who have
to offer thanksgiving: those who have crossed the sea, those who have traversed
the wilderness, one who has recovered from an illness, and a prisoner who has
been set free.[10]

42. Amulets

TALMUD

These days, we tend to think of amulets as superstitious or
charming at best. However, for our ancestors, the written
Name of God and the word of God had the power to heal.

Our Rabbis taught: What is an approved amulet? One that has healed [once], a
second time and a third time; whether it is an amulet in writing or an amulet of
roots, whether it is for an invalid whose life is endangered or for an invalid whose
life is not endangered. [It is permitted] not [only] for a person who has [already]
had an epileptic fit, but even [merely] to ward it off. And one may tie and untie it
even in the street, providing that he does not secure it with a ring or a bracelet
and go out therewith into the street, for appearances' sake. But it was taught: What
is an approved amulet? One that has healed three men simultaneously?—There is
no difficulty: the one is to approve the man; the other is to approve the amulet.

R. Papa said: It is obvious to me that if three amulets [are successful for] three people, each [being efficacious] three times, both the practitioner and the amulets are [henceforth] approved. If three amulets [are successful] for three people, each [being efficacious] once, the practitioner is [henceforth] approved, but not the amulets. If one amulet [is efficacious] for three men, the amulet is approved but not the practitioner. [But] R. Papa propounded: What if three amulets [are efficacious] for one person? The amulets are certainly not rendered approved: but does the practitioner become approved or not? So we say, Surely, he has healed him![11]

43. *Prayer for the Sick*

PRAYER BOOK, EIGHTEEN BENEDICTIONS

Jeremiah prayed in the singular, "Heal me, Lord, and I shall be healed. Save me and I shall be saved" (Jeremiah 17:14). The Sages, however, made this plea into a communal prayer recited every weekday. It serves to remind us that if we have health, there are others for whom it is one of the sweetest gifts on earth.

Heal us, O Lord, and we shall be healed; save us and we shall be saved; for thou art our praise. Grant a perfect healing to all our wounds. For thou, almighty King, art a faithful and merciful Physician. Blessed art thou, O Lord, who healest the sick of thy people Israel.[12]

44. *Thou Givest All, Taking Nought*

ANONYMOUS

One of the ways Jewish prayer helps the pray-er make a connection with God is through long sequences of synonyms, which may be a gateway to a meditative state, as in this prayer. This prayer was recited in the Jerusalem Temple late in the Second Temple period.

... sanctify, sustain, gather, govern, establish, glorify, confirm, pasture, raise up,
enlighten, pacify, administer, perfect—
the people which thou has established,
the peculiar people, the people which though hast ransomed,
the people which thou hast called, thy people, the sheep of thy pasture.
Thou art the only physician of our ailing souls,
keep us in thy joy,
heal us in sickness,
cast us not away as unfit to receive thy healing.
The word of thy mouth is the giver of health.
These things we beg of thee, Master:
remit whatever we have done amiss,
check whatever leads us to sin,
neither record against us all that we have done unlawfully.
Forgiveness of sin is the expression of thy long-suffering.
It is a fair thing, O Immortal, not to be wroth with mortals,
doomed to destruction, short-lived, inhabiting a toilsome world.
Never doest thou cease to do good, for thou art bountiful;
thou givest all, taking nought, for thou lackest nothing;
every righteous thing is thine, unrighteousness alone is not thine.
Evil is that which thou wouldst not, the child of our imaginations.—
Receive from us these psalmodies, these hymnodies, these prayers,
these supplications, these entreaties, these requests,
these confessions, these petitions, these thanksgivings,
this readiness, this earnestness, these vigils, ...
these couchings upon the earth, these prayerful utterances.
Having a kindly master in thee, the eternal King,
we beseech thee to behold our pitiful state.[13]

45. King David's Prayer

ZOHAR

*Every moment of life, even the last, offers an opportunity for
spiritual redemption.*

When King David pondered upon the judgments that a man [has to undergo] when he leaves this world, he said first of all "Bless the Lord, O my soul"— before you leave this world, and while you are still with the body; "and all that is within me bless His holy name"—that is you, all my bodily organs that partner my spirit while it is still with you, you bless the holy name now, before the time comes when you will be unable to bless Him or express your gratitude to Him.[14]

46. Confession by the Gravely Ill (May be read in one's behalf)

VIDUI

Before death, Jews confess their wrongs and make peace with the human beings whose presence they are about to leave.

My God and God of all who have gone before me, Author of life and death, I turn to You in trust. Although I pray for life and health, I know that I am mortal. If my life must soon come to an end, let me die, I pray, at peace.

If only my hands were clean and my heart pure! I confess that I have committed sins and left much undone, yet I know also the good that I did or tried to do. May my acts of goodness give meaning to my life, and may my errors be forgiven.

Protector of the bereaved and the helpless, watch over my loved ones. Into Your hand I commit my spirit; redeem it, O God of mercy and truth.[15]

47. Give Countenance to Caregivers

PRAYER

Caregivers have their own, human frailties. Recognizing that God works through their knowledge and effort, we should assist them by our prayers and encouragement.

May the one who blessed and led our ancestors give countenance onto those who provide help for the ill and troubled among us. May they be filled with fortitude and courage, endowed with sympathy and compassion, as they give strength to those at their side. May they fight against despair and continue to find within themselves the will to reach out to those in need. And in their love of others, may they feel the blessings of community and faith in each hour of the day's passing.[16]

48. Two Blessings for Healing

MARCIA FALK

The author of these prayers, a poet and translator, writes, "It has been suggested to me that all of us—no matter what our circumstances—would do well to accept what is to come without denial, for mortality is our common condition. I agree, yet I cannot help but feel that it is also human to hope for recovery when recovery seems possible, and that it is helpful to hear others wishing it for you as well. So I have written two different blessings for those who are ill, one of which asks, much like the traditional blessing, lirfu'at hanefesh v'lirfu'at haguf, / r'fu'ah sh'leimah, *literally, 'for healing of the spirit and for healing of the body/complete healing.' The other blessing asks for a different kind of wholeness—one that comes from a deep acceptance of one's place in the greater whole of being. I leave it to individuals to choose which variation serves their greater needs."*

FOR ONE IN NEED OF HEALING

As those who came before us were blessed
in the presence of the communities that sustained them,
so we offer our blessings
for one among us in need of healing.
_____ (name)
may you have comfort and relief
in the healing of body and mind,
and may you return in time
to health and wholeness and strength.

FOR ONE GRAVELY ILL

As those who came before us were blessed

111

in the presence of the communities that sustained them,
so we offer our blessings for one among us needing support.
_____ (name)
may your spirit be calmed
and your pain be eased,
may you receive comfort
from those who care for you,
and may you drink from the waters
of the ever-giving well.[17]

49. A Mother's Prayer

CHAVA WEISSLER

When a woman gives birth, she may say this with great de-
votion. Her prayer is a "tekhine," a class of late medieval Yid-
dish prayers popular among Ashkenazic women. Many of
these prayers, like this one and that which follows it, were col-
lected and translated by Professor Weissler.

Almighty God, righteous judge, with truth and with justice have you punished us women from the creation of human beings, that we women must bear our children with pain. It is within your power: whomever you punish is punished, and to whomever you show mercy is shown mercy, and no one can contradict you. Who would say to you, What are you doing? Merciful God, have mercy upon me, because of the merit of all the righteous men and all the pious women upon whom you have had mercy, and whose prayers you have heard. When they prayed and called upon your name, that you open their wombs, you opened them with great compassion and mercy. You let them be delivered, with compassion and mercy.

And you do not remember my sins at the time of birth. God, be praised, you were before the creation of the world, and bear the whole world until the end with great mercy. Reject my sins from before you, and let them not be brought before your court. And when the evil angels come and want to tell and recall my many misdeeds and untidy or bad works, do not permit them to stand before your court, and do not accept their voices, and stop up all the holes in your holy throne, so that their cry will have no way to come before your holiness. But the good angels, who speak well of your children Israel, and promise [? act as advocates?] for me, receive their speech, and hear their voice, be accounted before you like all the good promises[?] in your world. And take the key to the womb in your right hand, that which no one [undecipherable word], and open my womb without any pains or pangs. And let the infant be born without any harm or brokenness. Weaken the evil inclination in him, so that the child may be from its youth of a good nature. And protect me and the child from all evil spirits and evil people, and may no evil eye harm us.

Almighty God, hear my prayer, and accept my tears in your [undecipherable word], like the prayer which you accepted from Hannah, and you let her be told by the prophet, Go in peace, the God of Israel will give you your request which you desired of him—and the prayers of the other pious women which you have accepted and made to come true. You are the God who accepts the prayers of those who call upon you with a whole heart. May the word of my mouth and thoughts of my heart be acceptable before you, God, my creator and my redeemer.[18]

50. The Etrog

CHAVA WEISSLER

As with the use of amulets, Jewish folk medicine of previous eras may seem nonsensical or enchanting, depending on the tendencies of the reader. Certainly this tekhine linking the festival of Sukkot, which is replete with symbols of fertility, particularly the womb-shaped citron, with the desire for fertility is a logical extension of that holiday's practices.

This is the thing to say when biting off the stem of the *etrog*.

Lord of the World, because Eve ate of the apple, all of us women must suffer such great pangs as [almost] to die. Had I been there I would not have had any enjoyment from [the fruit]. Just so, now I have not wanted to render the *etrog* unfit during the whole seven days when it was used for a mitzvah. But now, on Hoshana Rabbah, the mitzvah is no longer applicable, but I am [still] not in a hurry to eat it. And just as little enjoyment as I get from the stem of the *etrog* would I have eaten from the apple which you forbade.[19]

51. Prayer for Those Having Difficulty Conceiving

NINA BETH CARDIN

Conceiving a baby today can be every bit as difficult as it was for our ancestors. Although technology can serve as an aid, prayer can also unlock these gates, which we so desperately want to be open. Rabbi Cardin is the author of Out of the Depths I Call to You, *a book of prayers for the married Jewish woman.*

"God heals the broken-hearted and binds up their wounds, counts the number of the stars and calls them all by name." —PSALM 147:3–4

This prayer is phrased in the plural and written in the voice of a married couple. It is easily adaptable for an infertile person to say on her or his own.

On our bed at night, we sought the one our hearts ached for;
we sought, but did not find, that one.
How lovely you would be, so we imagine, how lovely!
Every part of you would be fair; no blemish would mar your coming.
Who is the one that shines through like the dawn,
Beautiful as the moon,
radiant as the sun,
awesome as hosts draped in their colors?
Who is the one that our hearts wait for,
wait for, as the watchman for the morning light?
In you, God, our ancestors trusted,
In You they trusted, and You answered them.
We will trust in God, for God's goodness is never-ending;
God's mercy is without bounds.
We will trust in God, for God is our help and our shield.

May the God who made heaven and earth, hear our plea and
grant us a child.
—*Based on verses from Song of Songs and Psalm 22*[20]

52. *Prayer after a Miscarriage or Stillbirth*

SANDY EISENBERG SASSO

*While the loss of a pregnancy is every bit as real and painful
as any other death, there has been a tendency to overlook this
type of loss. Recently, however, pregnancy loss has been recognized liturgically in prayers such as this one. Rabbi Sasso
is an author of books for children and parents.*

"Seeing our days are determined, the number of our months are with You, You
set limits that we cannot pass."

God, we are weary and grieved. We were anticipating the birth of a child,
but the promise of life was ended too soon. Our arms yearned to cradle new
life, our mouths to sing soft lullabies. Our hearts ache from the emptiness and
the silence. We are saddened and we are angry. We weep and we mourn. Weep
with us, God, Creator of Life, for the life that could not be.

Source of healing, help us to find healing among those who care for us and
those for whom we care. Shelter us under wings of love and help us to stand up
again for life even as we mourn our loss.

Barukh attah adonai, zokher yetzurav lehayyim berahamim.

Blessed are You, Eternal our God, whose compassion renews us unto life
(from the High Holiday *Amidah* [standing prayer]).[21]

53. *Prayer after Safe Delivery*

FANNY NEUDA

*There is nothing to compare to the unique quality of a child's
first cry. For the mother, who has just endured (and will endure!) great pain, it is a healing unto itself, as expressed in this
prayer. Fanny Neuda is a nineteenth-century author of
prayers for Jewish women.*

115

How dark was everything around me but a few hours ago; anxiety filled my heart, and I was afraid of the results of my fears and pain. But when I called in my woe, the Lord heard me, and saved me from my troubles. The hours of anxiety have passed, and now joy and light surrounded me. Thou, O God! has safely led me through the dangers of the hour of delivery, Thou has done more unto me than I ventured to hope; Thou has fulfilled my prayer, Thou has given me a dear, healthful, well-formed child. Therefore, I praise Thy mercy, and shall never forget Thy benefits; my heart and mouth shall ever overflow with thanks and praises of Thy supreme power and loving-kindness.

And with filial confidence in Thy mercy I commit all my cares unto Thee, trusting that Thou wilt accomplish the work of grace which Thou has commenced. Thou will renew my strength, that I may be able to fulfill the duties of a good and faithful mother.

My God and Lord! Bestow Thy protection also upon my newborn infant, that it may thrive and grow, and be healthful in body and soul, to be a pleasure unto *Thee,* a delight unto me and my beloved husband, and honor unto all men. Yea, Eternal One! in Thee I place my trust, I wait upon *Thy* help; he who trusted in *Thee* shall never be put to shame. Amen.[22]

54. Mikveh Ceremony for Laura (1989)

LAURA LEVITT AND SUE ANN WASSERMAN

The mikveh, *the Jewish ritual bath, is one of Judaism's most powerful healing tools. It can be used not just for observance of family purity laws but to renew one's spirit and cleanse one from violation. Laura Levitt has trained in Jewish theology, and Sue Ann Wasserman is a congregational rabbi.*

The ceremony that follows was put together for me by my friend and my rabbi Sue Ann Wasserman after my rape in November 1989. The ceremony marks my particular experience and desire to heal. It is a ritual that speaks to the specific place I had come to in my healing on November 24, 1989. I went to the *mikveh* with Sue Ann and my mother a few days after my first period after the rape. It was the day after Thanksgiving during my parents' first visit. It was erev Shabbat. Since November I have had other ways of marking time since the rape. My body has overcome a multitude of diseases punctuated by visits to doctors. This has been ongoing. I just took my second HIV test. I have had to wait over six months for definitive results. Although I have maintained my professional life from the beginning, both teaching and studying, it has taken much time to recover other aspects of my life. I have slowly resumed having a fantasy life and a sex life, but I still long for a time when I will be able to live alone again.

SUE ANN: Although I grew up in a religious Reform Jewish home, *mikveh* was not a part of my background. I became interested in *mikveh* and the laws of family purity while in rabbinic school. My interest stemmed from my need and desire to find parts of my tradition that spoke to me as a woman. I read and wrote and thought about *mikveh* as a woman's ritual both past and present. My practical knowledge of *mikveh* has come through my work with people who are converting to Judaism. I became convinced of its power to provide a meeting place for people and God, through listening to my students speak about their experience and how significant the *mikveh* was as a conclusion to their formal study for conversion.

LAURA: Healing is a process. This *mikveh* ceremony is distinct in that it represents one of the few ways that I have been able to attend to my spiritual as well as my physical and emotional healing. Sharing this ceremony with other Jewish women is part of this healing. It is a way for me to give something of myself to other Jewish women, especially those who have been sexually abused. I want them to know that they are not alone. I also want them to know that there is a place for us and even our most painful experiences to be commemorated in Jewish community/ies.

My body was violated by rape. The *mikveh* offered me a place to acknowledge both that violation and my desire to heal. My need for ritual was very real. I needed to do something concrete to express my psychic and physical pain as a Jewish woman among other Jewish women I am close to.

For me, healing is not simply a return to some "wholeness" in the past; it is an experience of growth and change. Healing is the careful rebuilding of a life in the present that does not deny what has happened.

SUE ANN: When Laura was raped, I wanted to find a way to support her as a friend. As a rabbi, I needed to find a way for Judaism to respond to her. The *mikveh* seemed to be the most appropriate ritual for several reasons. (1) It was predominantly our foremothers' ritual. (2) It requires the whole body. (3) Its

117

waters flow in and out—symbolically flow from Eden, a place of wholeness. (4) Its waters symbolically flow from Eden, a place of wholeness. (5) The natural waters remind us of the constant intermingling presence of the Creator in our own lives. (6) Finally, water itself is cleansing, supportive, and life sustaining.

The task then was to find words that would give this ancient ritual meaning in the context of Laura's experience. I drew on the sources at hand and included my own words as well as asking Laura to bring whatever readings she thought would be healing for her.

LAURA: The poems I chose to read during the *mikveh* ceremony reflect these feelings. Like the narrator in Irena Klepfisz's "Di rayze aheym" (The Journey Home), I too wanted to return "home" but knew that the home I knew before the rape was no longer accessible to me. Nevertheless, I still needed a home. Healing has meant that I have had to rebuild a new life where I can attend to my scars while also experiencing joy again. I have had to rebuild my life "even from a broken web." These words, the poetry of contemporary Jewish women, have helped me articulate some of these feelings, but to speak them at the *mikveh* made them physically tangible.

Historically, the *mikveh* is a sacred space for Jewish women and our bodies. Through this ceremony, I was able to enter into that tradition. Sue Ann helped me reconstitute this place to attend to my own physical needs for healing. In a steamy room overlooking a pool of running water in a synagogue in Atlanta, we recited these words and I entered the water. In so doing, the violation of my Jewish female body was attended to. It was neither silenced nor ignored.

SUE ANN: We stood together at the *mikveh,* the three of us, reading a liturgy that had been created in a day, to prepare us to perform a ritual that has existed for centuries. It was a powerful and empowering experience, but it was only a first step in the creation of a new liturgy that will speak to those who seek healing after a rape or any form of sexual abuse.[23]

55. A Fertility Ritual

PENINA V. ADELMAN

Healing through text study, through making a certain passage your own and reading it over and over again to find your own

*meaning in it, is a quintessential form of Jewish healing. It al-
lows a connection with the past while making ancient texts
come alive in the present. The author is a storyteller and social worker.*

Conceiving a child did not come easily to me. Neither did the words to convey
my frustration, despair, and uncertainty to those who might have helped. But,
stories have been a source of strength and nourishment to me since I was a
little girl. I devoured the books of the Brothers Grimm and Andrew Lang like
hills of chocolate chip cookies. Myths of the Greek gods and goddesses were
more substantial, like roasted meat with gravy. In later years, I began to feast on
the tales of my biblical ancestors. When my life has presented a problem or
paradox, I have sought a solution in close study of the sacred text.

I learned to do this by studying Midrash, collections of rabbinic interpretations and parables which aim to clarify particular aspects of the *Tanakh* (compiled as early as the fifth century c.e.). One of my teachers, Judah Goldin,
explained that when the rabbis found something in the text which disturbed
them, from a grammatical deviation to a perplexing character flaw, they responded with a *midrash.*

When I lost my first pregnancy after trying to conceive for a prolonged
period of time, my sense of living harmoniously with Nature was sufficiently
disturbed to impel me to make a *midrash* in response. This *midrash* would be a
hybrid creature, part-story, part-ritual.

Nobody I knew well had ever lost a baby. I had heard horror stories of
friends of friends and their pregnancies-turned-nightmares, but these were
remote occurrences. When Death came to our household, my husband and I
had only each other. Our parents (the grandparents-to-be) seemed puzzled and
overwhelmed by this tragic break from the norm. They wanted to help, but how
could they give us a live child? While I was in the hospital recovering from the
laparotomy which removed the Fallopian tube where the pregnancy had been
trapped, phone calls and visitors kept coming. But when I was finally settled
once more at home, I looked at my husband, Steve and asked: What do we do
now? How do we start to live again?

What nobody could tell us was that we had experienced the real death of a
potential being. We were grieving, but we could not put words to it, we could

not invite people over to sit *shiva* for our dead baby. Then I remembered all those disgusting dead baby jokes I used to hear in fifth grade. Humor fills the vacuum caused by taboo. Talking about and mourning for the death of an abstract human being, one that was never held or touched, was taboo in our society and in Judaism.

This was intolerable to me. I had to find a way to mark this death or I would be grieving for the rest of my life. In the works of Elizabeth Kubler-Ross I discovered the notion that one's own experience with Death is the instructor to follow. I would look into my tradition to find what to do. I remembered the story of Hannah and Peninnah in the First Book of Samuel.

Hannah was the favorite wife of Elkanah, but she was unable to bear him any children. Peninnah, her co-wife, less favored, bore one healthy child after the other. Through much suffering, deliberation, humiliation, and prayer, Hannah was finally blessed with a son whom she named Samuel.

Here was my model. Hannah had lost hope and self-esteem. She even displayed symptoms of depression: she stopped eating and wept constantly (I Sam.1:7–8). This indicated how deeply she was mourning for the child she might never have.

Like Hannah I was paralyzed—by infertility and by my recent pregnancy loss. The Rabbis considered Hannah the paradigm of heartfelt prayer and unceasing faith. Therefore, I would consider her story to be a kind of prayer, and inspiration to survive this overwhelming period of loss and despair which was facing me. Accordingly, in the year following my pregnancy loss, I sat down daily with the story of Hannah and studied it from every possible angle. Each day I read another verse and pondered it. Then I read commentaries on the story, mostly in *Pesikta Rabbati,* to see what the Rabbis thought about Hannah and her rival, Peninnah. Finally I wrote a new version of the story, a synthesis of the original text, its commentaries, and my identification with Hannah through the experience of infertility.

The ritual of studying Hannah's story became a *kaddish* which I said each day for my dead child. In this way I was able to live through the loss instead of being consumed by it. Incidentally, my husband's response was quite different. Whereas I turned inward to find strength and renewed faith by studying texts, he used activity to overcome the loss and became a Jewish Big Brother. One year after the death, we created a joint ritual. [Their ritual is described in Penina V. Adelman, "Playing House: The Birth of a Ritual," *Reconstructionist* (January-February 1989.)] Before this could happen, however, we needed to do some individual preparation.

The more I studied, the more convinced I became that there was a ritual hidden there if I could only see it. However, this ritual lived between the lines of Hebrew text. No older wise woman was going to teach the ritual to me. Thus, part of the interpretive process would be uncovering this ritual for infertility.

My need to look into the sacred texts of my tradition in search of solace and hope echoed my desire to look life straight in the eye again after losing my baby and to find meaning in the experience. Magical thinking led me to believe that by studying Hannah intensely I would ingest some of her strength and that this strength was contained in the very letters of her story. Similar reasoning often lies behind the activity of Torah study. The *wachnact* or "night of watching" before a *brit milah* when there is communal study all night long to protect the newborn from the Angel of Death is a folk custom which illustrates the notion of study as a form of Jewish worship just as Torah readings in the synagogue during the week, on the Sabbath and holidays do. In addition, the *tefillin* and *mezuzah* which contain Hebrew prayers may be seen as types of amulets protecting those who use them. Thus, I believed that the study of Hannah's story might protect me from further loss and offer some guidance in becoming a mother.

Hannah's silent prayer became the basis of the ritual. It represented the silence of all those who had experienced such losses and could find no place within Judaism to mark them. By studying Hannah and identifying with her, I became another link on a chain of women who had had difficulty in conceiving or had lost children. This chain included all the matriarchs and extended back as far as Lilith (Adam's first wife, who was condemned to lose all her babies as they were born because she refused to submit to Adam's will). In this ritual, giving voice to the silence would be my goal.

I first sang and told the story of Hannah in my Rosh Hodesh group composed of women only, a safe forum for the initial public exposure of my experience. Then on the one year anniversary of the pregnancy loss, I performed the story as the *haftarah* on the first day of Rosh Hashanah, the time when Hannah's story is traditionally read.

Presenting my *midrash* in public before a group of men and women meant the experience was no longer my burden and my husband's alone. At last, I understood my compulsion to develop a ritual where there had been none. Ritual places personal experience in the public realm where it may be witnessed, dealt with, and shared. The loss of a child, potential or real, becomes bearable when the person sitting to your right and the person sitting to your left experience it with you and can say, "Finally I understand."[24]

56. After a Miscarriage

VICKI HOLLANDER

Miscarriages and stillbirths are deaths and should be mourned as such. This poem calls on God's creative powers for comfort. Vicki Hollander has served as a rabbi and spiritual leader to a Jewish Renewal Movement.

Naming is integral to healing. Naming the aspect of God we experience when we are ill is also a crucial step in healing. This poem recognizes God as the Creator, Giver, and Taker of life.

HAYOTZER, *one of seventy names of God, is translated as "One who fashions, forms, creates."*

Hayotzer,
One who shapes,
Who formed us out of moistened clay,
Who rolled and pinched and sculpted the world,
hold me now.

You who enabled wisps of seeds to grow,
Who partnered the life which grew inside me,
shelter me.

Life was gifted,
Life removed.

Hayotzer,
shape me a place where I can weep,

and mourn the loss,
and let the blackness inside
cry.
Help me say goodbye
to the child
who was growing within me,
to the dreams I bore,
to the love I held within for that budding soul,
plucked away.

Let my voice ring,
a mother's call,
wild to the universe,

And You,
stand by me,
stand at my side,
and watch my tear fall and touch the earth.
Hear my pain and
hold me.

Hayotzer,
You who shaped me,
Heal my body and my soul.
Mend my spirit.
Thread new life among my bones.

Help me to find ground again.
To feel the earth beneath my toes.
To smell the beckoning scent of rich soil.
To see shoots of green emerge through winter beds,
determined hands grasping life.
To hear the sap rushing within.

I kneel to plant.
A seed of life.

An act of faith.

Hayotzer,
Sower of life.
And act of faith.

Hayotzer,
Sower of life,
Take my hand and, for a time,
hold it tight.[25]

57. To Relax Spiritually

EARL A. GROLLMAN

> *Anger is, perhaps, an inevitable part of being ill. We just don't want what is happening to be happening. This poem shows us what may come after this consuming phase. Rabbi Grollman has written popular works on bereavement.*

Perhaps more than any other event
the loss of health
raises the most urgent issues
about

good and evil,
reward and punishment,
of why terrible things happen to a loved one.

Your religion may provide you
with a spiritual philosophy
that helps you make some sense of
sickness and health.

Beware.

Religion can be hazardous to your health,
when you believe you haven't prayed hard
enough,
and punishment is linked with illness.

Religion then becomes a tool
for denial of real emotions and
keeps you from releasing feelings of
helplessness, guilt, anger.

A mature, forgiving, open faith
encourages expression,
allows your angry cry to heaven—
    "How could you, God!"

Religion offers no absolute answers,
no guarantee of special treatment,
no extended length of time for your beloved.

For many,
faith *does*

help its believers
to accept the unacceptable,
and to ennoble
ignoble misfortune.[26]

The Jewish Healer

*It may truly be said that medicine (the medical man)
should be a man's constant companion. To be sure, this
holds good only in the case of a consummate physician
with a complete mastery of theoretical and practical
knowledge.*

Maimonides, The Regimen of Health

Introduction

n a time of illness, we entrust to a doctor that which is most precious to us. From that physician, we should look for excellence, but of what sort? We can take for granted that the physician has a high level of knowledge and technical competence because such skills are certified and licensed. But what is the importance to us of other less measurable qualities such as judgment, amiability, devotedness, empathy, integrity, and accessibility? Do we need someone who listens, who spends time with us, who is attentive, caring, honest, forthright, humble, and empowering; someone with whom we can enter comfortably into a longstanding personal alliance?

Such qualities, often critical to success in therapy, originate less from a physician's training and more from personality or character. It is these often frustratingly inscrutable attributes at the heart of our medical care that have concerned Jewish authors for fifteen hundred years. One of the most recent, Dr. Bernard Lown, recipient of a Nobel prize and renowned cardiologist, puts it this way: "Medicine has lost its way, if not its soul." What is being lost is a "three thousand-year tradition" of "special affinity and trust," and it is being replaced by technological procedures. Writes Dr. Lown, in his book The Lost Art of Healing *(Houghton Mifflin, 1996) about the roots of his own conviction:*

> *My philosophic outlook has been shaped by many elements: foreign birth, a Jewish heritage with a rabbinic tradition, a love of books, and above all a continuing romance with medicine. My more than four decades of medical work have only increased my fascination with the magical art of healing as espoused by the great twelfth-century philosopher-physician Maimonides, who prayed, "May I never forget that the patient is a fellow creature in pain. May I never consider him merely a vessel of disease."*

Great numbers of other Jewish physicians might have written the same.

The writings in this section represent a small sample of the ways in which Jewish writers have viewed healers. The section includes perspectives from non-physicians as well as consciously Jewish physicians as to what we should expect from the doctors who treat us. Despite the great differences among the authors in terms of expression and culture, as well as the technical capabilities of medicine in their times, Jews have insisted that ethics and behavior in medical care stem from basic Jewish values that command us to honor God's image in every human being.

58. Wellness and Holiness in the Bible

CAROL MEYERS

In an essay written for this volume, Professor Carol Meyers explains the attitudes underlying the references to healers in the Hebrew Bible.

One of the most ubiquitous features of human life is the presence of illness. The earliest known written languages, which evolved in the Near East in areas around ancient Israel, contain extensive medical literature. Identification of ailments and prescribed treatments appear in this ancient corpus of "scientific" documents. We would categorize many of them as magical or folkloristic, but we can also recognize the intuitive good judgment of the ancients in matters of hygiene and health care.

Ancient Israel participated in the general concern exhibited since antiquity of maintaining or recovering health. However, because the Bible does not contain the kind of extensive information found in the practitioners' handbooks of other ancient cultures, knowledge about Israelite conceptions of illness and healing has been difficult to obtain. But recently three developments in historical research together make it possible to understand the Israelite health care system: 1) the findings of medical anthropologists, who obtain information from the observation of existing premodern societies; 2) the discoveries of osteo-archaeologists, who subject human skeletal remains from the biblical past to paleopathological analysis; 3) the insights of comparativists, who bring the data found in Egyptian and Mesopotamian texts to bear upon an understanding of biblical passages. As a result, rather than conceptualize our biblical ancestors as living in a health care wilderness, it now seems appropriate to think of them as having a health care system. That is, they had resources and strategies for preventing or curing illnesses; and they had notions about the cause of illness and about options for treatment or therapy.

Most of the particulars of the Israelite health care system may seem unacceptable or alien to us because of its pre-scientific reasoning and because, as we shall see, of the way it links illness and transgression. Nonetheless, recognizing that the Israelites had a system of health care connects us to them, for any such system implies a concern for the suffering of the afflicted and an attempt to establish well-being for all.

In thinking abut illness and health in the Bible, it is important to realize that our modern category of "illness"—which denotes the psychological and social experience of an ailment—is more useful than that of disease, which refers to a biological (or psychological) condition. Diseases can sometimes be recognized or even identified in biblical texts, but more often they are obscure or have been erroneously mislabeled by traditional translations and commentaries. (A case in point is biblical "leprosy" [e.g., II Kings 5; Leviticus 13–14] , which is almost certainly not Hansen's disease.)

Ancient Israel's conceptions of the etiology of illness were fundamental to its health care system. For the most part, biblical texts indicate what scholars have identified as a "utopian" position. Any illness has a cause that can be understood by the patient. In the Bible, illness comes from God and is sent because of the sin or unrighteousness of the afflicted person (most clearly stated in Deuteronomy 28). This perspective implies that divine instrumentality in causing illness operates according to a principle of divine justice. Further, this concept implies that all illnesses are potentially curable, as long as the patient follows a procedure for the cessation of and atonement for sinful behavior.

Fortunately for those of us who cannot accept the idea of an intrinsic connection between the presence of illness and the committing of sin, the Bible is not a monolithic document. For the idea of illness, as for many other concepts and attitudes reflected in its texts, the Bible has different perspectives. The utopian model may predominate, but another "realist" model is also present, notably in Job. Job cannot understand the cause of his affliction, his ailments may not be curable, and his illness is the result of divine purposes that are not arbitrary but cannot be comprehended.

Because of the dominant biblical conceptualization of illness being a consequence of sin, a prominent set of biblical texts connects the idea of purity, or rather impurity, with illness. Those texts are mainly ones dealing with priestly matters and are found in the books of Leviticus and Numbers. "Purity," in biblical usage, is related to holiness (not cleanliness). "Purity" indicates fitness. It designates people and things that can be brought near to God, the epitome of purity and sanctity. Those persons and objects most closely approximating God's perfection could approach God's earthy abode, the temple. Members of the priestly family, or animals meant for sacrifice, that were in some way blemished or ill were disqualified from temple ritual. Similarly, infirm Israelites were denied access to the temple precincts.

The connection of impurity and sin with illness complicated the way in which health care assistance was delivered in ancient Israel. Because of the link between illness and sin, the health care system normally meant that what we would call religious personnel were the health care providers. Note that the term physician, sometimes applied to ancient medical practitioners, is inappropriate. Ancient practitioners indeed used procedures and substances *(materia medica)* that might broadly be designated medical. Yet their grounding in theological conceptions of illness and its etiology makes the use of "physician" misleading. More neutral is the term health care consultant—someone to whom an afflicted person, or that person's family, turned for assistance. Such consultants did not specialize in healing as such; rather they facilitated the patient's communication with God, the sine qua non of achieving and maintaining wholeness and health.

The health care consultants were thus individuals who could help a patient with the three major steps in the healing process. Because those aspects all involved what we would call "religious" behaviors, those consultants were typically prophets or priests—professionals familiar with the procedures for dealing with illness. However, because people with disabilities and blemishes could not come too close to any sanctuary of the Lord, and because, beginning in the seventh century B.C.E., there was only one legitimate temple for God (the one in Jerusalem), legitimate health care options were often hard to obtain. In many ways, as Psalm 88 suggests, people with illness were often marginalized. Health care was thus sometimes obtained through illegitimate means: by seeking out the magicians, prophets, or priests of local Canaanite healing gods. Otherwise health care involved self-help: carrying out procedures at home without the guidance of authorized professionals.

One can understand the possibility of the latter, self-care option by looking at each of the three steps of healing. The first was *petitionary:* it provided the patient with a set of prayers to be said or rituals to be performed in order to confess sins, beseech forgiveness, and request healing. If a patient had no access to the temple or standard liturgy, he or she could compose individual prayers (like Psalms 38 and 39) at home. The second step was the therapeutic one, which would have been the one most akin to modern medicine, for it involved physical procedures and the application or swallowing of "medicinal" substances. There is very little direct evidence for how procedures and substances would have been used in the Temple. But comparative data, as well as evidence about the presence of Moses' bronze serpent (cf. the AMA's caduceus), probably part of a *therapeutic* ritual for snake bites (see Numbers 21:5–9) until the eighth century B.C.E. (II Kings 18:4), suggest a wide repertoire of healing procedures that were part of priestly practice. At the same time, folk medicine probably made the use of various natural or herbal remedies, without recourse to an official consultant, frequent domestic events. An example would be Leah's use of "love plants" as an aphrodisiac to cure infertility, which was considered an illness (Genesis 30:14–16). Such self-medication would have been quasi-legitimate, so long as positive results were attributed to God and not the substance or the supplier of the substance.

The final step in the healing process—*thanksgiving*—is often overlooked. It was probably considered obligatory for a recovered patient to offer prayers and sacrifices at the Temple. The person cured of the skin ailments erroneously called "leprosy," for example, performed certain purification rituals and brought sacrifices (Leviticus 14). Just as for the other two steps of the healing procedure, this last one too could be carried out at home through private prayer and also by taking or dispatching offerings to the Temple. Being freed from illness meant regaining the status of ritual purity, providing these post-illness expressions of gratitude to God were made to the Temple.

Although the biblical focus is, for obvious reasons, on the use of health care consultants connected with the Temple, that option was not available to all. As for most societies, the home was undoubtedly the major locus for health care for the ill. Still, the religious dimension—the petitionary and thanksgiving prayers before and after treatment—was paramount. In ancient Hebrew thought, the human being was a whole entity, not a combination of discrete body and soul. Restoration to well-being was inconceivable without what we would call a holistic approach. The person as a whole was treated through appeal to God as well as by physical procedures. Health care consultants were clearly more than medical practitioners—they dealt with the moral and spiritual life of a patient as well as with the psychological or physical distress. The ultimate goal of the health care system was to achieve general well-being *(shalom)* and thus sanctity for all Israel.

59. The Comfort of Music

BIBLE

In this well-known story from the Bible, the young David calms the troubled soul of King Saul. The episode is, for the Bible, unique in that healing is affected by an ordinary mortal and without a miracle. On second glance, however, David was not so ordinary for, as we are told, "The Lord is with him." Saul was not healed by the music in and of itself, but by music flowing from the soul of a loved and loving companion, in touch with God.

Now the spirit of the LORD had departed from Saul, and an evil spirit from the LORD began to terrify him. Saul's courtiers said to him, "An evil spirit of God is terrifying you. Let our lord give the order [and] the courtiers in attendance on you will look for someone who is skilled at playing the lyre; whenever the evil spirit of God comes over you, he will play it and you will feel better." So Saul said to his courtiers, "Find me someone who can play well and bring him to me." One of the attendants spoke up, "I have observed a son of Jesse the Bethlehemite who is skilled in music; he is a stalwart fellow and a warrior, sensible in speech, and handsome in appearance, and the LORD is with him." Whereupon Saul sent messengers to Jesse to say, "Send me your son, David, who is with the flock." Jesse took an ass [laden with] bread, a skin of wine, and a kid, and sent them to Saul by his son David. So David came to Saul and entered his service; [Saul] took a strong liking to him and made him one of his arms-bearers. Saul sent word to Jesse, "Let David remain in my service, for I am pleased with him." Whenever the [evil] spirit of God came upon Saul, David would take the lyre and play it; Saul would find relief and feel better, and the evil spirit would leave him.[1]

60. Asa's Transgression

BIBLE

This brief comment about King Asa reflects the skeptical atti-tude of the Bible toward professional healers, translated "physicians." It may have been appropriate because at that time healers were often diviners and magicians, who were charlatans deserving the wrath of biblical writers.

The acts of Asa, early and late, are recorded in the annals of the kings of Judah and Israel. In the thirty-ninth year of his reign, Asa suffered from an acute foot ailment; but ill as he was, he still did not turn to the LORD but to physicians. Asa slept with his fathers. He died in the forty-first year of his reign and was buried in the grave that he had made for himself in the City of David. He was laid in his resting place.[2]

61. Honor the Physician

BEN SIRA

Ben Sira's aphorism "make friends with the physician" would become the textual basis of a more welcoming attitude toward physicians among the talmudic Sages. He advocated a bal-ance between using physicians and praying to God. Ben Sira was a Jewish scholar who lived in the Second Temple period.

Make friends with the physician, for he is essential to you;
    him also God has established in his profession.
From God the doctor has his wisdom,
    and from the king he receives his sustenance.
Knowledge makes the doctor distinguished

and gives him access to those in authority.
God makes the earth yield healing herbs,
    which the prudent should not neglect.
Was not the water sweetened by a twig
    that people might learn his power?
He endows humans with the knowledge
    to glory in his mighty works,
Through which the doctor eases pain
    and the druggist prepares his medicines;
Thus God's creative work continues without cease
    in its efficacy on the surface of the earth.

My son, when you are ill, delay not,
    but pray to God, for it is he who heals.
Flee wickedness; purify your hands,
    cleanse your heart of every sin.
Offer your sweet-smelling oblation and memorial,
    a generous offering according to your means.
Then give the doctor his place
    lest he leave; for you need him too.
There are times that give him an advantage,
    and he too beseeches God
That his diagnosis may be correct
    and his treatment bring about cure.

Whoever is a sinner toward his Maker
    will be defiant toward the doctor.[3]

62. Herbs, Baths, and Devils

JOSEPHUS

Remarks by the historian Josephus reflect prevailing beliefs, popular in his day (first century C.E.), that illness is caused by demons and cured through magic remedies, spells, ritual, and exorcism.

Now, within this place there grew a sort of rue, that deserves our wonder on account of its largeness, for it was no way inferior to any fig tree whatsoever, either in height or in thickness; and the report is, that it had lasted ever since the times of Herod, and would probably have lasted much longer, had it not been cut down by those Jews who took possession of the place afterward: but still in that valley which encompasses the city on the north side, there is a certain place called Baaras, which produces a root of the same name with itself; its colour is like to that of flame, and towards the evening it sends out a certain ray like lightning: it is not easily taken by such as would do it, but recedes from their hands, nor will yield itself to be taken quietly, until either the urine of a woman, or her menstrual blood, be poured upon it; nay even then it is certain death to those that touch it, unless any one take and hang the root itself down from his hand, and so carry it away. It may also be taken another way, without danger, which is this: they dig a trench quite round about it, till the hidden part of the root be very small, they then tie a dog to it, and when the dog tries hard to follow him that tied him, this root is easily plucked up, but the dog dies immediately, as if it were instead of the man that would take the plant away; nor after this need any one be afraid of taking it into their hands. Yet, after all this pains in getting it, it is only valuable on account of one virtue it hath, that if it only be brought to sick persons, it quickly drives away those called Demons, which are not other than the spirits of the wicked, which enter into men that are alive, and kill them, unless they can obtain some help against them. Here are also fountains of hot water, that flow out of this place, which have a very different taste one from the other; for some of them are bitter, and others of them are plainly sweet. Here are also many eruptions of cold waters, and this not only in the places that lie lower, and have their fountains near one another, but, what is still more wonderful, here is to be seen a certain cave hard by, whose cavity is not deep, but it is covered over by a rock that is prominent: above this rock there stand up two [hills or] breasts, as it were, but a little distant one from another, the one of which sends out a fountain that is very cold, and the other sends out one that is very hot; which waters, when they are mingled together, compose a most pleasant bath; they are medicinal indeed for other maladies, but especially good for strengthening the nerves. This place has in it also mines of sulphur and alum.[4]

63. Solomon's Wisdom

JOSEPHUS

It was said in ancient and medieval times that King Solomon received from God the secrets of healing and also that he had authored a book of medicine, which was subsequently lost. Here Josephus's account of one Eleazar suggests that there was a post-Solomonic tradition of magical healing among Jews.

Now the sagacity and wisdom which God had bestowed upon Solomon was so great, that he exceeded the ancients, insomuch that he was no way inferior to the Egyptians, who are said to have been beyond all men in understanding; nay, indeed, it is evident that their sagacity was very much inferior to that of the king's. He also excelled and distinguished himself in wisdom above those who were most eminent among the Hebrews at that time for shrewdness: those I mean were Ethan, and Heman, and Chalcol, and Darda, the sons of Mahol. He also composed books of odes and songs, a thousand and five; of parables and similitudes, three thousand; for he spake a parable upon every sort of tree, from the hyssop to the cedar; and in like manner also about beasts, about all sorts of living creatures, whether upon the earth, or in the seas, or in the air; for he was not unacquainted with any of their natures, nor omitted inquiries about them, but described them all like a philosopher, and demonstrated his exquisite knowledge of their several properties. God also enabled him to learn that skill which expels demons, which is a science useful and sanative to men. He composed such incantations also by which distempers are alleviated. And he left behind him the manner of using exorcisms, by which they drive away demons, so that they never return, and this method of cure is of great force unto this day; for I have seen a certain man of my own country whose name was Eleazar, releasing people that were demoniacal in the presence of Vespasian, and his sons, and his captains, and the whole multitude of his soldiers. The manner of the cure was this: —He put a ring that had a root of one of those sorts mentioned by Solomon to the nostrils of the demoniac, after which he drew out the demon through his nostrils; and when the man fell down immediately, he adjured him to return into him no more, making still mention of Solomon, and reciting the incantations which he composed. And when Eleazar would persuade and demonstrate to the spectators that he had such a power, he set a little way off a cup or basin full of water, and commanded the demon as he went out of the man to overturn it, and thereby to let the spectators know that he had left the man; and when this was done the skill and wisdom of Solomon was shown very manifestly: for which reason it is, that all men may know the vastness of Solomon's abilities, and how he was beloved of God, and that the extraordinary virtues of every kind with which this king was endowed, may not be unknown to any people under the sun; for this reason, I say, it is that we have proceeded to speak so largely of these matters.[5]

64. No Healing in Shrines

TALMUD

The Rabbis of the Talmud warned against believing in idolatrous healing. They were likely referring to the numerous healing temples of Asclepius, a healing cult dedicated to a Greek deity, and perhaps to Christian shrines.

[An Israelite named] Zunin said to R. Akiba: "We both know in our heart that there is no reality in an idol; nevertheless we see men enter [the shrine] crippled and come out cured. What is the reason?" He replied, "I will give you a parable: To what is the matter like? To a trustworthy man in a city, and all his townsmen used to deposit [their money] in his charge without witnesses. One man, however, came and deposited [his money] in his charge with witnesses; but on one occasion he forgot and made his deposit without witnesses. The wife [of the trustworthy man] said to [her husband], 'Come let us deny it.' He answered her, 'Because this fool acted in an unworthy manner, shall I destroy my reputation for trustworthiness!' It is similar with afflictions. At the time they are sent upon a man the oath is imposed upon them, 'You shall not come upon him except on such and such a day, nor depart from him except on such and such a day, and at such an hour, and through the medium of so and so, and through such and such a remedy.' When the time arrives for them to depart, the man chanced to go to an idolatrous shrine. The afflictions plead, 'It is right that we should not leave him and depart; but because this fool acts in an unworthy way shall we break our oath!'" This is similar to what R. Johanan said: "What means that which is written, And sore and faithful sicknesses?(Deuteronomy 28:59)— 'Sore' in their mission and 'faithful' to their oath."[6]

65. Incantations to Heal the Sick

JULIUS PREUSS

The Bible condemned magic in general, but the Sages accepted it for healing. This selection is from the classic work on medicine in the Bible and Talmud by Julius Preuss.

The treatment of a disease, in all generations, was dependent upon the understanding of the cause thereof. To treat the cause of the disease has been the desire and goal of therapists since times immemorial. As long as one believed that the illness was caused by the presence of a perilous evil spirit (demon, Satan) in the patient, it was natural to attempt to drive it out of the patient, in order to cure the sickness. It is noteworthy that the Talmud does not at all refer to actual exorcism. However, the word "incantation" *(lachash)* is used very often, which we interpret to represent a mild form of exorcism.

Concerning the basic question as to whether or not incantation is "a heathen practice", as is true of most aspects of superstition, and should therefore be prohibited, one can find supporters of both positions in the Talmud. Among the ancient Sages of the *Mishnah,* the *Tannaim,* there is not a single one who allows incantation, even if no names of idolatry are invoked during the incantation, and even if Biblical verses with God's name are recited. They declare that if someone "whispers a spell over a bodily illness" and says: *I will put none of these diseases upon thee, which I have brought upon the Egyptians, for I am the Lord that healeth thee, he is deprived of everlasting bliss* (i.e. the world to come). These Sages further prohibit one person from calling another to recite a Biblical verse to calm a frightened child, or to place a Bible or phylacteries on the child, in order that he fall asleep.

However, Rabbi Yochanan, the most prominent Palestinian Sage of the period of the *Amora'im* (sages of the *Gemara*), is not familiar in principle with this objection to incantation. In fact there exists a small but significant number of magical incantations from his Babylonian contemporaries, in which are even contained Biblical verses with God's name therein. It seems very doubtful, however, that these incantations originated with the Rabbis. In view of the numerous materials with cuneiform characters, it seems probably correct to assume that the Rabbis simply took them over from their heathen environment. Wherever necessary, the names of idolatrous deities seem to have been replaced with monotheistic designations.

Since incantation belongs to an occult science, the formulas used are mostly comprised of phrases unintelligible to us. Only the names of the patient and his mother are included in all incantations of antiquity. In some such incantations, the medicine man expectorated, and this spitting out occurred before or after a Biblical verse was recited which contained God's name. This practice was considered to be particularly offensive.

The use of incantations is a very ancient heathen custom. In Homer, blood flow is said to have been stopped in this manner. Cato is said to have bequeathed an incantation which is said to be helpful for dislocations; Marcus Varro has an incantation against podagra. The Druids sang (incantations) for the Gauls and the Alrunes for the Teutons. In Jerusalem, the 91st Psalm was sung as a *shir shel pega'im* or *shir shel naga'im*, as protection from evil spirits. In the "center of intelligence", even today, one can observe "incantations of the rose" recited by the most intelligent people.

One "whispered a spell" to ward off snakes and scorpions, and to guard against them, and for the healing of eye illnesses. It is related that Rabbi Meir used to hold discourses on Sabbath evenings, which were also attended by women. One husband, angry because his wife stayed out so late, swore that his wife could not return to the house unless she spat in the face of the speaker. When Rabbi Meir learned of this, he feigned an eye illness and asked that an intelligent woman *(chachama)* who understood the "whispering of spells" be brought. Such a woman was brought and she spat seven times in his face. Domestic peace was thus restored among the aforementioned couple.

Evidently, even in those days, women, in particular, made use of incantations, although the Talmudic Sages themselves were not frightened away from practicing this art. Thus, Rabbi Chanina went to visit the febrile Rabbi Yochanan and "uttered an incantation over him" whereby he was healed.

The use of incantations by physicians of antiquity is extolled by no less an authority than the great Galen. He states:

> Some people believe that incantations are equivalent to fairy tales of old women. I, too, thought this way for a long time. As time passed, however, I became convinced of the value of incantations, because of their apparent efficacy. I learned of their use for scorpion bites, and also for bones which remained stuck in the throat, and which became immediately dislodged following the enunciation of an incantation, *di'epodes.* The incantation formulas fulfill their purpose.

Incantation for a bone stuck in the throat, *bil'a,* is also mentioned in the Talmud and the disciples of Jesus revealed the power of their master to be *soter* or healing, in that, as the Talmud itself asserts, they whispered spells, using his name, with good results.

A special form of incantation includes the "placing of one's hands" on the patient. This is also a heathen custom. When the Syrian general, Naaman, came to Elisha in order to be healed of his leprosy, he thought that the prophet would stand before him and move his hand up and down over the leprous site, so that the leper (Naaman) would recover. Naaman did not expect a direct placing of the hand on his body, because touching a leper renders a person ritually unclean.

Placing the hands over a patient also played an important role in the legends about Jesus in which he healed the sick. Wolzendorff cites as proof that the miraculous healing of the people effected by Jesus was the result of "suggestion", the fact that his cures were not successful in Galilee; because there, he and his family were known. Jesus himself complained: *a prophet is not without honor, but in his own country, and among his own kin, and in his own house.*

Maimonides quotes the Talmudic decrees concerning incantations as follows: "if one was stung by a scorpion or a snake, it is permitted to whisper a spell over the affected part, so as to soothe the patient and give him reassurance. Although the procedure is absolutely useless, it has been permitted because of the patient's dangerous condition, so that he should not become distraught. One who whispers a spell over a wound, at the same time reciting a verse from the Torah, or one who recites a verse over a child to save it from fright or one who places a Torah scroll or phylacteries on an infant to induce it to sleep, are not only considered in the category of sorcerers and soothsayers, but are also included among those who repudiate the Torah itself; for they use its words to cure the body, whereas the Torah is only medicine for the soul."[7]

66. Permission to Physician to Heal

TALMUD AND MIDRASH

In the following selections from Talmud and Midrash, the Rabbis debated and tentatively accepted the validity of the healing craft. The famous statement of the Mishnah (second century) that physicians are destined for damnation is balanced by the assertion in rabbinic literature that God has given permission to the physician to heal. Many Sages themselves, notably Samuel, acquired reputations as healers. However, with this acceptance came concerns about the extent and limits of a physician's authority.

R. Judah says in his name: Ass-drivers are most of them wicked, camel drivers are most of them proper folk, sailors are most of them saintly, the best among the physicians is destined for Gehenna, and the most seemly among butchers is a partner of Amalek.[8]

On going in to be cupped one should say: "May it be Thy will, O Lord, my God, that this operation may be a cure for me, and mayest Thou heal me, for Thou art a faithful healing God, and Thy healing is sure, since men have no power to heal, but this is a habit with them." Abaye said: A man should not speak thus, since it was taught in the school of R. Ishamel: [It is written], *He shall cause him to be thoroughly healed.* From this we learn that permission has been given to the physician to heal. When he gets up [after cupping] what does he say?—R. Aha said: Blessed be He who heals without payment.[9]

Rabbi Ishmael and Rabbi Akiva were walking through the streets of Jerusalem and met a sick man who asked them: "How can I be cured?" They answered: "Do thus and such until you are cured." He said to them: "But who afflicted me?" "The Holy One, blessed be He," they answered. "So how can you interfere in a matter that is not your concern? God afflicted me and you wish to heal?" The rabbis then asked: "What is your vocation?" "I am the tiller of the soil. Here is a vine-cutter in my hand." They asked: "But who created the vine-yard?" "The Holy One, blessed be He." "Well you interfered in a vineyard which was not yours. God created it and you cut away its fruits?" they asked. "But were I not to plow and till and fertilize and weed, the vineyard would not produce any fruit," he explained. "So," they responded, "from your own work have you not learned what is written (Ps. 103:15): as for man his days are grass. Just as the tree, if not weeded, fertilized, and plowed, will not grow and bring forth its fruits, so with the human body. The fertilizer is the medicine and the means of healing, and the tiller of the earth is the healer."[10]

A sick person is fed at the word of experts. R. Jannai said: If the patient says, I need [food], whilst the physician says: He does not need it, we hearken to the patient. What is the reason? *The heart knoweth its own bitterness*. But that is self evident? You might have said: The physician's knowledge is more estab-lished; therefore the information [that we prefer the patient's opinion]. If the physician says: He needs it, whilst the patient says that he does not need it, we listen to the physician. Why? Stupor seized him.

Mar son of R. Ashi said: Whenever he says, "I need [food]" even if there be a hundred who say, "He does not need it", we accept his statement, as it is said: *"The heart knoweth its own bitterness"*. We learned in the Mishnah: If no ex-perts are there one feeds him at his own wish. That means only if no experts are there, but not if such experts are there?—This is what is meant: These things are said only for the case that he says, "I do not need it", but if he says, "I need it", then there are no experts there at all, [and] one feeds him at his own wish, as it is said: "The heart knoweth its own bitterness".[11]

67. Physician's Oath

ASAPH

The earliest writings of Jewish physicians have shown a ten-dency to fuse Jewish ethics with secular medical practice. Asaph's medical writings, which date from late antiquity (third to seventh century C.E.), are said to be among the earli-est by any Jewish physician. They include this oath, which has a distinctly Jewish overlay on the classic Oath of Hippocrates. That ancient oath (fourth century B.C.E.) enjoined the physician to act in the best interest of the patient, to maintain confidentiality, and it prohibited abortion, murder, assisted suicide, and sexual congress between physician and patient.

And this is the oath administered by Asaph, the son of Berachyahu, and by Jochanan, the son of Zabda, to their disciples; and they adjured them in these words: Take heed that ye kill not any man with the sap of a root; and ye shall not dispense a potion to a woman with child by adultery to cause her to miscarry; and ye shall not lust after beautiful women to commit adultery with them; and ye shall not disclose secrets confided unto you; and ye shall take no bribes to cause injury and to kill; and ye shall not harden your hearts against the poor and the needy, but heal them; and ye shall not call good evil or evil good; and ye shall not walk in the way of sorcerers to cast spells, to enchant and to bewitch with intent to separate a man from the wife of his bosom or woman from the husband of her youth.

And ye shall not covet wealth or bribes to abet depraved sexual commerce.

And ye shall not make use of any manner of idol-worship to heal thereby, nor trust in the healing powers of any form of their worship. But rather must ye abhor and detest and hate all their worshipers and those that trust in them and cause others to trust in them, for all of them are but vanity and of no avail, for they are naught; and they are demons. Their own carcasses they cannot save; how, then, shall they save the living?

And now, put your trust in the Lord your God, the God of truth, the living God, for He doth kill and make alive, smite and heal. He doth teach man understanding and also to do good. He smiteth in righteousness and justice and healeth in mercy and lovingkindness. No crafty device can be concealed from Him, for naught is hidden from His sight.

He causeth healing plants to grow and doth implant in the hearts of sages skill to heal by His manifold mercies and to declare marvels to the multitude, that all that live may know that He made them, and that beside Him there is none to save. For the peoples trust in their idols to succour them from their afflictions, but they will not save them in their distress, for their hope and their trust are in the Dead. Therefore it is fitting that ye keep apart from them and hold aloof from all the abominations of their idols and cleave unto the name of the Lord God of all flesh. And every living creature is in His hand to kill and to make alive; and there is none to deliver from His hand.

Be ye mindful of Him at all times and seek Him in truth, uprightness, and rectitude that ye may prosper in all that ye do; then He will cause you to prosper and ye shall be praised by all men. And the peoples will leave their gods and their idols and will yearn to serve the Lord even as ye do, for they will perceive that they have put their trust in a thing of naught and that their labor is in vain; (otherwise) when they cry unto the Lord, He will not save them.

As for you, be strong and let not your hands slacken, for there is a reward for your labours. God is with you when ye are with Him. If ye will keep His covenant and walk in His statutes to cleave unto them, ye shall be as saints in the sight of all men, and they shall say: "Happy is the people that is in such a case; happy is that people whose God is the Lord."

And their disciples answered them and said: All that ye have instructed us and commanded us, that will we do, for it is a commandment of the Torah, and it behooves us to perform it with all our heart and all our soul and all our might: to do and to obey and to turn neither to the right nor to the left. And they blessed them in the name of the Highest God, the Lord of Heaven and earth.

And they admonished them yet again and said unto them: Behold, the Lord God and His saints and His Torah be witness unto you that ye shall fear Him, turning not aside from His commandments and aid not the evildoers to shed innocent blood. Neither shall ye mix poisons for a man or a woman to slay his friend therewith; nor shall ye reveal which roots be poisonous or give them into the hand of any man, or be persuaded to do evil. Ye shall not cause the shedding of blood by any manner of medical treatment. Take heed that ye do not cause a malady to any man; and ye shall not cause any man injury by hastening to cut through flesh and blood with an iron instrument or by branding, but shall first observe twice and thrice and only then shall ye give your counsel.

Let not a spirit of haughtiness cause you to lift up your eyes and your hearts in pride. Wreak not the vengeance of hatred on a sick man; and alter not your prescriptions for them that do hate the Lord our God, but keep his ordinances and commandments and walk in all His ways that ye may find favour in His sight. Be ye pure and faithful and upright.

Thus did Asaph and Jochanan instruct and adjure their disciples.[12]

68. The Good Physician

ISAAC ISRAELI

*The medical writings of the tenth-century Moroccan physi-
cian Isaac Israeli served as universal medical texts for centuries. His set of instructions for physicians includes ethical
injunctions, which stemmed in part from Jewish religious con-
victions and in part from ancient Greek medical writers.*

1. Man, more than other living creatures, seeks to maintain himself. It is more
so since he is an image of God and has the obligation to make use of all things
to ensure his being, his continuance, and his preservation. This is before he
becomes preoccupied with other knowledge and tasks with which he may be
concerned. Because man himself is important, it is therefore obligatory and
compulsory that, before all else, comes the use of a practical art of medicine.

6. The best physician is that one who has delved into the works of most
ancient physicians, especially in the work of Galen, the Prince of Physicians,
whose exposition is extraordinary and who constantly handled therapeutics
with the greatest exhaustiveness. Those people err who say, "Do not go to the
master physician but to the practical healer." The ignorant do not know his
attempts, how he kills thousands before he heals one person. He says, however,
"Rely on me for I have looked into it." Do not listen to him for life is too short to
depend on uncertain trial to cure an illness or to know the nature of a plant
[drug]. It is worth while to accept the experience of thousands of past years
which we have inherited in writings so considerately prepared for us.

11. The physician does not effect the cure; he prepares and paves the way
so that nature, the real worker, may effect it.

13. Practical medicine, in its goal, is concerned only with the possible
rather than with the necessary. Death, however, is certain and unavoidable; it is
outside the power of the physician who considers people as good and worthy.

14. Like the study of all works on practical medicine, it is necessary to
have a knowledge of that which is pertinent to the principles of the natural
sciences, of which medicine is only one branch. It is valuable to have experience
in logical methods in order to refute the charlatans with reason, to intimidate
them, and to command respect.

15. The necessity for the physician to maintain health and to do away with illness is twofold; the latter is of less importance than the former. It is better for man that he not become ill rather than he become sick and then be cured.

16. If a sick one under a physician's care recovers, the physician should not conclude that he is a skillful specialist; it is possible that he could have been healed by another means, for example, by nature, without a doctor.

25. For your therapy, do not rely upon miracle means which often consist of stupidity and superstition.

30. Be especially concerned with visiting and treating the poor and needy sick for you cannot assume a more rewarding work.

31. You should calm the patient, concentrate on his improvement in outlook. If you are not convinced of it, then you should support his psyche.

43. A practice which is too large confuses the decision of the physician and permits incorrect orders to be prescribed.[13]

69. Rambam the Physician

MAIMONIDES

In his last two decades of life, Moses Maimonides, the greatest Jewish medieval theologian, devoted himself to medical practice and to medical writing. He was chief physician to the great Sultan Saladin and his successors. In his lifetime he was considered a leading medical authority in the Islamic world. Today medical historians, including Islamic scholars, consider him to be an exemplar of a remarkable era in the development of Western medicine. Of his ten medical treatises, half were letters to individuals who solicited medical advice. Passages from these and from other private correspondence give a unique glimpse of the man and of his medical practice in the twelfth century. As they make clear, he was deeply devoted to his patients and to the profession, and he himself battled with illness and grief.

Now God knows that in order to write this to you I have escaped to a secluded spot, where people would not think to find me, sometimes leaning for support

147

against the wall, sometimes lying down on account of my excessive weakness, for I have grown old and feeble.

With regard to your wish to come here to me, I cannot but say how greatly your visit would delight me, for I truly long to commune with you, and would anticipate our meeting with even greater joy than you. Yet I must advise you not to expose yourself to the perils of the voyage, for beyond seeing me, and my doing all I could to honor you, you would not derive any advantage from your visit. Do not expect to be able to confer with me on any scientific subject, for even one hour either by day or by night, for the following is daily occupation. I dwell at Misr Fostat and the Sultan resides at Kahira 'Cairo'; these two places are two Sabbath days' journey about one mile and a half distant from each other. My duties to the Sultan are very heavy. I am obliged to visit him every day, early in the morning; and when he or any of his children, or any of the inmates of his harem, are indisposed, I dare not quit Kahira, but must stay during the greater part of the day in the palace. It also frequently happens that one or two of the royal officers fall sick, and I must attend to their healing. Hence, as a rule, I repair to Kahira very early in the day, and if nothing unusual happens, I do not return to Misr until the afternoon. Then I am almost dying with hunger. I find the antechamber filled with people, both Jews and Gentiles, nobles and common people, judges and bailiffs, friends and foes—a mixed multitude, who await the time of my return. I dismount from my animal, wash my hands, go forth to my patients, and entreat them to bear with me while I partake of some slight refreshment, the only meal I take in the twenty-four hours. Then I attend to my patients, write prescriptions for their various ailments. Patients go in and out until nightfall, and sometime even, I solemnly assure you, until two hours and more in the night. I converse and prescribe for them while lying down from sheer fatigue, and when night falls, I am so exhausted that I can scarcely speak.

In consequence of this, no Israelite can have any private interview with me except on the Sabbath. On this day the whole congregation, or at least the majority of the members, come to me after the morning service, when I instruct them as to their proceeding during the whole week: we study together a little until noon, when they depart. Some of them return, and read with me after the afternoon service until evening prayers. In this manner I spend that day. I have here related to you only a part of what you would see if you were to visit me.[14]

In Egypt I met with great and severe misfortunes. Illness and material losses came upon me. In addition, various informers plotted against my life. But the most terrible blow which befell me, a blow which caused me more grief than anything else I have experienced in my life, was the death of the most perfect and righteous man who was drowned while traveling in the Indian Ocean. For nearly a year after I received the sad news, I lay ill on bed struggling with fever and despair. Eight years have since passed and I still mourn, for there is no consolation.[15]

Let not our Master censure his minor Servant for what he has mentioned in this his treatise about the use of wine and song, both of which the Law abhors, because this servant has not commanded that this ought to be done, but mentioned what his Art determines. The lawgivers have already known, as the physicians have known, that wine can be of benefit to mankind. The physician, because he is a physician, must give information on the conduct of a beneficial regimen, be it unlawful or permissible, and the sick have the option to act or not to act. If the physician refrains from prescribing all that is of benefit, whether it be prohibited or permissible, he deceives, and does not deliver his true counsel. It is manifest that the Law commands whatever is of benefit and prohibits whatever is harmful in the next world, while the physician gives information about what benefits the body and warns against whatever harms it in this world. The difference between the edicts of the Law and the counsels of Medicine is that the Law commands compliance with what benefits in the next world and compels it, and forbids that which harms in the next world and punishes for it, while Medicine recommends what is beneficial and warns against what is harmful, and does not compel this or punish for that, but leaves the matter to the sick in the form of consultation; it is they who have the choice.[16]

70. King Francis and the Converso Physician

STORY

In his book, Jews, Medicine, and Medieval Society, *Professor Joseph Shatzmiller writes the following:*

In the countries of Mediterranean Europe during the High or Late Middle Ages (1250 onward), one can hardly find a Jewish community that did not count at least one medical doctor among its members. Next to moneylending, medicine seems to have been the preponderant profession among Jews. . . . A minority group accounting for less than 1 percent of the population and representing at most 5 or 8 percent of the population in great cities occupied such a significant place in this profession, at times accounting for 50 percent or more of the practitioners. . . .[17]

The following story shows how great was the reputation of Jews as physicians in Europe during the Middle Ages.

When Francis de Vales, king of France, was seized with a very tedious sickness, and that the physicians of his house and court could give him no ease, he said that every time the fever returned, that it was not possible for any Christian physician to cure him. . . . He ordered a courier to be dispatched to Spain, to desire the Emperor Charles the fifth, to send a Jew doctor, the best of all the court. . . . There was no little laughing in Spain at his request, and all concluded that it was no other than the conceit of a man in fever. . . . They sent him a physician newly turned Christian, hoping thereby to comply with the king's curiosity. But the physician being arrived in France and brought to the king's presence, there past between them a most agreeable dialogue, wherein it was discovered, that the physician was a Christian, and therefore the king would take not physic at his hands. [Huarte relates the dialogue between the two about the nature of the messiah, whereby the doctor indicates his belief in Jesus Christ. The king is incensed by his response and orders him to leave.] . . . Then said the king, be gone to your own country in good time, for I have Christian physicians in my own court and house. I took you to be a Jew, who in my opinion are those that have a natural ability for cures. And so he took leave of him without allowing him to feel his pulse or examine his urine, or mingle the least word concerning his distemper, and forthwith sent to Constantinople for a Jew who recovered him only with Asses-milk.[18]

71. The Art of Healing

DAVID B. RUDERMAN

Abraham Yagel, an obscure sixteenth-century physician, left some personal manuscripts, which have been summarized by Professor David B. Ruderman in his book, Kabbalah, Magic and Science. *The following selection shows that Dr. Yagel saw no boundary between physical and spiritual health nor between the physician and spiritual counselor.*

Despite his literary and business interests, Yagel saw himself primarily as a physician. His distinguished contemporaries in the Jewish community of north-central Italy knew him both in this capacity and as an authority on astronomy and astrology. As we saw earlier, no less a religious authority than Menahem Azariah da Fano acknowledged him as "unique in our generation in the knowledge of the spheres" and as an "expert in all fields of learning." Yagel's patients were no less generous in their praise of his intellectual gifts and professional abilities. Solomon Forli, in requesting Yagel's medical intervention, proclaimed: "Who is greater in knowledge and in love for us than you, master? ... For from you is the source of life." On another occasion he wrote, "I have known you for some time by the name of one who is wise and discerning, a master of numerous fields and qualities." Daniel Modena, another of Yagel's patients, addressed him as "noble of the doctors"; Hananiah Finzi, one of Yagel's closest friends, panegyrized him as "a wise man preferable to a prophet," to whom "God bestowed wisdom in his heart to know how to find a cure for a blow." For Finzi, Yagel also represented the Solomon of his generation: "I refer to you in this generation: 'He was the wisest of all men' [Kings 5:11]."

No doubt Yagel appreciated such adulation. His voluminous scientific writings, his encyclopedic interests, and his bold educational plan offering to his Hebrew readers a vision of the overarching unity of all knowledge all testify to the seriousness with which he viewed himself and his prodigious accomplishments. Although he rarely referred to himself as "doctor," in one instance he signed a medical prescription in Latin characters with the name "Doctor Yagel." His medical title clearly provided him with intellectual status and spiritual authority among his coreligionists, a situation he earnestly sought and one that partially compensated for his incessant financial difficulties....

Yagel's position of respect in the Jewish community was attributable to a great extent to the obvious human needs for which he claimed to offer remedies. Jews of the sixteenth century lived in constant insecurity not only because they were a beleaguered minority but also because, like other human beings, they were constantly subject to pain, illness, and premature death. As Keith Thomas and others have shown, the hazards of coping with limited food supplies, bubonic plague, overcrowded living quarters, and poor sanitation affected all sectors of the population. Despite the high ratio of doctors practicing in northern Italy by the sixteenth century, the region was no less immune to the daily tragedies of life and death than the rest of premodern Europe.

Yet the claims and self-image of medical practitioners far outstripped their ability to effectuate reliable cures. Physicians, despite their sincere intentions, had little control over sanitary conditions. Even in dire emergencies such as plagues, they faced insurmountable difficulties in influencing public health policy. Their quarantines were bitterly resisted; they could not control the accompanying violence and looting; nor could they adequately cope with the putrid conditions of urban squalor that facilitated the virulent spread of the disease. Most important, they lacked appropriate conceptual knowledge. Most graduates of university medical schools were still trained according to the Galenic principles of humoral physiology, principles perfectly logical and internally consistent but unfortunately wrong....

Although the Galenic system continued to dominate medical learning throughout the sixteenth century because of the sheer weight of its authoritative tradition and appealing logic, it clearly required supplementation and refinement. The patient could be treated conventionally according to the principles of humoral physiology and simultaneously exposed to other forms of therapy—astrological medicine, magical healing, clerical counseling, or a combination of them all. In an intellectual universe structured by correlations and analogies between the corporeal, social, and cosmological, the appeal to supernatural forms of healing therapy appeared intellectually justifiable and self-evident. Medical science was holistic; the physician attempted to integrate his remedies within the cosmic reality he assumed to exist. He thus could prescribe natural remedies of diet control, evacuation, clean air, exercise, and sleep while charting the patient's horoscope and examining his religious and moral behavior....

By ascribing a variety of causes—natural, astral, and divine—to the patient's ailment, the doctor appeared less vulnerable or culpable if the patient failed to be cured; for although the physician was clearly responsible for the specific natural remedies he prescribed, he could hardly assume total responsibility for a condition astrologically determined, nor could he expect to be blamed for illness engendered by divine intervention. Moreover, as medical science was seen to encompass an astrological, magical, and religious dimension, the physician might prove more effective than his finite and faulty medical knowledge would ordinarily allow him to be. As an interpreter of the heavenly design, as a pastoral counselor, as a magical healer with a grab bag of prayers, charms, and talismans, the physician assumed a critical role as a kind of psychotherapist. Though generally helpless in the face of disease, he could offer psychological and pastoral care; he could heal by the power of suggestion; and he could help alleviate the anguish of his patient by regulating an individual's particular pain to a cosmic or divine source. Thus the physician—part scientist, part occultist, part clergyman—assumed a vital role within a society in constant urgent need of the services he purported to offer....

As a Jewish physician caring primarily for Jewish patients, Yagel understood his calling in a similar manner, with one added dimension: he came to his practice fully armed with the rich traditions of rabbinic medical wisdom and the imaginative speculations of kabbalistic theurgy and magic....

Since Yagel regards pathology as the study of divine, astral, and natural causes of illness, some revealed and some hidden, the physician must function with all three kinds of causes in mind. In a chapter of *Beit Ya'ar ha-Levanon* devoted to general remedies for illness, he offers specific guidelines for the patient and the physician, based mainly on a Zoharic text. When one becomes ill, he should first ask God's forgiveness, but then seek out a physician to effectuate a cure. The physician, in turn, should offer prayers to God, by whose agency the doctor is able to heal. Then the physician should examine his patient and offer his diagnosis. After determining what ails his patient, he should take blood from him, "since the majority of human illnesses arise from the increase of the blood when bloodletting is not performed at the appropriate time," "attempt to weaken the power of the illness through liquids and other [purgative]

153

drugs," and "protect him [the patient] by a good regimen of eating and drinking" in order to diminish the patient's pain. The physician must also "marshal his words prudently according to the conventions of medicine" in order to put his patient at ease, taking into account the quality of the patient's natural composition, his disease, and the specific conditions that led to the illness. Yagel also cautions against excessive bloodletting. If the patient becomes weak, he must be nourished immediately to restore his strength. Thus far, Yagel's interpretation of the *Zohar* text accords with the conventions of Galenic medicine.

What follows, however, surpasses the parameters of conventional Galenic treatment. The physician must record the details of the patient's horoscope, noting especially the precise time and circumstances of the beginning of the illness. He should also place around his bed substances that emit smoke; herbs and fragrances "will oppose the nature of the patient's constellation, since it is explained to masters of occult knowledge that smoke emissions engender miracles by bringing down the effluvia or the stars and conjunctions from evil to good." If the strategy is of no avail, the physician must then prepare his patient to accept death.

Yagel also points out three cardinal errors of physicians recorded in rabbinic literature. A physician might not suspect that the illness is attributable to sin and might consider "that everything evolves only from nature and the increase of the elements." Or he might jeopardize his patient's life "in his wish to do experiments on the bodies of human beings with his wisdom," or he simply will make mistakes in failing to be conscientious in his treatment. Finally, he might show favoritism in treating the wealthy and ignoring the poor.

Yagel's ultimate cure of illness lies in the realm of divine healing. He emphasizes that patients are sometimes cured by various charms and for this opinion he enlists the authority of the author of the *Sefer Ha-Zohar* regarding a mysterious Jewish medical book that contains, in Yagel's phrase, "words of medicine supported by the secrets of the Torah": "For some holy names emerge from verses written in the prophetic books that are employed by masters of amulets to heal known illnesses. Moreover, it [the book] contains medical advice that should be performed only by a sin-fearing person."

These procedures, Yagel explains on the basis of the *Zohar*, are similar to those employed by Balaam the magician "whose entire strength was in his mouth and in the spirit of his lips" in curing the ill through miracles. He is careful to warn, however, that many such charms are diabolical and can be performed only by "a person fearful of sin and clinging to God." All other charms, performed by less worthy practitioners through black magic, are prohibited. Yet the distinction between acceptable and forbidden charms is not clearly elucidated. The leap in Yagel's instructions from purgation and good diet to reciting holy names in the manner of Balaam from a mysterious Jewish source is both sudden and surprising. . . .

Yagel is neither confused nor agitated by the revolutionary pace of the new pharmaceutical discoveries, for it is the divine prerogative, he concludes, to determine when and how new dimensions of the natural world are revealed: "He [God] watches well over all the great things He created in revealing to us in our days things that nature covered from them [earlier generations] for thousands of years, even when He had disclosed them in other lands. For everything God does, He does in his own time, for there is a time for every desire and every act of creation, and according to the need for things and the time, God reveals them." As in the case of Yagel's fascination with other aspects of the natural world, the extraordinary discoveries confirmed and animated his belief in God's omnipotence and omniscience. Thus he proclaims: "For blessed is the wise man of secrets [God], to whom all mysteries are revealed."

Yagel's faith was tested more profoundly, however, by the severity of some of the cases he treated. His correspondence with his patients reveals the existence of a personal bond between the physician and patient. The relatively small sampling of *consilia* preserved by Yagel is insufficient to indicate whether the patients and cases they describe were typical of his practice. They provide little sense of the volume of his case load, of the proportion of Jewish or Christian patients he treated, and, like most *consilia* of other physicians, of the outcome of the treatment. The few cases Yagel copied were probably some of the most interesting he had treated, both from his perspective and our own. His patients, in the main, were well-to-do, respected members of the Jewish community. A number were learned in their own right in rabbinic and secular disciplines, such as Menahem Azariah da Fano and Hananiah Finzi. Yagel also treated the wife of Mordecai Dato and once assisted the widow of Judah Moscato. One of his most notable cases was the son of Daniel Modena of Sassuolo, the wealthy banker who apparently offered Yagel employment late in his career. In short, the patients Yagel describes were well connected, forming an

155

interesting cross section of the Jewish intellectual elite and the affluent from Mantua and Modena.

Almost all of Yagel's recorded cases concern some form of psychological disorder, which he usually subsumes under the general category of melancholia. In a letter to Menahem Azariah da Fano, for example, he describes the illness of Hillel of Viadana as a black, charcoal-like bilious humor affecting the brain and the heart that distorts the imagination and results in the patient's morbid depression. He prescribes soothing liquids and a tranquil atmosphere of prayer and personal support. Yagel also diagnoses the disease of Daniel Modena's son as a form of melancholia. Despite the special pleadings of the father to effectuate a cure, Yagel is soberly realistic about the slim chances for successful treatment. Yagel honestly informs his patron: "A man should know and be prepared for difficult illnesses that are sent [from heaven], which the doctor is not given permission to heal until the time of their order [to heal] arrives."

Nevertheless, Yagel prescribes a full regimen of purgatives and bloodletting. He prepares a chart for his patient listing the recommended order of purgations as well as supplementary astrological data. He orders his patient to hold in his hand a specially crafted copper amulet immediately after the purgation. He also offers an abundance of herbs and drugs as well as "hands outstretched to heaven" in prayer. Yagel's final letter to the father offers consolation on the son's death. In a remarkably compassionate and personal tone, Yagel laments the loss as his son and decries the misery of an old father who is obliged to mourn for his young son's premature death, whereby "the world order is overturned and the order organization is changed." Armed with an unwavering belief in divine justice, he failed to save the young man's life: "For high upon the high is the righteous judge; with scales and balances of justice, he weighs everything and will act with justice concerning everything that is hidden, for good or bad."

In another case Yagel encourages an unnamed patient to reduce his medication: "I saw your tears regarding your prolonged illness on your sickbed. You doubled and tripled your medication and still [the way] is long." He gently recommends limiting the number of purgations "and letting nature perform its function, since it is a wise worker." He soothes his patient with an entertaining story and encourages him to concentrate on his diet, to seek the support of his wife, and to pray.

Yagel's correspondence offers a fuller view of his treatment of psychological disease in two unusual cases. The first involved a young man of Mantua whose symptoms an anonymous observer carefully and clinically described to Yagel.

Mordecai Ongri . . . of Mantua, twenty-one years old. In the winter, after midnight, when he was alone by the fire looking at a small holy notebook, he claims he heard a sound in the room above as if something had fallen. The young man made a loud and frightening noise. A tremendous fear overcame him and he cried loudly for his father and brothers. When they searched the room above, they saw nothing and told him that it was the sound of cats running from one house to the next and that it was a natural occurrence. Yet from that moment, he remained like a man traumatized and petrified, lying down and incapable of getting up. He continued in this manner until they dressed and washed his face and hands as if he was a small infant . . . The doctor-bloodletter performed purgations and bloodletting on him . . . and this helped him somewhat [in curing] his disease, so that, when threatened, he returned to eating by himself and to taking care of his own bodily needs . . . He also did not trust himself to venture out alone from the house even during the daytime . . . Sometimes he reaches out his hand to take an object but his arm remains extended, for he claims that he is unable to [withdraw] it, as if another person's hands restrains him and does not allow him to take the food or clothing. So with great force and threats, he is encouraged to get up, to dress himself, to eat and drink. Also, in the beginning of his illness he cried a lot. He presently is not alert as he was during the beginning of his illness, when he prolonged his prayer by weeping, made confession, and found satisfaction by standing in the corners [of the room] afraid, alone, like a person who is astonished, surprised, and silent.

Yagel's relatively brief response to this inquiry transparently reveals his inability to offer adequate advice to effectuate a cure. He diagnoses the condition as melancholia. He prescribes sweet foods, chicken soup, and various purgatives. To these he adds Torah, worship, and charitable acts, the ultimate rabbinic prescription. He also suggests an arrangement of prayers with pleasant melodies and songs, all intended to calm the delirious soul. He obviously cannot promise any dramatic remedy for the young man's phobia.[19]

72. Physician's Oath

AMATO LUSITANUS

Amato Lusitanus, said to be the "single greatest medical fig-
ure of the Renaissance," was a physician to a pope, ambas-
sadors, and church officials and a prolific medical writer. His
oath, like that of Asaph, combines Jewish general ethics, a con-
servative medical approach, and Hippocratic injunctions.

"I swear by God the Almighty and Eternal [and by his most-holy Ten Commandments given on Mount Sinai by Moses the lawgiver after the people of
Israel had been freed from the bondage of Egypt], that I have never in my
medical practice departed from what has been handed down in good faith to
us and posterity; that I have never practiced deception, I have never overstated
or made changes for the sake of gain; that I have ever striven that benefit
might accrue to mankind; that I have praised no one, nor censured anyone to
indulge private interests, but only when truth demanded it. If I speak falsehood, may God and His Angel Raphael punish me with Their eternal wrath
and may no one henceforth place trust in me. I have not been desireful for the
remuneration for medical services and have treated many without accepting
any fee, but with none the less care. I have often unselfishly and firmly refused
remuneration that was offered, preferring through diligent care to restore the
patient to health, to being enriched by his generosity. [I have given my services
in equal manner to all, to Hebrews, Christians and Moslems.] Loftiness of
station has never influenced me and I have accorded the same care to the poor
as to those of exalted rank. I have never produced disease. In stating my opinion, I have always told what I believed to be true. I have favored no druggist
unless he excelled others in skill in his art and in character. In prescribing
drugs I have exercised moderation guided by the physical condition of the
invalid. I have never revealed a secret entrusted to me. I have never given a
fatal draught. No woman has ever brought about an abortion with my aid.
Never have I been guilty of base conduct in a home which I entered for medical service. In short, I have done nothing which might be considered unbe-
coming an honorable and distinguished physician, having always held
Hippocrates and Galen before me as examples worthy of imitation and not

having scorned the precepts of many other excellent practitioners of our art. I have been diligent and have allowed nothing to divert me from the study of good authors. I have endured the loss of private fortune, and have suffered frequent and dangerous journeys and even exile with calmness and unflagging courage, as befits a philosopher. The many students who have come to me have all been regarded as though they were my sons. I have used my best efforts to instruct them and to urge them to good conduct. I have published my medical works not to satisfy ambition, but that I might, in some measure, contribute to the furtherance of the health of mankind; I leave to others the judgment of whether I have succeeded; such at least has always been my aim and ever had the foremost place in my prayers."[20]

73. Prayer of Maimonides

MARCUS HERZ

The misnamed "Prayer of Maimonides" is the best known
Jewish statement on medical ethics. Its language is ecumenical,
and it omits the prohibition against abortion. It was not au-
thored by Moses Maimonides but most likely by Marcus Herz,
a prominent eighteenth-century German Jewish physician.

Almighty God, Thou has created the human body with infinite wisdom. Ten thousand times ten thousand organs has Thou combined in it that act unceasingly and harmoniously to preserve the whole in all its beauty—the body which is the envelope of the immortal soul. They are ever acting in perfect order, agreement and accord. Yet, when the frailty of matter or the unbridling of passions deranges this order or interrupts this accord, then forces clash and the body crumbles into the primal dust from which it came. Thou sendest to man diseases as beneficent messengers to foretell approaching danger and to urge him to avert it.

Thou has blest Thine earth, Thy rivers and Thy mountains with healing substances; they enable Thy creatures to alleviate their sufferings and to heal their illnesses. Thou hast endowed man with the wisdom to relieve the suffering of his brother, to recognize his disorders, to extract the healing substances, to discover their powers and to prepare and to apply them to suit every ill. In thine Eternal Providence Thou has chosen me to watch over the life and health of Thy creatures. I am now about to apply myself to the duties of my profession. Support me, Almighty God, in these great labors that they may benefit mankind, for without Thy help not even the least thing will succeed.

Inspire me with love for my art and for Thy creatures. Do not allow thirst for profit, ambition for renown and admiration, to interfere with my profession, for these are the enemies of truth and of love for mankind and they can lead astray in the great task of attending to the welfare of Thy creatures. Preserve the strength of my body and of my soul that they ever be ready to cheerfully help and support rich and poor, good and bad, enemy as well as friend. In the sufferer let me see only the human being. Illumine my mind that it recognize what presents itself and that it may comprehend what is absent or hidden. Let it not fail to see what is visible, but do not permit it to arrogate to itself the power to see what cannot be seen, for delicate and indefinite are the abounds of the great art of caring for the lives and health of Thy creatures. Let me never be absent-minded. May no strange thoughts divert my attention at the bedside of the sick, or disturb my mind in its silent labors, for great and sacred are the thoughtful deliberations required to preserve the lives and health of Thy creatures.

Grant that my patients have confidence in me and my art and follow my directions and my counsel. Remove from their midst all charlatans and the whole host of officious relatives and know-all nurses, cruel people who arrogantly frustrate the wisest purposes of our art and often lead Thy creatures to their death.

Should those who are wiser than I wish to improve and instruct me, let my soul gratefully follow their guidance; for vast is the extent of our art. Should conceited fools, however, censure me, then let love for my profession steel me against them, so that I remain steadfast without regard for age, for reputation, or for honor, because surrender would bring to Thy creatures sickness and death.

Imbue my soul with gentleness and calmness when older colleagues, proud of their age, wish to displace me or to scorn me or disdainfully to teach me. May even this be of advantage to me, for they know many things of which I am ignorant, but let not their arrogance give me pain. For they are old and old age is not master of the passions. I also hope to attain old age upon this earth, before Thee. Almighty God!

Let me be contented in everything except in the great science of my profession. Never allow the thought to arise in me that I have attained to sufficient knowledge, but vouchsafe to me the strength, the leisure and the ambition ever to extend my knowledge. For art is great, but the mind of man is ever expanding. Almighty God! Thou has chosen me in Thy mercy to watch over the life and death of Thy creatures. I now apply myself to my profession. Support me in this great task so that it may benefit mankind, for without Thy help not even the least thing will succeed.[21]

74. Laws of the Physician

SHULḤAN ARUKH

The Shulḥan Arukh, one of Judaism's most important law codes, outlines attitudes toward healing and the medical profession, which evolved many centuries after the time of the Mishnah. Expanding on the Talmud, it decrees that the physician has not merely permission, *but an* obligation, *to heal; and it adds the requirements that physicians must be trained and licensed by properly constituted authorities. This rule acknowledges the development of schools, professional societies, and civil codes for physicians after the twelfth century.*

1. The Torah has granted the physician permission to heal, and it is a religious duty which comes under the rule of saving an endangered life. If he withholds [treatment] he is regarded as one who sheds blood; and even if there is someone else who can heal him; for not from every one does one merit to be healed. Nevertheless, one should not occupy himself with medical treatment unless he is an expert and there is none other greater than he; for if not so, he is regarded as one who sheds blood. If one administered medical treatment without the permission of the Jewish Court, he is subject to payment of indemnities, even if he is an expert; and if he administered medical treatment, having the permission of the Jewish Court, and erred, causing [thereby] injury [to the patient], he is exempt by the laws of man and is held responsible by the laws of Heaven. If he caused death and it became known to him that he acted inadvertently, he is banished on account of him.

2. The physician is forbidden to take payment for his wisdom and learning but he may receive payment for his trouble and lost time.[22]

75. Satires on Physicians

HARRY FRIEDENWALD

Popular doggerel in the sixteenth century suggests that physicians did not always live up to the ideals of their profession.

The two following poems appeared in a collection of short poems published in Constantinople in 1577.

I am astonished at the physicians of our time,
When I behold their deeds and their deceit!
I saw them assembled near one (who called)
For their help and for relief from his ills;
When they cure they boast of the glory of their work,
But when they take life they say that God has killed;
They lay blame upon the sick who are innocent,
Yea in vain "they make long their furrows." (Ps. 129)
They demand great pay for shedding blood and
Fill their money bags with silver!
Is there anything like their evil in the world?
Can the earth endure their insolent arrogance?

Give thanks, oh reader, to the Lord, your Creator,
That you never fell into the hands of this doctor.
For you would not now read this poem
If while he lived, he had been your doctor.[23]

76. The Jewish Hospice

SAMUEL S. KOTTEK

The Jewish hospital is in the span of Jewish history only a recent arrival. Its medieval precursor was, as Professor Samuel Kottek writes, the "Hekdesh," a hospice for the poor and the stranger.

In the Middle Ages, the care of the sick in the Jewish communities was usually in the hands of sick care societies, one of their preoccupations being the so-called "Hekdesh." This was a kind of hospice, usually a single room or a little house near the Jewish cemetery. Its aim was to serve as a shelter for wandering peddlers and for strangers having no family connection in the town and eventually for sick people of poorer segments of society.

In those times, and until late in the eighteenth century, none of the middle class, and certainly none of the more affluent economic groups, would ever have dreamed of "hospitalizing" any member of their family in the Hekdesh. The sick were treated at home, even remote relatives being taken in by their kinsmen. Stress was laid on the commandment of "visiting the sick" and on strengthening family ties. For these reasons, the necessity of a hospital was not felt in the Jewish population. On the other hand, the constant persecutions and the frequent spoliations of the Jews led to poverty and migrations and created the need for communal shelters.

The term Hekdesh originally meant something dedicated to the Temple (it comes from a root meaning "holy"), and it implies that the hospice was supported by religiously motivated charity. (It should be noted that the first French Christian hospital was called Hôtel-Dieu, a shelter dedicated to God.)

The first recorded hospice in Germany was apparently in Regensburg in A.D. 1210. Such hospices were also recorded in other places of the Jewish Diaspora such as Yugoslavia, Sicily, and Spain, and are known to have existed throughout the thirteenth and fourteenth centuries. As late as the sixteenth century, every Jewish community of some importance had its Hekdesh.

The Hekdesh was administrated by the so-called "Hevrah Kadishah," a brotherhood that cared for the sick and for the dead. Sometimes this responsibility was shared by the community or even taken over by it. Unlike Christian hospitals of that time, the Hekdesh played no central role in the charities and had no autonomy until late in the eighteenth century.

The Hekdesh was located either in the synagogue building or near the cemetery. The reason for this peculiarity was the chronic lack of space for building and housing in the ghetto. Some hospitals were outside the walls of the city (in Berlin, Halberstadt, and Hanover), which was of course the case for the lepers' hospital and the so-called "Blatterhaus" (hospital for syphilitic patients), whenever and wherever there was such a Jewish institution. There was usually only one hospital for each Jewish community, but in larger communities, such as Posen, Berlin, Breslau, and Vienna, there were two hospitals. In Frankfurt, there were as many as three hospitals for some time.

How long did people stay in the Hekdesh? Usually, strangers were taken in for only a single night and then went somewhere else, but occasionally they stayed for a few days. A sick stranger, however, was allowed to stay until his recovery. In the Hekdesh there was usually only a single room with a few beds. Even in 1765 in a community as important as Wilna, there were only 18 beds available, ten for men and eight for women. The Jewish hospital built in Frankfurt in 1796 had no kitchen or bathing facilities.

The new hospital built in Vienna and opened in 1793 to replace the old Hekdesh, which had offered only six beds, comprised a cellar with laundry and pantry; a ground floor with the flat of the manager and his aides, the kitchen and a reserve sick room; and a first floor with two wards for men and women, five small rooms for two or three patients, an operating room, and a small synagogue. This seemed very large at the time and was indeed exceptional.

The care of the sick was in the hands of a beadle, who was in charge of the men, and a widow or the beadle's wife, who cared for the women. A physician or a surgeon was entrusted by the community with the duty of treating the poor without charge and was obliged to make sick calls in the hospital once or twice a day. The necessary funds were raised in two different ways, either by personal grants or by alms put into special boxes during the prayers at the synagogue on Mondays and Thursdays. In ancient times, these were market days; a short section of the Torah was read, and alms were collected, a tradition carried on to this day.

The sanitary conditions were usually dreadful, with little cleanliness or room and were aggravated by lack of funds and lack of education among the poor. The situation was not different in Christian hospitals.

Special problems existed in the care of women in labor and of the insane. In 1722, for instance, the Jewish community at Fürth was compelled to restrict the right of local poor women to enter the hospital for lying-in. If such a woman did appear, she would be accepted, but her family would get no further aid for the following three years, except in the case of sickness. In 1770, these regulations were extended from people living in the vicinity of eight to 10 miles (as stipulated in 1722) to those living at a distance of 14 miles. It appears, thus, that the sick-care establishment still remained a xenodochion and was not yet a nosocomion. The insane were sheltered in special rooms, often in the attic of the hospital, and the conditions in their quarters were even worse than in those of the other patients. However, in these times, the Christians often held the insane in dungeons and towers.

Servants had a right to a special status and to a kind of social insurance. For instance, a regulation made in the community of Kraków as early as 1595 stated that whenever a maid-servant fell ill, her employer had to pay for her stay in the Hekdesh and for food and drugs for a period of two weeks. Then, if she was still ailing, the costs were equally divided between the maid and the employer for an additional month. After that period, she had to pay all the costs, and if she could not, the "Hevrah Kadishah" took her in charge. Similar regulations, differing only in details, existed in several other communities.[24]

77. Principles of Administration of the Hospital

HARAV Y. HALBERSTAM

How can Jewish law be put to practical use in the administration of a hospital, not only in the individual actions of isolated patients and caregivers? A nineteenth-century Jewish hospital in Posen, which survived until the Holocaust, declared that it would be governed by the following nine principles.

1. The Kiryat Sanz Hospital shall be established as a holy institution with the aim of bringing benefit and healing to those who suffer, in accordance with the commandments of the Torah as stated in Tractate Nedarim 41, and in the Shulchan Aruch, Yoreh De'ah 336.

2. The Hospital shall accept every patient without distinction of sex, religion or race.

3. The Hospital shall be established on the basis of complete faith in the Creator of the Universe, Who grants life to every living creature, and in Whose hand is every living soul. Its doctors and medical staff shall have a firmly based faith in this basic principle, and all their practices shall be in accordance with a spirit of faith in the Creator and in His Holy Torah.

4. In this Hospital all the commandments of the Torah shall be observed, as laid down by the *Shulchan Aruch* and by our great Rabbis. A Rav learned in

Torah shall be appointed, to whom all questions shall be put concerning religious practice, and his decisions shall be final and binding upon all the Hospital staff. In the matter of the observance of the Sabbath, the permission granted in the Torah to instruct non-Jews to carry out certain classes of work under certain conditions shall be made use of. Care shall be taken that the clothing worn by persons in the hospital shall be modest in accordance with the traditions of the Torah and Judaism.

5. Every effort shall be made to employ doctors and medical staff who are highly qualified in their profession, and who also possess good qualities in their mode of behavior and in their attitude to life. They should be persons who are full of love for their fellow Jews and for every other human being. As it is stated in the Torah: "Thou shalt love thy neighbor as thyself."

6. All staff shall endeavor in every possible way to lessen the pain and suffering of the patients and seek to improve their inner feelings and spiritual condition, as this will also assist in their healing, as the *Shulchan Aruch* states.

7. Every effort shall be made to be very particular in the observance of the commandments relating to the treatment of one's fellowman, with special care not to do any wrong to any person who works in the Hospital, or comes into contact with the Hospital, and to be especially careful that all wages are paid at the correct time, without any delay.

8. The atmosphere in the hospital among the staff, and in their dealings with all whom they come into contact, shall be based on friendship, peace and brotherly love.

9. A Torah research institute shall be established to carry out research on solutions to medical problems in the light of the rulings of the Torah, in order to assist Jewish people who observe the commandments of the Torah.[25]

78. Studies of Jewish Physicians in the Warsaw Ghetto

ISRAEL MILEJKOWSKI

It would be hard to find a more moving example of the devotion to the healing professions than this statement. Dr. Israel Milejkowski, the head of the department of public health in the Warsaw ghetto, discusses his colleagues' medical research on the ravages of malnutrition in the ghetto.

The torture of words ... I have never felt it as strongly as now when I have to write an introduction to this work. This is an unbelievable moment since the work was originated and pursued under unbelievable conditions. I hold my pen in my hand and death stares into my room. It looks through the black windows of sad empty houses on deserted streets littered with vandalized and burglarized possessions. It is difficult under such conditions to collect one's wits and even more difficult to express one's feelings. My tongue is too pallid to present the magnitude of the defeat. I am looking for suitable words—it is torture.

This work was never finished. It was interrupted on July 22, 1942. This was a crucial day in the history of the Warsaw ghetto—the day when the deportations, the mass murder, began. Yes, deportations, mass murder, synonymous words in the history of the ghetto. The monstrosity of it will be fully understood only in the future.

Let us be silent—as silent as the empty houses in the empty streets of our ghetto. In this prevailing silence lies the power and the depth of our pain and the moans that one day will shake the world's conscience.

The history of the Warsaw ghetto can be divided into two periods—before July 22, 1942 and the period following. The first period was characterized by general hunger, the second period by massive death. It is not surprising, therefore, that when the second period started, the work on hunger stopped. The hospitals and laboratories were destroyed and, most important, the human element, our workers and the subjects of our work, were gone. Work was stopped but not liquidated. When the first horrible shock of the deportations was over, the accumulated scientific material was studied again and organized. This is the work being published now. It is an "unfinished symphony" full of meaning, written by Jewish doctors in 1942. One detail should not be omitted: the work on the manuscript is being carried out in one of the undestroyed rooms of the cemetery buildings. This is the symbol of our living and working environment.

The work on hunger started in February 1942. Hunger was the most important factor of everyday life within the walls of the Warsaw ghetto. Its symptoms consisted of crowds of beggars and corpses often lying on the streets covered with newspapers. Mortality data on hunger and its two companions, tuberculosis and typhus, were collected from orphanages and refugee centers and from specific hospital material.

167

A group of medical colleagues, themselves living constantly with the hunger problem, decided that the reality of their everyday grim life should become the subject of our scientific work. Disregarding the terrible conditions, which were completely unsuitable to the work in progress, all of these doctors labored with utmost devotion and fervor. The hospitals were located in temporary buildings not suitable for the purpose, and lack of apparatus, reagents, and other equipment made the research even more difficult. Many of our physician colleagues themselves suffered from hunger. In spite of this, nobody interrupted the work and quietly, modestly, without any advertising the work was done. The material collected during five months would have required at least a year under normal conditions. It was as if we knew subconsciously that the work could be interrupted at any minute.

The tops of the walls of the Warsaw ghetto were covered with broken glass. Their purpose was singular: mass extermination by mass starvation. That was the reason for this odious brick and glass structure. But the creator of this monstrosity was somehow frustrated; a new unpredicted power arose in Warsaw: smuggling. Smuggling, a rather shameful occupation, was our salvation. Night and day the smugglers fought the diabolic forces that built the walls. Smuggling food from the Aryan part of Warsaw curtailed the prevalence of hunger, its spread, its tempo, and its irreversibility. No changes in the structure of the walls—no bricks, no maiming broken glass—could prevent some supplies from trickling into the ghetto. Therefore the enemy had to find another more efficient means of extermination. After 18 months of struggle our conqueror, seeking our possessions, our blood, and our lives, discovered a better way and hunger was replaced by deportation.

Deportation became the curse of the ghetto. Where to? How? People were chased from the streets, from apartments, from basements and attics. They were chased with guns and with whips into the unknown. Packed into cattle-trains, children separated from parents and wives from husbands, masses of people without water or bread. People driven in inhuman chaos, disorganized, the old, the young, the healthy, and the mortally sick together; a trip without return. This system of extermination was much more efficient than hunger; we have the data to prove it.

The closing of the ghetto walls resulted in 43,000 deaths; in two months deportation resulted in 250,000 deaths. Therefore I emphasize once more the role of the unknown smuggler, who with his own blood and sweat made our scientific work in the ghetto possible.

I must mention here two men who helped us to start and to continue our research, the head of the Jewish council, Adam Czerniakow, and the head of the economic council, Abraham Gepner.

A last few words to honor you, the Jewish doctors. What can I tell you, my beloved colleagues and companions in misery. You are a part of all of us. Slavery, hunger, deportation, those death figures in our ghetto were also your legacy. And you by your work could give the henchman the answer "Non omnis moriar," "I shall not wholly die."

Dr. Israel Milejkowski
Head, Department of Public Health
Jewish Council in Warsaw
Warsaw, October 1942[26]

79. The Sacredness of Human Life

SHIMON M. GLICK

Israeli physician Dr. Shimon Glick argues for a fundamental distinction between the basic premises of Jewish medical obligations and those of current western ethics based on patient rights and autonomy.

Unlimited Human Autonomy—A Cultural Bias?

Autonomy has become a dominant bioethical value in the Western world. It is the basis of many ethical decisions, and considerations of autonomy influence legislators, judges, and the public alike. The predominance of autonomy has been described by one of its critics as verging on the "tyrannous."

In this essay I describe three recent events in Israel that run counter to this trend. They include court decisions and the enactment of laws that clearly place Israel in a unique, and perhaps lonely, position in the Western world. The most recent event was a decision by a district judge who ordered the force-feeding of a group of political prisoners engaged in a hunger strike that, in the opinions of physicians in the prison service, was endangering their lives. The judge stated clearly that when there is a conflict between life and dignity, the preservation of life takes precedence.

By coincidence, one of the prisoners was hospitalized in the department of internal medicine that I head. Since this was a most unusual and delicate situation for the entire staff, I decided that rather than have the house officer proceed immediately to the admission history taking and physical examination, I would first meet with the prisoner to discuss the issues. He was a pleasant, articulate young man in his 20s who had the usual appearance of an ultra-orthodox Jew, with a beard, side locks, and a large skullcap. He was engaged in reading a religious tract.

After a few pleasantries, I explained that he had been sent to the hospital to be fed, even against his will. I pointed out that I was under two sets of orders, one from the legally constituted Israeli court, and the other, since I am an orthodox Jew, from a divine edict that commands me not to let a fellow human die if such an event can be prevented. He responded quite calmly that he rejected the authority of the court, since he regarded it as part of the corrupt system against which his protest was directed. With respect to the divine edict, he pointed out that there are situations in which one is commanded by this same divine authority to sacrifice one's life for a greater cause. He indicated that he would not be dissuaded from this firmly held position.

I indicated that we had the will and the ability to feed him even against his will and that it would be much more pleasant for all concerned if he did not resist being fed through a nasogastric tube. He asked for time to think it over and shortly thereafter stated his position. He requested assurance that the tube feeding meet his particularly high standards for kosher food and that he be permitted to deposit a letter, with copies sent to a list of government authorities, indicating that he was being fed against his express wishes and that I would bear the legal and criminal consequences. When this was accomplished, he offered no resistance and accepted the feeding "under protest."

The decision by this Israeli court stands in striking contrast to a recent situation in Turkey in which at least 12 hunger strikers died; to previous political hunger strikes in Ireland and South Africa; and to the generally accepted position of Western bioethicists, as reflected in the Tokyo Declaration. I am convinced that my particular hunger striker was ultimately pleased with the turn of events. He received the necessary attention, yet he was prevented from dying by a superior power. In essence, he was able to have his cake and eat it too.

The second event, which took place a month earlier, was the enactment of a patients' rights bill by the Knesset, Israel's national legislature. Much of the law was relatively noncontroversial, but one clause in the original bill created considerable debate. It required that informed consent be obtained before treatment, as in most Western countries, and it spelled out in some detail the information to be provided to the patient. The legislators were faced with a major dilemma, however: what to do when a patient refuses a treatment that is clearly lifesaving. The government's chief legal counsel convened a meeting of about 30 physicians, philosophers, lawyers, and clergy to discuss this issue. The civil libertarians in the group, of course, took the standard Western position — namely, that under no circumstances could therapy be rendered against the will of a competent patient, unless the patient's illness threatened the welfare of others, as in the case of certain communicable diseases.

But others in the group would not accept this position. As one of Israel's leading philosopher-ethicists stated dramatically: "I simply am incapable of standing idly by and watching while someone lies on the railroad tracks waiting for an approaching train in order to commit suicide, without making an effort to prevent that person's death, even against the person's will." The final compromise, a bit unusual by any standard, permits a competent patient to be treated against his or her expressed will if the legally constituted hospital ethics committee is convinced that there is "reason to believe that after receiving the treatment the patient will give . . . retroactive consent."

This compromise might legitimately be seen as a bit of Talmudic legerdemain to justify physician's paternalism and disregard of patient's wishes. But I would contend that it allows a less simplistic approach to a patient's refusal of therapy than does the conventional Western view. Indeed, on occasion, patients who are fully competent in the legal sense refuse lifesaving therapy, but the reason for the refusal may well be an irrational fear, which is not always overcome even by repeated attempts at persuasion. One might perhaps see forcing people to undergo lifesaving therapy as an action that does respect their autonomy and for which they may be temporarily compromised by irrationality, although they remain within the bounds of legally defined competence. Such overriding of patients' expressed wishes should be rare, and indeed is so in

Israel, but the Israeli system now provides an avenue of escape from rigid adherence to the constraints of laws based on autonomy, which may lead to needless deaths.

The two events I have described were preceded by a landmark decision in 1993 by the Israeli Supreme Court that perhaps best articulates the Israeli position on autonomy. In the decision, which concerned the treatment of a child with Tay-Sachs disease, the vice-president of the Court described Israeli law and society as an amalgam of two values that may at times conflict. On the one hand are the values of Jewish tradition, which place great emphasis on the sanctity of human life. On the other hand are the values of Western democracy, which stress human autonomy. These two fundamental principles may conflict when questions about ending a patient's life at the patient's request are raised. The vice-president therefore enunciated precedent-making position that, in accordance with the principle of the sanctity of human life, unequivocally ruled out any action that could be construed as active euthanasia or physician-assisted suicide, even when it was taken in response to a patient's express wishes. At the same time, the decision recognized, out of respect for human autonomy, the right of a terminally ill, suffering patient to reject intrusive and uncomfortable therapy that cannot cure the basic illness.

These three examples provide a glimpse into how a society that by many standards is an integral part of the Western scientific and medical world deviates considerably from Western norms in certain fundamental respects. The reasons are multiple and complex. Clearly, however, Jewish faith and culture place enormous emphasis on the value of human life. This position has been expounded in terms of what I call the "mythology" of the infinite value of human life.

The biblical admonition "Do not stand idly by your friend's blood" creates an imperative for extensive involvement in the affairs of others, for their benefit—more so than is generally accepted in the West. In addition, the concept of mutual responsibility among Jews has been clearly articulated: "All Jews are responsible for each other's deeds." Furthermore, the trauma of the Holocaust, whose survivors abound in Israel, is often remembered in terms of the failure of the nations of the world to take action to prevent the death and suffering of others. There are a few factors that, I believe, contribute to the Israeli ethos, which calls into question a policy of nonintervention when human life is at stake.

The conventional Western view says to competent people who wish to end their lives, "If that is your autonomous desire, we will not obstruct you in any way." Indeed, most Western countries have abolished the criminality of suicide. The traditional Jewish view says, "You are so valuable to us, beyond what you mean to yourself, that we simply cannot permit you to die. We care so much about you that we are willing even to violate your human rights in order to save your life." These two contrasting approaches represent, on the one hand, an individualistic view of society, and on the other hand, a perception of society more as a community, even a family. It is perhaps no coincidence that one of the chief proponents of the communitarian movement in the United States is a former Israeli.

Classic Western bioethics and law do not accept unlimited human auton-omy, either. They override individual autonomy when respecting it would en-danger others, as when antituberculous therapy must be imposed, but they respect autonomy almost totally when others are not directly affected. The Israeli view described here may be seen as a rejection of the idea that a person's actions in ending his or her life affect only that person. Instead, it asserts that a person's death diminishes others as well and that therefore society is permitted to intervene.

The widely accepted Western approach by which a hunger striker's expressed desire to die is accepted at face value and by which society is absolved of any responsibility for preventing such a death seems somewhat simplistic, as is clear from the story of the hunger striker I have told here. A Western court would have had no difficulty deciding not to feed him, and in-deed the issue would probably not have been brought to a court, but that might have been a tragic error.

Even the strongest advocates of autonomy would do well also to consider the possibility that some of the most articulate, seemingly determined hunger strikers may not be fully autonomous in their actions. Pressures from politically like-minded colleagues, the need to save face, and other factors may preclude a totally autonomous decision. An error by which dignity is denied in favor of life may be remediable, but one that denies lifesaving action is irreversible.

In describing the case of this hunger striker, I do not in any way mean to assert that people do not have the right to sacrifice their lives for a higher cause. The world is a better place because of many such martyrs. Nor do I countenance the complicity of physicians with totalitarian regimes when they force-feed fasting protesters in a manifest attempt to break the resistance of legitimate protest movements. But I do think that the issue is much more complex than is suggested by the politically correct view that feeding hunger strikers by force is always unethical.

Israel is not alone in limiting autonomy in favor of preserving life. At a 1992 conference on the cross-cultural dimensions of medical ethics, a speaker described the prosecution and conviction in India of a physician who allowed a patient to die because he did not impose treatment against the patient's will.

There is deep disagreement in the West about many bioethical issues, whether they are classic ones such as abortion and euthanasia, or issues related to advances in biology and medicine, such as genetic engineering and new techniques of reproduction. But there is a fairly strong consensus about the respect given to patients' autonomy in a wide range of ethical situations, and about the priority that autonomy should be accorded. The consensus may create the illusion that this Western approach is almost canonical truth. It is important, however, to be aware of and sensitive to trends that run counter to prevalent Western axioms and dogma and that may contribute significantly to bioethical thinking.[27]

The Caring Sage

*Then the word of the Lord came to Isaiah: "Go and tell
Hezekiah: Thus said the Lord, the God of your father
David: I have heard your prayer. I have seen your tears.
I hereby add fifteen years to your life."*

Isaiah 38:4

Introduction

*S*ince biblical times, Jewish clergy—whether priest, rabbi, rebbe, or sage—have helped to care for the sick. Until this century, the community believed in the Sage's ability to comfort and help the ill and in the Sage's great spiritual power to look inside individuals and diagnose their illnesses, whether mortal or moral. What we would call medical knowledge was part of a Sage's tool kit. The Sages understood that the realms of body, emotion, intellect, and spirit were all linked together and that pain and illness in one could result in sickness in the others. Therefore, the Sages endeavored to care for people by helping them in all four of these "worlds." They provided information on hygiene and diet and could name the disease or the demon that was causing the symptoms. They offered counsel and help in decision-making. The Sages developed a curriculum of enlightening texts to study, which would give sick persons and their families succor. And they offered a framework for existence that included a life after death, which could comfort the dying and their kin.

Today, rabbis, cantors, and laypersons continue to practice the rabbinic tradition of visiting the sick. It is one of a clergy person's central tasks: to ease suffering through companionship and prayer. These acts of caring are all the more potent when performed within Judaism's framework of concern for the sick.

80. Solomon Overcomes the Devils

TESTAMENT OF SOLOMON

*In ancient times, King Solomon was believed to have received
from God the knowledge of healing, which he brought to the
Jewish people.*

The Testament of Solomon *(probably a late third-century
work of uncertain provenance and authorship) offers a detailed picture of King Solomon as seen in the culture of the
day. In this selection, King Solomon learns about thirty-six
heavenly bodies, divisions of the Zodiac, that cause disease.
Angelology, demonology, and astrology were popular parts of
Judaism until recent times and were considered integral forms
of the knowledge needed to cure illness.*

Then I commanded another demon to appear before me. There came to me
thirty-six heavenly bodies, their heads like formless dogs. But there were among
them (those who were) in the form of humans, or of bulls, or of dragons, with
faces like the birds, or the beasts, or the sphinx. When I, Solomon, saw these
beings, I asked them, saying, "Well, who are you?" All at once, with one voice,
they said, "We are thirty-six heavenly bodies, the world rulers of the darkness of
this age. But you, King, are not able to harm us or to lock us up; but since God
gave you authority over all the spirits of the air, the earth, and (the regions) beneath the earth, we have also taken our place before you like the other spirits."
    Then I, Solomon, summoned the first spirit and said to him, "Who are you?"
    He replied, "I am the first decan of the zodiac (and) I am called Ruax. I
cause the heads of men to suffer pain and I cause their temples to throb. Should
I hear only, 'Michael, imprison Ruax,' I retreat immediately."[1]

81. What's in a Name?

TALMUD

*After the destruction of the Temple, the Rabbis took on some
responsibilities formerly reserved for the Priests, as in the following case of the diagnosis of the skin condition* tsara'at,
often translated as leprosy.

Having the knowledge and ability to differentiate among diseases and give them a name is a crucial step in the healing process. To this end, Jewish texts throughout history emphasize the importance of diagnosis. In the following excerpt skin diseases are addressed in a detailed way. The crux of this text, however, is not the details, but the importance of having an authorized person give a name to an illness, and thus begin the healing process.

R. Hanina the Prefect of the Priests says: The colours of leprosy-signs are sixteen. R. Dosa b. Harkinas says: The colours of leprosy-signs are thirty-six. Akabya b. Mahalaleel says: Seventy-two. R. Hanina the Prefect of Priests says: They may not inspect leprosy-signs for the first time the day after the Sabbath since the end of that week will fall on the Sabbath; nor yet on the second day of the week since the end of the second week will fall on the Sabbath; nor [do they inspect leprosy-signs] in houses on the third day of the week since the end of the third week will fall on the Sabbath. R. Akiba says: They may inspect them any time; and if [the time for inspection at the end of the seven days] falls on a Sabbath they leave it until after the Sabbath. This may bear either with leniency or with stringency.[2]

82. Rabbinic Remedies

TALMUD

If one were to look for a treatise on folk cures in the rabbinic era, one would have to go no farther than the Babylonian Talmud, tractate Gittin, folios 68b–70b. Here is a short example of the sorts of healing arts that were part of a Sage's repertoire. Not only was the Sage learned in spiritual healing, he also had to care for the bodies of those in his community.

For blood rushing to the head the remedy is to take *shurbina* and willow and moist myrtle and olive leaves and poplar and rosemary and *yabla* and boil them all together. The sufferer should then place three hundred cups on one side of his head and three hundred on the other. Otherwise he should take white roses with all the leaves on one side and boil them and pour sixty cups over each side of his head. For migraine one should take a woodcock and cut its throat with a white *zuz* over the side of his head on which he has pain, taking care that the blood does not blind him, and he should hang the bird on his doorpost so that he should rub against it when he goes in and out.[3]

83. Samuel the Healer-Sage

TALMUD

One of the Sages, Samuel, was a well-known and accomplished physician. The bifurcation of body and soul was a foreign concept to the Sages. Healing and empathy were part of Torah in the broadest sense.

Samuel Yarhina'ah was Rabbi's physician. Now, Rabbi having contracted an eye disease, Samuel offered to bathe it with a lotion, but he said, "I cannot bear it." "Then I will apply an ointment to it," he said. "This too I cannot bear," he objected. So he placed a phial of chemicals under his pillow, and he was healed. Rabbi was most anxious to ordain him, but the opportunity was lacking. "Let it not grieve thee," he said. "I have seen the Book of Adam, in which is written, 'Samuel Yarhina'ah shall be called "Sage", but not "Rabbi", and Rabbi's healing shall come through him.'"[4]

84. Hasidic Home Treatments

JOEL BA'AL SHEM

Bloodletting was a common practice until very recently, and it was considered crucial that Sages have some knowledge of it.

Blood Letting

He who is cupped should not eat any apples that day. I have found it in an old book and it is already well-known that he who is cupped should not partake of milk, cheese, onions or cress. They have also said that he who has been bled should not move from his place until he has first drunk, and he should not eat until he has waited as much time as it would require to walk one-half mile. If much blood comes forth due to cupping, take an herb called *tiringita*, boil in old, strong wine, drink for three days each morning, and the blood will return to its former strength. During the boiling you must keep the vessel covered.

Blood (Nose Bleed)

For nose bleed, take at the apothecary's *urtica* juice, dip cotton in the juice and place in the nostrils. Also dip a cloth in the juice and lay on the temples and forehead.

It is also good to cut an onion in two parts, take half and seal the nostrils.

The Kabalists have written that whoever smells the leaves of myrtles causes the flow of blood from the nose to cease.

In the works of Nahmanides, I found it prescribed to write the patient's name backwards with his blood, or to mix lime with the white of a hen's egg and place it on the forehead, or to burn the droppings of a pig (male pig for man, etc.) in a new pot, and put the ashes in the nose. These cure.[5]

85. Adding a Name

HASIDIC TALE

Changing a sick person's name in order to facilitate healing is a ritual practiced to this day. This is not meant as a superstitious rite but as a profound redirection of the person's life. The new name must be accompanied by a new mission and vision—a renewal of spirit that is meant to speed the renewal of body.

My brother once was very, very sick when he was a child. My father went into the Boyaner Rebbe. He told him then to change his name. There is a certain thing of changing—not changing—but adding on a name. That's what they do. And he promised him he would be better. He started getting better then.[6]

86. Simhah and Healing

REBBE NACHMAN OF BRESLOV

Judaism has long recognized the connection between body, emotion, intellect, and spirit. Bringing joy and meaning to life also adds to health. Rebbe Nachman, a nineteenth-century Hasidic scholar, wrote the following from his own experience with illness.

It's a great mitzvah to be happy all the time, and to make every effort to avoid gloom and depression. All the illnesses people suffer come only because of lack of joy. For there are ten basic types of melodies, and these are the foundation of true joy. Thus it is written, "[It is good to give thanks to God, and to sing to Your Name, O Most High. . . .] With an instrument of *ten* strings. . . . For You have made me *joyous*, O God, through Your work" (Psalm 92:2–5). These ten types of melody enter into the ten different pulses of the human body, giving them life. For this reason, when a person is lacking in joy, which consists of the ten types of melody, his ten pulses become weakened because of the flaw in the ten types of melody, giving rise to illness. For all the different kinds of illnesses are included in the ten kinds of pulse, and all the different kinds of songs and melodies are included in the ten types of melody. The particular illness that arises corresponds directly to the flaw in the joy and the song. Eminent medical authorities have also spoken at length about how all illness is rooted in depression and gloom.

And joy is the great healer! And in time to come there will be tremendous joy. For this reason our Rabbis said, "The Holy One, blessed be He, will be the Head of the dance circle of the tzaddikim in time to come." That is to say, God will form a dance circle of the tzaddikim, and He will be the Head of the circle *rosh choleh*. For the Divine Presence is above the head of the head *(rosh)* of the sick person *(choleh)*, as our Rabbis learned from the verse, "HaShem will sustain him on the bed of sickness" (Psalm 41:4, *Nedarim* 40a). For the invalid has no vitality at all: it is only the Divine Presence that gives him life. Through the joy that will reign in time to come, all sickness will be remedied. The sickness of the invalid, the *(choleh)*, will be turned into *(choleh)*, a dance circle, and then God will be the *(rosh choleh)*, Head of the dance circle, because joy is the remedy for the invalid. This is the reason that joy and dance are called *choleh*: because they are the remedy for illness.

The main point is that one must make every effort and put all one's strength into being happy at all times. Man's natural tendency is to let himself become depressed and discouraged because of the vicissitudes of life. Everyone has his full share of suffering. For this reason one has to force oneself to be happy at all times and to bring oneself to a state of joy in whatever way possible, even with good-natured fun and jokes. It is true that true contrition over wrongful behavior is a good thing, but only for brief periods. One should set aside time each day to examine oneself and regret any wrong one may have done and open one's heart to God. But one should then be happy for the whole of the rest of the day. The dangers of grieving over one's sins, which can easily lead to depression, are much greater than those of veering from joy into light-headedness. Contrition is far more likely to lead to depression. One should therefore always be happy, and only at set times feel regret for any wrongdoing.[7]

87. Rabbi Sofer Visits the Sick

AARON LEVINE

Even rabbis are human and have limits on their time, strength, and patience. How can one authentically perform the mitzvah *of visiting the sick without wreaking havoc on the rest of one's life? Rabbi Akiva Eger (1761–1837, Germany) provides a role model for delegating this duty to those who are trained to perform it. The selection is from a contemporary Hasidic manual on visiting the sick.*

Rabbi Shlomo Sofer relates how his great-grandfather, Rabbi Akiva Eger, dearly loved the *mitzvah* of *bikkur cholim.*

Whenever he heard that any Jew was sick, he would personally visit him and bring him tasty foods to restore his spirit. This present from such a holy, pious man was as sweet to the palate of the sick man as refreshing cold water to the thirsty soul. My grandfather was accustomed to explaining the verse, *"veazvu l'acherim chailum"* (Psalm 49:11)—that the word *"ve-azvu"* means to help, similar to the verse *"ezov ta-azov emo"* (Shemos 23:5) meaning, what a man does to help his friend and others, this is his wealth, his portion and his possession, which will remain for him as an everlasting merit.

Many times he would sleep at night near the *choleh* and do his best to consult with the doctors and urge them to do their utmost for the *choleh.* He would record the patient's name and the name of his mother, so that he could pray for him. For many years he did this every day without neglect, and without letting his heavy schedule prevent him from performing this very dear *mitzvah.*

Similarly did he conduct himself when he became Rabbi of Posen. Each day he visited the sick to see for himself and to determine clearly their conditions, so that he could do something to improve their welfare and to pray for them. When he went to another city, he visited the hospital there. If he found any good ideas which were lacking in his city, he made mental notes and made sure to introduce them in his city. Conversely, when he noticed something lacking in another city, he attempted to the best of his ability to make sure it was implemented there.

However, after being in Posen a long time, he realized that the extent of his numerous involvements rendered it absolutely impossible for him to continue performing this *mitzvah* to the same extent as before. He had to find other ways. Therefore, he chose two trusted individuals, appointed them as his personal representatives, and paid them out of his own pocket to visit the sick each day, to enquire on his behalf and in his name concerning their welfare and their condition, to bring them presents, and to ascertain their names and the names of their mothers—and then he himself prayed for them.[8]

88. *An Authentic Encounter*

LEVI MEIER

How can any visitors make true contact with a person who is ill without having experienced the illness themselves? Jewish law provides guidelines that help break down the barriers between people. Then, the genuine contact which leads to healing can take place. Rabbi Meier has written extensively about medical ethics.

As Chaplain of Cedars-Sinai Medical Center, I take care of four major areas: religious institutional policy and procedures, religious services, seminars on Jewish medical ethics, and pastoral visitation. This volume has focused on the difficult and complex decision-making processes involving physicians, patients, and family members.

Another major area of medical ethics is the *routine* care of patients. This requires that the professional give adequate time to the patient, and see him or her as a *person*. Most of my time at the medical center is devoted to pastoral visitations in situation of presurgery anxiety, postsurgery depression, and major illness. In the course of this experience I have developed guidelines formulated to assure that the visit be of maximum benefit to the patient, and these are here described.

Within the range of human relationships, the "classical medical model" and the "authentic engaging encounter" are at opposite poles of the continuum. The classical medical model draws a sharp division between the doctor and the patient. The doctor metacommunicates that he knows more about the patient than the patient himself does. Frequently, medical theory and technology take precedence over direct interaction with the patient. This position allows the doctor to evaluate, diagnose, judge, and disclose the patient's illness to the patient. The patient frequently feels helpless in that he must rely on the doctor's expertise.

Contrary to this approach is the "authentic engaging encounter," which can come about between any two people, regardless of their professions or any supposedly hierarchical relationship. In a medical encounter of this type, both the doctor and patient realize that all humans must ultimately face similar life situations. The quality of the relationship between the two is one of reciprocal mutuality—each party declares what he really is all about. The doctor is willing to unmask himself and share with the patient his own fears and trepidations. Within this intimately engaged encounter, the patient realizes that his recovery, or more specifically, his will to recover, is a responsibility shared by doctor and patient. A common encounter situation that has not been widely dealt with from the point of view of Jewish law is that of visiting the sick. Psychological insights into the *Halakha* (Jewish law) of visiting the sick (Shulhan Arukh, Yoreh Deah, 335), clearly indicate that the relationship between the visitor and patient share life's uncertainties and fears, and the visitor must strive for the ability to demonstrate genuine empathy.

The fact that the relationship both prior to and during a person's illness is the basis of and related to the efficacy of the visit is demonstrated by detailing which friends are allowed to visit immediately, and which after a 3-day period (Shulhan Arukh, Yoreh Deah, 335.1).

Those people who have had a prior relationship with the patient can visit immediately. However, those people who are merely acquaintances, who ordinarily see the patient sporadically or incidentally can only visit after the first 3 days of illness. If a relationship exists, it makes sense to continue it during a difficult and trying period. The patient feels comfortable enough to share some of his inner thoughts with such a confidant. However, a period of illness is no time to intensify a relationship with a casual acquaintance. This attempt would probably only make the patient uncomfortable.

In addition to specifying on which days it is permissible to visit, the *Halakha* also recommends which hours in the day are most suitable for the effectiveness of the visitor-patient relationship. The visitor should not visit during the first 3 or the last 3 hours of the day. During these time periods, the patient will appear, respectively, too well or too sick, and the visitor will not be moved to pray on behalf of the patient either because he looks so healthy, or because he looks so sick that prayers are too late (Shulhan Arukh, Yoreh Deah, 335:4).

During the course of the day, however, the health status of the patient will appear such that the visitor will be emotionally moved to pray on his behalf. Thus, the day and time specifications for visiting the sick reflect a genuine caring relationship between patient and visitor.

The visitor should not conceal his intention to pray on behalf of the patient. The visitor should pray for divine mercy in the language that the patient understands, despite the fact that prayers are generally recited in Hebrew. When the patient hears and understands what is being requested on his behalf, his feelings of isolation and of being forsaken are alleviated.

The reciprocal relationship between visitor and patient is so crucial that the visitor must consider on which occasions it is inappropriate to visit the sick. Any visit that would possibly cause embarrassment or impose other hardship is forbidden (Shulhan Arukh, Yoreh Deah, 335:8).

For example, visiting one who has an intestinal disease that might cause him embarrassment, or one who suffers from headaches, making speech difficult, should be avoided. A visitor is not just paying a visit to an object, but to a subject—a person with a specific condition and unique feelings.

The *Halakha*'s concern about the I-Thou relationship (Buber, 1970) between patient and visitor is not limited to the here and now, wherein one person is sick and one is healthy. The vicissitudes of life dictate that one day the visitor will be the patient and the patient will be the visitor. Our common human frailties are at once recognized by both visitor and patient in an authentic encounter.

Throughout "healthy life," unspoken differences are usually noted between people of different socioeconomic status (SES), as reflected in peer socialization.

In contrast to this approach to social behavior are the halakhic guidelines for visiting the sick. Since man is finite, all aspects of SES vanish in the face of illness. A person of prestige is obligated to visit a youngster, and all other human differences are set aside during a person's health crisis (Shulhan Arukh, Yoreh Deah, 335:2).

We are all vulnerable to illness. A powerful person may tomorrow be in the throes of death. Illness is the equalizer of all human beings. Since we are all in the same boat, genuine empathy for the pain and suffering of the patient must be felt and understood.

In the course of a visit to the sick, clichés and trite statements are usually inappropriate and change the relationship from an I-Thou to an I-It encounter. It makes no sense to quote theological truths to a person in agony. The Midrash relates:

> Rabbi Hanina once fell ill. Rabbi Yohanan went to visit him. He said: "How do you feel?" Rabbi Hanina replied: "How grievous are my sufferings!" Rabbi Yohanan said: "But surely the reward for them is also great!" Rabbi Hanina said: "I want neither them nor their reward!" (Song of Songs, Rabbah 2:16:2).

Yes, the reward for suffering is great (Talmud, Brachos 5A). But this Talmudic opinion, which Rabbi Hanina obviously knew, was meaningless at that time. A dictum that is appropriate in a classroom may be totally inappropriate for consoling a person in anguish. A suffering person desires to be understood. His pain, his anger with God, his blasphemies, must not be challenged but must be accepted at this time. An illustration of this situation is given in the Midrash:

> Rabbi Simeon ben Yohai used to visit the sick. He once met a man who was swollen and afflicted with intestinal disease, uttering blasphemies against God. Said Rabbi Simeon: "Worthless one! Pray rather for mercy for yourself." Said the patient, "May God remove these sufferings from me and place them on you ..." (Abot de Rabbi Nathan 4:1).

A sick person desires the visitor to be able to demonstrate genuineness, warmth, and empathy. Again, it is these qualities that create an I-Thou rather than an I-It relationship.

How should the visitor feel about himself after he has accomplished his task? Lest he feel grandiose and view himself as the provider of health, the

Halakha dictates that he feel humble and recognize the efficacy of the only Healer—God. This end is served by regulating where the visitor may sit. He should not sit higher than the sick person, because the Shekhinah is above the head of the sick (Shulhan Arukh, Yoreh Deah, 335:3); that is, the restoration of health is dependent upon God.

The *Halakha* recognizes that no human relationship can ever be dictated. What can be *suggested* are guidelines making possible human relationships of an I-Thou nature. Most discussions of this precept detail three responsibilities involved in visiting the sick: performing tasks for the patient; encouraging the patient; and praying for his or her recovery. These acts, however, are merely outward manifestations of the precept. Behind them lies the "essence" which has been described. If the visit is performed in bad faith, it is antithetical to its purpose. The visitor is challenged to open himself up—to recognize his own deficiencies and weaknesses.

Visiting the sick requires one to recognize and share our common fears, as well as to empathize, and be authentic. In contrast, when one is in the presence of mourners, the only response is total silence and, before departing, the recital: "May the Omnipresent comfort you amongst the other mourners of Zion and Jerusalem" (Ha-Siddur).

Visiting the sick is a difficult commandment to perform. It is among those acts the fruit of which man eats in this world while the principal remains for him for the world to come (Talmud, Shabbos, 127b). It requires an authentic and genuine response between the visitor and patient. The concrete guidelines that the *Halakha* sets before us offer us a way to realize this authentic encounter, the essential component of the visitor-patient relationship.[9]

89. Is the Rabbi a Psychotherapist?

ROLAND B. GITTELSOHN

What is the boundary between psychological and spiritual counseling? A modern congregational rabbi examines his own practice.

"Rabbi, forgive me for disturbing you. My father's in the intensive-care unit of Newton-Wellesley Hospital ... brought here by ambulance last night ... another massive heart attack. He's being kept alive on machines. The doctor has just told my sister and me he doesn't think there's any chance that Father will regain consciousness or be able to breathe again on his own and has asked whether we want him to 'pull the plug'. We feel torn to pieces, Rabbi . . . we can't make that kind of decision alone . . . we need your help."

I dropped the work I had been doing, canceled the day's remaining appointments, and within minutes was on my way to the hospital, where I remained with the young man and his sister through the dinner hour and into the evening. How could I refuse? I had confirmed both of them, had only a few months before officiated at their mother's funeral, had married the man and his wife.

There was a time when I would have had no resource other than my own intuition with which to help them. During my student years, the curriculum of the Hebrew Union College contained not a single course in what has since become known as pastoral psychology. It did not take long after ordination to realize what a glaring gap this left in my professional competence. The gap had to be filled. I read avidly, attended many lectures, studied psychiatry at the Karen Horney Institute. All of which has stood me in good stead.

We rabbis sometimes quip that we're the poor person's psychiatrists. True . . . and false. Some men and women do indeed come to us because they can't afford a psychiatrist's fees. Others, because they foolishly suppose that seeking psychiatric help is a sign of weakness rather than the symptom of strength it really is. Still others, because they are afraid or ashamed of being labeled mentally ill. Studies show that more emotionally disturbed Americans turn to their clergy-persons for primary help than to any other profession. Whatever their reasons, congregants do approach us in large numbers for personal therapy, and we must know what to do with them.

We must also know our own limitations. I have at times been horrified to hear colleagues tell of the extremely complicated cases of emotional pathology they undertook to "cure." As well might they, without medical training, try to remove an infected appendix with a rusty knife! Rabbis as well as Christian clergy must know enough psychiatry to know that they are not psychiatrists. They must see themselves as general practitioners, able to distinguish between anxieties they are competent to treat and those requiring referral to a specialist.

There are qualitative as well as quantitative differences between the kinds of therapy that can be provided respectively by psychiatrists and psychologically oriented religious leaders. Neither is entirely right or totally wrong; at their best they complement each other. Psychiatry concentrates on the individual, especially on his or her relationship in early childhood with both parents, and on memories and impressions that were repressed because acknowledging them would have been too painful. Religious counseling, while it can never afford to ignore this dynamic, attempts to provide also a larger framework of meaning for the troubled individual.

As a rabbi, I am convinced that for human beings to attain a comfortable measure of mental health, in addition to releasing childhood repressions and fears into consciousness, draining our psyches of their festering poisons, we must see ourselves as pieces fitting into a jig-saw puzzle. My analogy, of course, is inadequate. We are more than inert matter being manipulated by external forces. Having discerned an overall pattern, we must then, by our own initiative, take deliberate steps to fit ourselves into it.

A chassidic rabbi once prayed: "Lord of the world, how could I venture to ask why everything happens as it does? Why are we driven from one exile to another? Why do our foes torment us so? I do not beg you to reveal to me the secret of Your ways. How could I endure the weighty burden of this awesome knowledge? Ah, it is not why I suffer that I long to know, but only whether I suffer for Your sake."

Even for those who may not believe in God, in sheer psychological and emotional terms this is our most compelling need: to know that the insults and pains we inevitably suffer serve a purpose larger and more lasting than ourselves. For some, a humanistic purpose will suffice. Others yearn for cosmic meaning too. All of us can pay the necessary price in discomfort and distress only if we understand it as the means to an important and enduring end. I shall return to this thought later.

Secular psychiatry risks intensifying the narcissism that is part of the patient's illness in the first place. We see this at its worst in the flood of self-help books and cults that threaten to inundate us. At every turn we are bombarded by *how to's: how to* get rich quickly, *how to* enjoy sex more, *how to* relieve tension and live happily. The religious counselor insists that this obsessive concentration on *me,* far from being the cure, is part of the disease.

Yes, each of us who is emotionally ill must begin by identifying the responsible factors in his or her past. We cannot be cured, however, until we learn to include the Other as a part of the Self. I have had psychiatrists and psychologists, thoroughly familiar with all the theories and techniques of their own professions, come to me for help. This is the "plus" I have sometimes been able to give them.

Over a period of years, I led groups of twenty or twenty-five individuals on what Catholics call retreats; my preference was to label them Shabbatons, a term derived from Shabbat, the Hebrew word for Sabbath. We secluded ourselves on each such occasion in a small New Hampshire inn where we could study and search together from Friday to Sunday. The combination of a quiet rural setting, withdrawal from the turmoil and tension of ordinary life, and an opportunity to relate intimately with friends, including one's rabbi, often worked magic. At the conclusion of several such experiences, a participant burst out with a variation of the following: "I don't know why, but I have disclosed things about myself to you fellows that I have never told my psychiatrist!"

As we sat in a circle under the sun at one Shabbaton, summarizing what the weekend had meant, a man in his later seventies suddenly exclaimed between tears, "I realize for the first time that through the years I have given the least of my energy and time to the things which have meant most to me!"... The husband of a woman in public life expressed profusely—probably for the first time in his life—what it meant for him to be the spouse of a woman so much more prominent in the community than himself.... An adult son was able to voice resentments against his father that had been repressed since childhood.

Did these weekends produce effective therapy? For some, I have little doubt they did. Can forty-eight hours cure deep-seated neuroses, untangle the knots in twisted personalities? Most probably, no. But they can offer priceless opportunities to ventilate stuffy psychiatric attics that had never before been opened. Men and women have been able to expose things about themselves that they had previously suppressed, expose them to others who would understand and accept without condemnation. This can be and often is a first step in successful therapy. Call it preventive therapy if you will—minor, not major, emotional surgery. It illustrates a kind of psychological help that a religious leader may be uniquely able to give.[10]

90. A Memoir of a Hospital Visit

JAMES RUDIN

Though rabbis and laypersons today are trained to visit the sick, sometimes there seems to be an unbridgeable gap between visitor and patient. When rabbis fall ill, they can occasionally span this chasm and provide insight. Rabbi Rudin co-authored the book Why Me? Why Anyone? *with Rabbi Jaffe.*

My best friend, Hirshel Jaffe, has leukemia.

I found out a few days ago and I still can't believe it.

We have been rabbis and friends for more than twenty years, and in all that time I've never seen Hirshel sick or even tired. He had boundless energy, always in perpetual motion, never still. He could play three sets of tennis on the hottest day and later go out and run six miles to channel his enormous natural enthusiasm and nervous energy. Running was his real passion. Even Hirshel's Hebrew name, Zvi, means "deer" or "swift runner."

I'll never forget the day he ran in the New York City Marathon.

It was a beautiful late October afternoon in 1978, so warm that the marathon participants were complaining. I was in Central Park with my wife, Marcia, and our two daughters, watching thousands of long-distance runners cross the finish line after their grueling twenty-six-mile course had touched each of New York City's five boroughs. But we were really there to cheer on our good friend Hirshel. He had been training for ten years. How many miles he must have run to prepare for this day!

Although jammed in a huge crowd, by some miracle we saw Hirshel bounding toward the finish line. He was sporting a T-shirt with bold blue-and-white letters proclaiming him "The Running Rabbi." Amazingly, it seemed as if he had energy to spare even after running twenty-six miles. Hirshel was smiling triumphantly, and as he ran across the finish line we could hear him shout, "I did it! I did it!"

Hirshel paced back and forth to cool his body down gradually. One of the marathon officials threw a silver foil insulating cape around him to prevent his body heat from escaping too quickly. Hirshel's wife, Judi, and their children,

Nina and Rachel, ran over to him and threw their arms around their personal champion.

We all walked together and sat down under a large tree. I urged Hirshel to lie down in the shade and rest, but he said, "No, I'm fine. I'm hardly tired, Jim. I feel so great I think I could run the whole thing all over again."

We laughed as Hirshel started to nibble on the snack food provided to all who finished the grueling race. Little groups of exhausted but happy runners and their admiring families and friends were scattered, some standing, some sitting, all over the Sheep Meadow in Central Park. The rays of the bright autumn sun reflected off the hundreds of silver capes. The runners reminded me of medieval knights in their shining armor, resting after a long and strenuous battle. "I did it, I did it! I made it!" Hirshel repeated over and over again, as if he couldn't believe it. He was beaming.

Now, less than three years later, that same tall, trim, highly conditioned body is out of control, wracked by insidious killer cancer cells Hirshel Jaffe didn't even know about until it was almost too late. My active, aggressive, energetic friend—only forty-six years old—always so forceful and in such control of his own life, is now waiting in a hospital, at the mercy of physicians and a medical technology that may not be able to help him. The first hint Marcia and I received that something was wrong with Hirshel came only a few weeks ago. The Jaffe family was spending the day with us at our vacation home in the Poconos. Our favorite pizza place was closed, so we all had dinner that night at a family restaurant we had never eaten in before. Our mistake. The food was terrible, but we were managing to gag it down until Judi found a dead fly in her baked potato. After we got over the shock and stopped laughing we called the waitress over to show her the fly. She went to get the manager. When we complained to the manager, he said he wasn't responsible for the dead fly in the potato. "God must have put it there," he conjectured. However, he did subtract fifty-nine cents, the estimated cost of the potato, from our total bill.

We were still talking about the incident as we walked out to our cars, but when I casually asked Hirshel if he'd been playing any good tennis lately, he said, "No, I don't have enough energy for both tennis and running." His answer caught Marcia and me by surprise. It was so unlike Hirshel to have to ration his energy. He has always been so healthy and vigorous. And we noticed a slight edge in his voice. Little did we know that that very morning, when he and Judi picked up their girls from camp, he could hardly walk in the heat and couldn't carry the children's trunks.

Tomorrow the doctors are going to take out Hirshel's spleen. Marcia and I and our daughters, Eve and Jennifer, have traveled to the hospital to visit him and to cheer him on, just as we cheered him over the marathon finish line that sunny day that now seems so long ago. But, I ask myself, what can I say to Hirshel today that will cheer him? Will I be able to give him the emotional support he's going to need? I'm one of his best friends, so if I can't help him, who can?

As a rabbi, Hirshel Jaffe has always been there to comfort others when they need it. But who will comfort Hirshel? Who will be his rabbi? Hirshel has always been like a shepherd to his flock of congregants. Who will be Hirshel's shepherd now?

Most of us turn to our religion in times of emotional crisis because it provides meaning to our lives and helps us. Will our Jewish tradition bring solace to my friend? I wonder. Will all the things he has been telling his congregants, when they come to him with their agonizing pain, comfort Hirshel now that *he* is the one that needs it? Or will he find the words we rabbis have learned to say over the years just glib, empty clichés?

I spot Hirshel at the end of the hospital corridor. He is wearing cutoff pajamas, a short bathrobe, bright sweat socks, and his well-worn Nike running shoes. His incongruous outfit makes me laugh. But as he walks toward me, my amusement fades when I see how pale he is. He's lost a lot of weight, which makes him look even taller and more gaunt than usual, and makes his dark-brown mustache seem too large for his face.

Hirshel grasps my hand and steers me toward his hospital room. "Jim, so good to see you!" He is smiling, obviously trying to be cheerful. But behind his heavy tortoiseshell glasses his eyes have a haunted look, a look of desperation. Like the look in the eyes of my brother, Bert, when he realized he was going to die of Hodgkin's disease. I'll never forget those eyes. Hirshel has them now. My brother had his spleen removed also in a vain attempt to stop his cancer. This whole scenario is agonizingly familiar to me.

Hirshel has tried to make the room cheerful. There are dozens of cards and bouquets from his congregants at Temple Beth Jacob in Newburgh, New York. He's very well-known and liked, and the news of his illness has shaken the synagogue and the community. Above his bed he's taped a photo of himself finishing the 1978 New York Marathon in his "Running Rabbi" T-shirt. Nearby is a giant funny card some congregants made to cheer him up. On the other wall are pictures of Judi and the children. Judi has put a *Playboy* pinup, X-rated cartoons, and Murphy's famous law that proclaims, "When one thing starts to go wrong, everything will go wrong." Judi, a nurse, knows about mix-ups in hospitals.

But no matter how many cards and flowers fill a patient's little space, no matter how humorous the pinups and comforting the mementos from home, hospital rooms are always grim. As a rabbi I have been visiting patients for twenty-five years, and I know the rooms are always somehow the same. They're hot and stuffy, and stale odors left over from a thousand unappetizing and often uneaten meals hang in the air.

Trying to hide my discomfort, I smile as I sit down on the hard chair next to his bed.

"You look good, Hirshel," I begin, lying a little.

"I'm very up, Jim. A little nervous, of course. I've never had surgery before. Now I just want to get it over with. The doctors said it's a routine operation. 'A piece of cake,' they told me. My blood count is dangerously low now, but it should bounce back right after the spleen comes out. So you know me, Jim, I'm an up person, and I feel hopeful.

"Tell me what happened, Hirshel. We're still so confused. When did you find out ...?

"It all happened so fast, Jim, that's what's so unbelievable. Suddenly I started to feel really fatigued and listless. That was the beginning of July—about a month ago. Weary, hardly any energy. I felt sleepy in the middle of the day, and sometimes I had to leave the temple and go home to lie down. And I couldn't run as far or as fast as usual. My running buddies started to notice. I tried to keep running, but the hills felt like mountains to me. I was fighting sleep at the wheel of my jeep, and I was afraid I'd have an accident. I just felt so drained.

"I complained to Judi about how bad I felt and finally in her blunt, direct way she said, 'You better go to the doctor, Hirshel, it could be something very serious.' But I still didn't make an appointment.

"One day a friend flew me in his plane up to Martha's Vineyard for the day so I could check on our summer house. We went running on the beach, and when we were finished I noticed a bruise on my ankle. I knew I hadn't fallen down or hurt it—I had just been running as usual. I was really scared because the bruise was such a visible sign. Like a stigma. And I couldn't shake the fatigue. Finally, I asked a friend to recommend an internist. You know, Jim, I didn't even have a doctor. I hadn't been to one in years.

"Well, the internist wasn't too concerned at first about my fatigue, but I pushed him to give me a blood test. The counts came out really low. He must have been hoping for a simple explanation like mononucleosis or a virus, but I knew my body well enough to sense something was very wrong. My blood counts kept dropping, and they kept redoing the tests. Meanwhile I started scanning Judi's medical textbooks to see if I could find out what was wrong.

"The internist knew we were leaving soon for our month on Martha's Vineyard, and he said, 'Rabbi, why don't you go on your vacation? I'll see you in a month. You should bounce right back.' But I said, 'No, I don't want to go away not knowing what's the matter.' Then he said very quietly and seriously, as if he knew I thought I had cancer, 'All right, we'll look further. Let's examine your bone marrow.'

"They didn't see anything abnormal in the bone marrow biopsy, but by now my blood count was alarmingly low. My fears grew when the internist called and said, 'Rabbi, we want you nearby where we can watch you. Maybe it would be better to postpone your trip.'

"But they still weren't coming up with a diagnosis. Luckily I have a friend who's a pathologist, and he said, 'Why don't you come up to my lab and let me take a look at your blood?'

"There was my friend peering through his electron microscope. He told me later he saw the weird-looking cancer cell growing in me from his very first look. His mind must have been racing, but he was trying to carry it off calmly. He asked me if anyone had examined my spleen. I didn't realize the significance of his question at the time. He called a hematologist friend. Judi and I sat in the hematologist's office a few days ago and heard everything confirmed. I have hairy-cell leukemia."

"Harry?"

"H-a-i-r-y. Like on your head. The cells look like a hair under the microscope. That's how the disease got its name. They don't know much about it. It's very rare. There are only about two hundred cases a year in the United States, less than two percent of all leukemias, the physicians told me. So here I am, Jim, the indestructible Hershel Jaffe, never sick a day in my life. My spleen is very enlarged, and that's dangerous so they have to get it out. A splenectomy is the first step in battling this strange leukemia. I dread surgery, but I have to have it. We'll lick this! We'll use every medical technique we have. Do I have any choice?"

"Will they give you chemotherapy after the surgery?"

"No. Aggressive chemotherapy doesn't seem to help hairy-cell leukemia. The doctors explained that they don't like to do anything except take out the spleen until absolutely necessary because sometimes the disease can be chronic and progress very slowly."

"Are your parents here, Hirshel?"

"No, they're still up in our house on the Vineyard. Why should they break up their vacation? It's a long trip. And my doctor said I'll be up there in a week and they can see me there. I can recuperate lying on our deck watching the surf … By the way, we really appreciate you and Marcia taking our girls this week. It gives Judi a chance to breathe and visit me. I can't thank you enough. I realize now how much it means to have friends who care about you."

"Didn't you already know that?"

"I guess it never came home to me before that I needed anybody that much. I was always worrying about everyone else's problems. Now for a change I have to worry about myself. I still haven't gotten over the shock of my diagnosis yet. A lot of things are racing through my mind. I am thinking, 'My God, you're vulnerable, Hirshel, you've really got something wrong with you.'

"I thought I'd always have my perfect health. You know me, Jim, I've always had so much energy. I was running six or seven miles a day. It became my second religion. My body was conditioned so well it responded to all my demands. I always ate the right food, never smoked or drank except for wine on Shabbas. Judi used to tease me about my health fetishes.

"I guess I thought if I jogged I'd live forever. I remember once, about two years ago, I made a kind of bargain with God. I was feeling great, running alone on South Beach in front of our house on Martha's Vineyard. The surf was awesome. It was a gorgeous day. I could run six or eight miles on the wet sand right on the edge of the water and keep up with those high school track athletes training there. I was feeling indestructible, and I looked up to the heavens and said, 'Hey, I'm going to live to be one hundred and twenty, maybe more.' I was saying, 'Well, God, I'll just take care of my body. You want human beings to be healthy, don't you?'"

"Pacts with God can be dangerous, Hirshel."

"It wasn't really a Faustian bargain because I didn't agree to give very much back to God. I was just being selfish. I felt so triumphant. You know, the *Rocky* image. The waves were coming in, and there were lovers on the beach, and I'm thinking I'll push death away.

"For years Judi's been trying to warn me. She said, 'Hirshel, with all your running, you think you're going to live forever? You could get a stroke or cancer, anything can happen.' I used to get so angry at her I'd go out and run ten more miles. All the while she was saying to me, 'Hirshel, don't think you're indestructible.' Well, now I've discovered she was right. Judi is so right about nearly everything."

"I'd feel indestructible too, Hirshel, if I were in your shape. You're young, lots of life ahead of you. We never expect anything like this to happen to us. It always happens to somebody else. God, why does it have to be you? It's just not fair. I would be so angry!"

"I'm really not angry, Jim. Maybe being a rabbi makes me more accepting because I deal with illness all the time. That's part of my job. I know I can't will or wish away this disease. Besides, it won't do me any good to be angry."

"I don't know. Maybe it would make you feel better if you got angry. Do you feel guilty instead?" Am I being tactless in asking my friend this question? I wonder. But I push ahead anyway. "You know, Hirshel, some people feel guilty when they find out they're sick. That's their first reaction, almost like a reflex. They think God is punishing them for something they've done. One woman said to me years ago when her husband died, 'I guess I should have kept a kosher home.' I had another congregant who thought his daughter was killed because he had been cheating on his wife. He actually half-believed it. I told him I don't think God works like that. But do you think God is punishing *you* Hirshel?" Is this the time or the place for questions like this? I wonder again. Probably I should stop asking these heavy question, but I'm very curious about what Hirshel thinks now. We've struggled with these issues together for so long as rabbinical students and as rabbis.

"You mean do I think God has sent me this illness, like that restaurant manager's theory that He put the dead fly in Judi's baked potato? No, I don't think my illness is part of some divine plan. It can happen to anyone. Maybe it's just chance. I don't think I was fated to have leukemia. You know Jews don't believe in blind fate, Jim.

"My congregants have been asking me these questions for twenty years. I've always told them, 'God doesn't single out people because they've been good or bad. Illness is just part of human vulnerability.' Of course, I'm not all that calm about it. When I heard I had leukemia, half of me said, 'O.K., you've got it, who are you to complain?' Maybe that was the rabbi half of me who has seen so much illness and buried so many people and who knows this can happen to anyone. But the other half of me, the human side, was already screaming out to someone, something, maybe to God, to save me."

"But didn't you scream out, 'God damn it for bringing this on me,' or 'Damn God for letting this happen to me?'" I press. "Jim," I tell myself, "stop grilling Hirshel. He probably hasn't even had time to think about these things yet. Don't sound so harsh. I should be more sensitive to his feelings. But maybe if I force him to confront these questions, he'll be able to express his anger, and that will help him. I am here to offer my support to Hirshel, and I don't want to fail him. I hope I'll know the right thing to do."

"No, I don't curse God, Jim. And I want to tell people that. I want to say to my congregants, 'All the things I've been telling you all these years are true. We don't curse God.'"

I think, "Well, Jim, I hope you're proud of yourself. You've managed to thoroughly depress your friend instead of cheering him up. Let's change the subject." I point down to his Nike running shoes. "You know, Hirshel, you look like an imprisoned jogger."

Hirshel laughs. "Yeah, these sneakers do look a little funny with my pajamas, don't they? I guess I'm just trying to cling to my 'Running Rabbi' image. I threw that picture into my suitcase to remind me of my better days. I've been out in the halls just pacing around. I can't stand being cooped up in this room ..."

My wife walks into the room. Marcia immediately sees how pale and thin Hirshel is, and our eyes meet. I know she's thinking of my brother, too, remembering the doom in Bert's eyes the last time she saw him in his hospital room.

"I'd better leave now, Hirshel," I tell my friend. "They only allow one visitor at a time up here. We'll be thinking of you tomorrow. Everything will be fine. We'll call you a day or so after your operation when you'll feel like talking."[11]

91. How to Pray in the Hospital

JOSEPH S. OZAROWSKI

Jews are seldom trained to pray spontaneously. More often, we look for a text in a book to recite. Yet, when we are ill and when we visit those who are ill, the most effective prayers may come directly from the heart. This selection is from Rabbi Ozarowski's book on illness and bereavement, To Walk in God's Ways.

Rabbinic sources underline prayer as a major goal of the *bikur holim* visit.

> When R. Dimi came he said, "Whoever visits the sick causes him to live, and whoever does not visit the sick causes him to die." How does one "cause" this? Does this mean that whoever visits the sick will ask mercy [pray] that he may live, and whoever does not visit the sick will ask mercy that he should die? Would you think this? But [it must mean] that whoever does not visit the sick will not ask mercy, neither that he should live nor die.

> Raba, on the first day of his illness said, "Do not reveal this to anyone, lest it affect my fortune." Afterward, he said, "Go tell of my illness in the market so that whoever hates me will rejoice ... while those who care for me will ask mercy for me."

The above sources do not tell us of the content of these prayers. While the Talmud elsewhere offers some of the themes of prayer on behalf of the ill (as we will shortly see) and these are formalized in many of our own prayers for the ill, there are no "official prayers for the ill" from the talmudic period. This leads me to believe that there was once a tradition of spontaneous prayer for the sick in Judaism. Many Christian hospital chaplains, ministers, and priests will offer a prayer at the bedside of a patient. Christian liturgy is not as fixed as traditional Jewish liturgy, and many Christian patients will expect or at least appreciate prayer with a clergyperson. I have worked with ministers who developed this into an art—using the prayer as a summary of the visit and the person's feelings. For example, after a session dealing with the patient's apprehensions about entering a nursing home after surgery, the following dialogue ensued:

Pastor: I'd like to share a prayer with you. Will that be all right?

Patient and wife [simultaneously]: Yes, please do.

Pastor: Dear God, we thank you for this opportunity to get acquainted and to share in our common faith. May you go with P. through the hard places and undergird him in the power of your spirit. Be with his family, and undergird them in faith. May Your love and grace be sufficient for all these things. Amen.

I remember at the time how impressed I was with this technique, assuming it was simply not a part of Jewish tradition. But I thought I would try it out with a congregant.

Congregant: Well, I am looking forward to getting out of here.

Rabbi: I know you are, and we look forward to having you back at *shul*. Well, it has been good seeing you. Do you mind if I pray with you here for your recovery?

Congregant: Why would you want to do that?

Rabbi: Well, er, um, I just hope that the *Ribbono Shel Olam* [Master of the Universe] smiles upon you and guides you as you face the future back at home.

It appears that Jews do not expect or seem to need spontaneous bedside prayer. This may be true because Jews are used to prayer from a fixed liturgy and assume pastoral care deals only with the personal dimensions of the visit, as described earlier.

After discovering the numerous talmudic references to praying or "asking mercy" for the patient, as the rabbinic sources literally put it, I now believe that at one time there was a tradition of spontaneous, unfixed prayer for the ill. While my experience still leads me to assume that many Jewish patients do not care about it, perhaps we ought to attempt to retrieve this tradition, whether in the presence of the patient, or privately. I have started using, when appropriate, the closing moments of a pastoral visit to summarize the feelings I have heard expressed in the form of a quasi-prayer or blessing such as:

Rabbi [after, say, a session where the patient expressed apprehension for the future]: It has been good seeing you. Let us hope and pray that the *Ribbono*

Shel Olam [Master of the Universe] will strengthen you and guide you through the times to come; and know that all of us are with you.

Patient: Thank you so much, Rabbi.

Another related clinical issue surrounding liturgy is the need for specifically rabbinic prayer on behalf of or with the patient. I was always led to believe that Judaism frowned on the need for clergy assisting someone in prayer. The following is typical of my early encounters with this issue:

Patient: Rabbi, would you say a prayer for me?

Rabbi: There really is no prayer that I can say that you could not say yourself.

Judaism is indeed a people's religion in the sense that one does not need a rabbi for a service. Having grown up in the sixties and seventies, and personally sharing this attitude, I have always felt my role to be that of a teacher rather than an intermediary to God. I saw myself helping to facilitate others' observance and growth. "Praying for them" did not fit into my *weltanschauung*. I was therefore rather surprised to come across the following passage in the Talmud during my research for this work.

> R. Pinhas Ben Hama expounded: One who has an ill person in his home should go to a wise man [Heb. *Hakham*] [so that] he may ask mercy for him, as it says (Proverbs 16:14), "The anger of a King is like messengers of death, but a wise man will pacify it."

The commentaries explain that the King is the Divine King whose messengers (or angels, another translation) inflict illness, especially severe life-threatening illness. For these maladies, the prayer of the wise is especially helpful in saving the patient. Thus, classical Jewish thinking teaches that prayers of a wise or righteous person have special efficacy in the eyes of the Almighty. This is not merely folklore, theology, or philosophic theory. It is codified in Jewish Law and also cited as practical guidance in the following medieval commentary: "... this is the custom in France. All those who have a sick person would seek the presence of the rabbi who holds forth, that he [the rabbi] may bless him."

Today, most people, Jews as well as non-Jews, believe that the prayers of or at least the presence of clergy add an extra dimension of aid to the invalid.

Jewish patients find it reassuring to have a rabbi who represents Jewish wisdom, practice, and history, at their bedsides. Encountering this passage has changed my own personal approach to pastoral care. I know and recognize that my congregants need to see me at their side, both for their therapeutic needs and because Jewish tradition demands that of me. Since I have studied these passages, I have also become particularly careful to publicly recite the traditional prayer for the sick in the synagogue on the Sabbath.[12]

92. Acceptance

SIDNEY GREENBERG

> *According to this homily of Rabbi Greenberg, the experience*
> *of suffering can be made to enrich the texture of our souls.*

Oriental rugs which are found in many homes are all woven by hand. Usually there will be a group of people weaving a single rug together under the direction of an artist who issues instructions to the rest. He determines the choice of colors and the nature of the pattern.

It often happens that one of the weavers inserts the wrong color thread. The artist may have called for blue and instead black was used. If you examine an oriental rug carefully, you may be able to detect such irregularities. What is significant about them is that they were not removed. The skillful artist just proceeded to weave them into the pattern.

Here is a wise procedure that we can follow in life. We should like the pattern of our lives to be woven exclusively of bright colored threads. But every now and then a dark thread steals into the fabric. If we are true artists of life we can weave even this thread into the pattern and make it contribute its share to the beauty of the whole.[13]

93. A Holy Thing

CHAIM STERN

> *To grieve is to love, to be loved, and to be worthy of love.*
> *Rabbi Stern is the editor of* Gates of Prayer, *the new Union*
> *Prayer Book.*

It is a fearful thing
to love what death can touch.

A fearful thing
to love, hope, dream:
to be—
to be,
and to lose.

A thing for fools, this
and
a holy thing,
a holy thing
to love.

For your life has lived in me,
your laugh once lifted me,
your word was gift to me.

To remember this brings painful joy.

'Tis a human thing, love,
a holy thing,
to love
what death can touch.[14]

94. Death at Its Turning

WILLIAM CUTTER

*In an essay written for this book, Rabbi William Cutter reflects
on several of the selections.*

Death is what makes us mortal; recognizing death may be what makes us
human. A consequence of this neat thought is that much good writing is done
around the event of death and death's companion, illness. Some of that "good
writing," the moving personal perspectives, is in the chapters of this book. We

spend our greatest efforts in the hope of conquering death—not forever, to be sure, but for "the time being," for some period of time that equates duration with value. When we write, we challenge our mortality.

Two phrases of recognition enliven my thoughts whenever I think of death. The first is Henry James's elegant greeting as cited by Max Lerner in one of our essays: "The distinguished thing," he called death, a description that captures a sense of sudden recognition, the respect and resignation when we look directly at the thing. The other thought, more closely allied to the tradition that prompts our book, comes from the Book of Samuel. Agag, the Amalekite enemy, notes King Saul's arrival and states with confidence: "Surely the bitterness of death had turned" *(Akhen, sar mar hamavet)*. Agag, the reader knows, is on the threshold of receiving his death blow from Saul, but may himself believe that his liberation is about to come. Will death be turning toward him or will it be turning away from him? And should it turn away, will it not with equal surety visit again—a second time more persistently? The "turning of death" is adopted by Nathan Alterman, a great poet of Israel's literary renaissance in his major poetic collection: "The Joy of the Poor." Here the poet employs irony to comment on an old talmudic expression, that the poor person is as good as dead. The "joy" in the title suggests that death frees one from the torments and constraints of life. A stanza from this gathering of poems about joy, poverty, and death might be translated as follows:

Said a man to his brothers, "dear friends
As I see it, life surely ends."
While another is sure, bitter death and its sorrow
Will invite us today, or at least on the morrow.
"The dawning of hope," for a third, quite delighted
"Is the joy in the fact that we're all invited."
(my translation)

The irony of death's turning is matched by the irony of hope's dawning.

The articles in our book flow from the ironic fact of death. That we are mortal no one doubts. Death turns toward us all. But what surprises and troubles us is that it turns toward us when we do not expect it or when its arrival does not seem fair. In any instance when we can read the line as "death does turn from us" we know intellectually that it is only for a while, and that the distinguished thing, having made her overture without being received, will come back again.

Every recovery is accompanied by the ominous possibility that redemption is only partial. Views of paradise as a permanent condition are somewhat different from the "lived life" as we know it. (The "lived life" was also a phrase coined by James.)

The essays here are stories of partial recovery from personal loss, but the true recoveries recorded here point to the moral fortitude of the authors. Each "survivor" in these chapters—whether from one's own disease and loss, or whether from the disease and loss of another—has come to represent the human potential for flourishing in death's shadow. That is why, in my own essay, I spoke of writing to live, and why the kinds of people who expressed themselves here found the opportunity in their experience to create anew— both for their physical lives, and for the words which they bequeath as part of their estate.

One of the most elegant statements about "Mr. Death," as I once humorously translated "Mar haMavet" comes from the great Hebrew poet Zelda:

When the bitterness of death turns
the soul parts
with trembling
from its earthly hopes.
The soul is torn from
limbs
and blood.
Every
Thing
sinks.

The delicate sense of sight
is cast
into the ice sea
And its wondrous riches
sink.

Every thing
sinks.
The play of fire ends
Along with light
And time,
And no more wall separates the soul from Nothingness.
Not lust,
Nor color.
And the world is complete.

May not one read these words with the same ambiguity suggested by the original biblical passage?

What is clear is that thinking of death has caused each of our authors to affirm life.

There is a fuller relationship awaiting the courageous: the firm faith of Gluckel, the playful sense of Max Lerner that the world can't live without him, the Shabbat memories of Rachel Cowan's even as she finds a sinking in her beloved husband's decline.

Our new acceptance of the inevitable may have consequences for social policy in the future. Or, one may say, the pressure to reconsider social policy may be influencing our willingness to accept the inevitable. Through all of this change, this collection is important because in each essay death is a powerful presence. Life and death are implicated as partners, located in rooms facing each other.

It seems to me that a phrase from a complex homily by Nachman of Breslov might be suitable at this point: "It often happens that the life of one thing may be dependent upon the death of another" (Moharan on Parashat Bo). Each of us who has lived the death of a beloved "other" has had to face this paradox: In order to live fully, we have had to find blessing in our losses. The clichés that harmonize deep sense of loss with optimism are less convincing, and certainly less interesting than the reality that death distinguishes us, even when it wounds; what turns *toward* us is death; what turns *away* from us may be bitterness. And that dual turning is what may distinguish death from every other experience—may we say—in life.

Rules and Ethics

Do not shrink from visiting the sick;
In this way you will make yourself loved.

Ben Sira 7:35

Introduction

*M*uch of Jewish concern for the sick has taken the form of ethical discussions and rules. Traditionally, Jewish medical ethics has consisted mostly of discussions regarding the need to balance the requirements of religious observation with the needs of the ill, the community's responsibility for the sick, the personal ethics of physicians, and certain specific topics such as abortion, suicide, and end of life issues. Ethical insights into modern medical choices as seen through the prism of traditional Jewish values is, as ever, today a lively, vital area of scholarship and debate.

It would be so easy if the decisions we had to make about ethical issues were black and white! But the issues are far from obvious when we love someone who is ill and don't want him or her to suffer. We know we should visit the sick, but we dread it. We have only so many financial resources and do not know upon whom to lavish them and to what effect. When someone we love has died, we may have the opportunity to help someone else continue living through organ donation, but we may not know what our loved one—or our religion—would say about it. These are some of the ethical issues we face in healing today.

Jewish tradition recognizes that there are few straightforward responses to such issues. What Judaism gives us is a process whereby we can examine the situation, balance the values we hold dear, and come to a solution that allows us to keep as much of our most dearly-held values as we can. While no solution will be perfect, one may be sufficient. Creatively reaching a conclusion that allows us to maintain the greatest degree of the greatest portion of those values is a solution we will be able to live with and justify to ourselves and to God. This is what the ethical process is about.

There are many great Jewish legal decision-makers today, in every band of Judaism's spectrum, from the halakhic pronouncements of Tsits

Eliezer, the authority at Hadassah Hospital in Israel, to the Reform Responsa Committee, and everything in between. Those searching for guidance in a particular situation should consult the authorities with whom they have a connection.

95. Illness and Shabbat

TALMUD

Values do not exist in a vacuum. We must constantly balance one against another. We see this clearly when someone is ill on Shabbat and the procedures used for healing violate the laws of that day of rest. The Sages perform this "juggling act" repeatedly in the following passage.

Mishnah: If one bathes in the water of a pit or in the water of Tiberias and dries himself even with ten towels, he must not fetch them in his hand. But ten may dry their faces, hands, and feet on one towel and fetch it in their hands. One may oil and [lightly] massage [the body]. But not knead or scrape. You must not go down to a wrestling ground, or induce vomiting, or straighten an infant's limbs, or set a broken bone. If one's hand or foot is dislocated, he must not agitate it violently in cold water but may bathe in the usual way. And if it heals, it heals.

One may not induce vomiting on the Sabbath. Rabbah b. Bar Hanah said in R. Johanan's name: They learnt this only [when it is effected] by a drug, but it may be done by hand. It was taught, R. Nehemiah said: It is forbidden even during the week, because of the waste of food.

Or straighten an infant's [limbs]. Rabbah b. Bar Hanah said in R. Johanan's name: To swaddle an infant on the Sabbath is permitted. But we learnt: You may not straighten?—There it refers to the spinal vertebrae, which appears as building.

One may not reset a broken bone. R. Hana of Bagdad said in Samuel's name: The *halachah* is that one may reset a fracture. Rabbah b. Bar Hanah visited Pumbeditha. He did not attend Rab Judah's session, [so] he sent Adda the waiter to him and said, "Go and seize him." So he went and seized him. When he [Rabbah] appeared, he found him [Rab Judah] lecturing. One may not reset a fracture. Said he to him: Thus did R. Hana of Bagdad say in Samuel's name: The *halachah* is that one may reset a fracture. Said he to him, Surely Hana is one of ours and Samuel is one of ours, yet I have not heard this; did I then not summon you justly?

If one's hand is dislocated, etc. R. Awia was sitting before R. Joseph, when his hand became dislocated. How is it thus? asked he. It is forbidden. And how is it thus? It is forbidden. In the meantime his hand reset itself. Said he to him, what is your question? Surely we learnt, if one's hand or foot is dislocated he must not agitate it violently in cold water, but may bathe it in the usual way, and if it heals, it heals. But did we not learn: one may not reset a fracture, he retorted, yet R. Hana of Bagdad said in Samuel's name: The *halachah* is that one may reset a fracture—Will you weave all in one web? he replied; where it was stated it was stated, but where it was not stated it was not stated.[1]

96. One Can't Heal Oneself

TALMUD AND MIDRASH

Visiting the sick has been an obligation for Jews since the talmudic period. Many stories in Talmud and Midrash underscore, as in this excerpt and the two passages that follow it, the Rabbis' belief in the therapeutic value of visiting. They made the duty to visit the sick into a sacred commandment. Talmudic discussions were reduced later to a simple code of rules by Maimonides and then made obligatory for Jews who follow traditional laws in the Shulḥan Arukh. How to make the visit of greatest value to the ill person is the subject of essays by Rabbi Cowan in this section and of Rabbis Levine, Meier, Gittlesohn, Rudin, and Ozarowski in the previous section.

That feedeth among the lilies. R. Johanan had the misfortune to suffer from gallstones for three and a half years. Once R. Hanina went to visit him. He said to him: "How do you feel?" He replied: "My sufferings are worse than I can bear." He said to him: "Don't speak so, but say 'The faithful God'." When the pain was very great he used to say "Faithful God", and when the pain was greater than he could bear, R. Hanina used to go to him and utter an incantation which gave him relief. Subsequently R. Hanina fell ill, and R. Johanan went to see him. He said to him, "How do you feel?" He replied: "How grievous are my sufferings!"

He said to him: "But surely the reward for them is also great!" He replied: "I want neither them nor their reward." He said to him: "Why do you not utter that incantation which you pronounced over me and which gave me relief?" He replied: "When I was out of trouble I could be a surety for others, but now that I am myself in trouble do I not require another to be a surety for me?"[2]

R. Hiyya b. Abba fell ill and R. Johanan went in to visit him. He said to him: Are your sufferings welcome to you? He replied: Neither they nor their reward. He said to him: Give me your hand. He gave him his hand and he raised him.
R. Johanan once fell ill and R. Hanina went in to visit him. He said to him: Are your sufferings welcome to you? He replied: Neither they nor their reward. He said to him: Give me your hand. He gave him his hand and he raised him. Why could not R. Johanan raise himself?—They replied: The prisoner cannot free himself from jail.[3]

97. Visiting, Healing, and Love

MIDRASH

One-sixtieth, in rabbinic literature, is considered the smallest amount of a thing as, for example, one second is one-sixtieth of a minute. We can take away just this much of a person's illness by sharing our presence with them.

If thy brother be waxen poor (xxv, 25). This bears on the text, *Happy is he that dealeth wisely with the poor; the Lord will deliver him in the day of evil* (Ps. XLI, I). Abba b. Jeremiah in the name of R. Meir said that this refers to one who enthrones the Good Inclination over the Evil Inclination. Isi said that it refers to one who gives a *perutah* to a poor man. R. Johanan said that it refers to one who buries a *meth mizwah*. Our Rabbis say that it refers to one who [assists a person] escaping from tyrants. R. Huna said it refers to one who visits the sick. For, said R. Huna, if a person visits the sick, a reduction of one-sixtieth part of his illness is thereby effected. They pointed out an objection to R. Huna: If that is so, let sixty people come in and enable him to go down into the street? He answered them: Sixty could accomplish this, but only if they loved him like themselves. But in any case they would afford him relief.[4]

98. Our Obligation to Visit the Sick

TALMUD

This passage from Talmud Tractate Nedarim is the clearest and longest one in the Talmud that outlines the duty to visit the sick. Such acts of kindness are among the highest obligations in Judaism.

It was taught: There is no measure for visiting the sick. What is meant by, "there is no measure for visiting the sick"? R. Joseph thought to explain it: Its reward is unlimited. Said Abaye to him: Is there a definite measure of reward for any precept? But we learnt: Be as heedful of a light precept as of a serious one, for thou knowest not the grant of reward for precepts? But Abaye explained . . . even a great person must visit a humble one. Raba said: [One can visit even a hundred times a day]. R. Abba son of R. Hanina said: He who visits an invalid takes away a sixtieth of his pain. Said they to him: If so, let sixty people visit him and restore him to health.

R. Helbo fell ill. Thereupon R. Kahana went and proclaimed: R. Helbo is sick. But none visited him. He rebuked them [the scholars], saying, "Did it not once happen that one of R. Abika's disciples fell sick, and the Sages did not visit him?" So R. Akiba himself entered [his house] to visit him, and because they swept and sprinkled the ground before him, he recovered. "My master," said he, "you have revived me!" [Straightway] R. Akiba went forth and lectured: He who does not visit the sick is like a shedder of blood.

When R. Dimi came, he said: He who visits the sick causes him to live, whilst he who does not causes him to die. How does he cause [this]? Shall we say that he who visits the sick prays that he may live, whilst he who does not prays that he should die!—"That he should die!" Can you really think so? But [say thus:] He who does not visit the sick prays neither that he may live nor die.

Whenever Raba fell sick, on the first day he would ask that his sickness should not be made known to any one lest his fortune be impaired. But after that, he said to them [his servants], "Go proclaim my illness in the market place, so that whoever is my enemy may rejoice, and it is written, *Rejoice not when thine enemy falleth . . . Lest the Lord see it, and it displeases him, and he turn away his wrath from him*, whilst he who loves me will pray for me."

Rab said: He who visits the sick will be delivered from the punishments of Gehenna, for it is written, *Blessed is he that considereth the poor: the Lord will deliver him in the day of evil* (Psalm 41:2). "The poor" *[dal]* means none but the sick, as it is written, *He will cut me off from pining sickness [mi-dalah]* (Isaiah 38:12): or from this verse: *Why art thou so poorly [dal] thou son of the King* (II Samuel 13:4)? Whilst "evil" refers to Gehenna, for it is written, *The Lord hath made all things for himself: Yea even the wicked for the day of evil.* Now, if one does visit, what is his reward? [You ask,] "what is his reward?" Even as hath been said: "he will be delivered from the punishment of Gehenna!"—But what is his reward in this world?—*The Lord will preserve him, and keep him alive, and he shall be blessed upon the earth; and thou wilt not deliver him unto the will of his enemies* (Psalm 41:3). *The Lord will preserve him,"*—from the Evil Urge. *"And keep him alive"*—[saving him] from sufferings; *"and thou wilt not deliver him unto the will of his enemies"*—that he may procure friends like Naaman's who healed him from his leprosy; and not chance upon friends like Rehoboam's, who divided his kingdom ...

R. Shisha son of R. Idi said: One should not visit the sick during the first three or the last three hours [of the day], lest he thereby omit to pray for him. During the first three hours of the day his [the invalid's] illness is alleviated; in the last three hours his sickness is most virulent.

Rabin said in Rab's name: Whence do we know that the Almighty sustains the sick? From the verse, *The Lord will strengthen him upon the bed of languishing.* Rabin also said in Rab's name: Whence do we know that the Divine Presence rests above an invalid's bed? From the verse, *The Lord doth set himself upon the bed of languishing* (Psalm 41:4). It was taught likewise: He who visits the sick must not sit upon the bed, or on a stool or a chair, but must [reverently] robe himself and sit upon the ground, because the Divine Presence rests above an invalid's bed, as it is written, *The Lord doth set himself upon the bed of languishing.*

Samuel said: Only a sick person who is feverish may be visited. What does this exclude? It excludes those concerning whom it has been taught by R. Jose b. Parta in R. Eliezer's name, viz., One must not visit those suffering with bowel [trouble], or with eye disease, or from headaches. Now the first is well, the reason being through embarrassment; but what is the reason of the other two?— On account of Rab Judah's dictum, viz., Speech is injurious to the eyes and to [people suffering from] headaches.[5]

99. *Without Measure*

TALMUD

This passage is so important a guide for righteous living that it was chosen to be studied every day. The portion of the passage in brackets is what is added to the talmudic text in our daily prayers. This passage demonstrates how caring for others can yield blessings in this world and the next.

These are the obligations whose fruit a man eats in this world and the principle is saved for him in the World to Come and these are they:

To honor father and mother;
to perform acts of loving kindness;
[to attend the house of study daily;
to welcome the stranger;
to visit the sick;
to help new brides and grooms;
to bury the dead;
to pray with sincerity;]
to make peace between a man and his friend.

And the study of Torah is equal to them all.[6]

100. *Rules of Visiting the Sick*

MAIMONIDES

Rambam, a physician in his own right, knew the value of spiritual healing and communal care, and he set forth the obligation in his code of law, the Mishneh Torah. *In it, he concisely summarized the ethical injunctions found in Talmud Tractate Nedarim (see 98 above).*

All are in duty bound to visit the sick. Even a man of prominence must visit a less important person. The ill should be visited many times a day. The more often a person calls on the sick, the more praiseworthy he is, provided that he does not inconvenience the patient. He who visits the sick is as though he would take away part of his sickness and lighten his pain. Whoever does not call to see the sick is as though he would shed blood.

A sick person should not be visited before the third day. If his illness came on suddenly and his condition is growing worse, he may be called on forthwith. He should not be visited either during the first three hours or during the last three hours of the day, because (during those hours) they who look after him are busy attending to his needs. Those who suffer from intestinal trouble or have eye trouble or headaches should not be visited, because it is hard for them to see callers.

One who visits a sick person shall not sit upon the bed, or in a chair or on a bench or any elevated place, or above the head side of the patient, but should wrap himself up and sit below the head side, pray for his recovery and depart.[7]

101. Laws of Visiting the Sick

SHULḤAN ARUKH

The Shulḥan Arukh is one of the most authoritative Jewish legal codes. Following Maimonides, it sets forth one's obligation to visit sick persons and make this a "religious duty." It adds the obligations to pray at the bedside and to visit sick "Gentiles."

Chapter 335: When to Visit the Sick; Which Sick Persons Should Be Visited; How to Pray for the Sick

1. It is a religious duty to visit the sick. Relatives and friends may enter at once and strangers after three days. If the sickness overtakes him both may enter forthwith.

2. Even a prominent person must visit a humble one; even many times a day and even if the visitor is of his affinity. One who increases [his visits] is considered praiseworthy, provided he does not trouble him. *Gloss: Some say that an enemy may visit a sick person. However, this does not seem plausible to me; but he should not visit a sick person nor comfort a mourner whom he hates, so that [the latter] should not think that he rejoices at his misfortune, and thereby feel depressed. Thus seems to me [to be the correct view].*

3. One who visits the sick may neither sit upon a bed, nor upon a chair, nor upon a stool, but must [reverently] wrap himself and sit in front of him [the

invalid], for the Divine Presence is above the top-side of his bed. *Gloss: [This applies] only if the sick person lies on the ground so that he who sits [near him] will be on a higher level; but when he lies upon the bed, it is permissible [for the visitor] to sit on a chair or a stool. And thus is our accepted practice.*

4. One must not visit the sick during the first three hours of the day,—for every invalid's illness is alleviated in the morning and [consequently] one will not trouble himself to pray for him; and not during the last three hours of the day, —for then his illness grows worse and one will give up hope to pray for him. *Gloss: One who visited [a sick person] and did not pray for him has not fulfilled the religious duty [of visiting the sick].*

5. When one prays for him, —if in his presence, one may pray in any language one desires; if one prays, not in his presence, one should only pray in Hebrew.

9. One must visit the sick of the Gentiles in the interest of peace.[8]

102. Learning to Cheer the Sick

RACHEL COWAN

What helps? The answer will be different in every situation, but here are some truly practical suggestions for helping healer and healed physically, emotionally, intellectually, and spiritually.

Taught by the bitter experience of caring for her husband, Paul, in the last six months of his life, Rabbi Rachel Cowan elaborates on the talmudic injunction to visit the sick.

I learned much about visiting the sick during the year when my late husband Paul fought so valiantly against leukemia. I had always thought that visiting sick people was important, and I tried to do it when I could. But, like most Jews, I didn't see it as a mitzvah in the sense of "commandment"; instead I preferred to translate mitzvah as "good deed"—something a nice person did when she felt up to it.

The year I spent with Paul during his illness—six months of that time in hospitals, sleeping in his room many nights, keeping him company and boosting his spirits—made me understand the importance of the mitzvah. If people do not have visitors, they find it that much more difficult to mobilize themselves to heal, to engage in the desire to overcome their illness, or to live as fully as possible in the face of it.

I mastered the art of living in a hospital—I developed a strategy for getting space on the perpetually overcrowded elevators so as to get the food I was heating up in the microwave oven in the basement lounge back up to Paul before it cooled off. On the other hand, I learned a deep spiritual truth—that through love and attention to small details and through learning to listen and to hold hands in silence, you can help a person transform fear and terror into hope and occasional peace of mind.

What are small details?

Clothes: Paul hated hospital pajamas, hated lying in bed dressed unnaturally, so I went out and bought colorful sweat pants, sweat shirts, cheerful T-shirts, and he felt like a normal person.

Music: We discovered that some tape decks can play continually, and we learned that some New Age music is very soothing. He played these tapes, and a guided meditation tape of Bernie Siegel's all night long, so he wasn't so frightened when he woke up in the middle of the night, and could eventually get back to sleep.

Food: Paul hated the airplane-packaged kosher meals at the hospital, so our friends cooked for him, and froze the food, and I brought it down and heated it in the microwave. Each meal he'd ask, "Who cooked this?" and then feel pleased to know he was eating Sharon's chicken, or Jackie's pea soup, or Doris's rice and beans.

Domestic routine: I brought a coffee pot and made him tea, poured him juice, cleaned up the room. I brought bright pillow covers and a pretty bedspread. I hung up all the cards he got and had a few photographs of the kids blown up to poster size for the walls. I constantly tidied up, and made him feel that he was living in our space, not theirs.

Books: Friends sent him books, or went out to buy him new ones. Several of us researched what books on the experience of cancer patients were helpful, which ones were too flaky, or too gloomy.

An interesting project: He worked on projects he cared about, so that he was a productive writer, not just a patient. He also invented a hospital project— a trivia quiz book on the 1960s which entertained him and our friends, and gave them all something cheerful and distracting to talk about.

A telephone tree: Patients and their families get overwhelmed by always having to report on their illness. Several friends organized telephone trees to let people know how things were developing, to answer questions people might have and to get people to donate blood, or to bring food, or to send cards. Paul came to feel that the perfect hospital call was a two minute chat, in which his friend Judy told him a bit of gossip, told him she was thinking about him, and hung up, without expecting him to rehearse his symptoms or take his emotional temperature.

Letting people help: Many people react to illness by drawing into themselves, feeling ashamed of their illness. They have always been used to the idea of having control; now they feel powerless. They are afraid of feeling dependent, of being needy. They are reluctant to ask other people for help. They keep telling people not to bother, they'll be all right. They should be encouraged to let people into their lives, to understand that people like to be able to help, if there are specific things that they can do.

Rituals and holiday celebrations: We celebrated Shabbat with challah and kiddush and a special meal every week. We even made Shabbat in the emergency room while waiting for the diagnosis—we shared a kosher hospital meal, and made kiddush over grape juice from a vending machine and a motzi over a piece of white bread. We also decorated the room for Sukkot, conducted two seders, ate blintzes on Shavuot, and davened with tapes of the High Holiday services. A friend came to blow the shofar. Again, all these celebrations helped Paul to retain his identity and integrity as a human being, not a patient. Paul laid tefillin every morning, too, looking out over the East River as the sun came up, sharing a quiet time in prayer before the nurses came in to begin the day's bustle of activity. Paul was able to maintain firm belief that God was with him in that room, that God cared about him.[9]

103. The Last Moments

M. REMA

Rabbi Moshe ben Yisrael Isserles, a halakhic authority of Cracow, Poland (1525–1572), summarized Jewish law on the last moments of life in the following manner.

It is forbidden to cause the dying to die quickly, such as one who is moribund over a long time and who cannot die. It is forbidden to remove the pillow from under him on the assumption that certain birdfeathers prevent his death. So too one cannot remove the keys of the synagogue from beneath his head, or move him that he may die. But if there is something that delays his death such as a nearby woodchopper making a noise, or there is salt on his tongue, and these prevent his speedy death, one can remove them, for this does not involve any action at all, but rather the removal of the preventive agent.[10]

104. Suicide

SEFER HASIDIM

There is a temptation, when death is inevitable and suffering is great, to end the pain through suicide. Jewish ethical sources are nearly unanimous in their rejection of this concept. Even a day of life with great pain is to be treasured.

If a person is suffering terrible pain, and he tells someone: "You can see that I am not going to live; kill me, as I cannot suffer anymore"; one may not touch him … whereas Saul was permitted [to shorten his life] to prevent a desecration of the divine name before Israel.

If a person suffers great pain, and he knows he cannot live, he may not commit suicide. This we learn from R. Haninah ben Tradyon, who did not want to open his mouth. But if there are factors preventing a speedy demise—such as a man chopping wood in the vicinity of a dying man's home, and the noise of the chopping prevents the soul from escaping—we remove the chopper from there. Likewise we do not place salt on his tongue to prevent his death. But if he is dying and he says, "I cannot die until you put me in a different place," they may not move him from there.[11]

105. Faith Healing in Jewish Law

IMMANUEL JAKOBOVITS

Immanuel Jakobovits is one of this century's great Jewish legal decision-makers. Here, he reflects Judaism's balance between faith healing and superstition.

The belief in the curative powers of religious shrines and saintly relics is unknown among the Jews. To be sure, it is reported that to this day sick people are carried to the synagogue in Cairo bearing the name of MAIMONIDES to sleep there hoping to obtain healing through the spirit of the great physician, but our information is that these pilgrims are mainly Arabs. A similar custom is known among Moslems who visit the tomb of AVICENNA at Hammadan where "cures are said to be not uncommon". The nearest Jewish parallel to this outlook is to be found among the Hassidic "wonder-rabbis" in modern times. Some of these occasionally resorted to faith-healing, but—as a leading medical historian has testified—"their cures were generally limited to moral or hygienic prescriptions and to the use of certain prayers, formulae or cryptograms. . . . Their medical system was of only the mildest sort; its suggestive therapy was often educational, always fantastic, but certainly not dangerous."

The relevant references to prayer in the codes of Jewish law are few but significant. A prayer for the sick, based on the wording of Jeremiah *xvii*.14, is to be recited three times every weekday among the *Nineteen Benedictions* (*O.H., cxvi*); this is included in the statutory Jewish prayer-book. Provision is also made for the insertion of a special intercession for the recovery of a sick relative or other specified individual (*O.H., cxix.I*). The purpose of these petitions is to "seek mercy" from God. That is also the principal object of the obligation to visit the sick; "and whoever visits the sick without pleading for mercy has not fulfilled the precept" (*Y.D., cccxxxv*.4, gloss). The law also lays down a formula for the success of medical treatment about to be administered: "May it be Thy will, O Lord our God, that this treatment shall be a healing unto me, for Thou are a gratuitous Healer" (*O.H., ccxxx*.4). Upon the safe deliverance from any illness it is obligatory to recite a special benediction of thanksgiving in public (*O.H., ccxix.I* and 8); but ISSERLES limits this to the restoration from dangerous diseases (*ib.*, gloss).

Detailed regulations governed the proclamation of special fasts, accompanied by the blowing of the *Shofar* horn, whenever a city was struck by an outbreak of the plague or other diseases in epidemic proportions, such as diphtheria, delirious fever and certain types of skin infection (*O.H., dlxxvi*.2–5). We have already noted that the obligation to fast in times of pestilence was subsequently revoked. There are also records of special prayers against the pestilential scourge, such as the plague-prayer written by R. SOLOMON BEN R. MORDECAI of Meseritz (printed in 1602 with the approbation of MORDECAI JAFFE and other rabbis). Another rabbi composed a liturgical poem against the threat of smallpox among children; published thirteen years later, it was included in the penitential liturgy of the Polish rite.

Apart from these public appeals for divine intervention to stave off disease and to secure relief, Jewish law also provides for the resort to more mystical media. Following the ancient Jewish belief that the prayers of the righteous are especially efficacious, ISSERLES records the view of some medieval authorities advising people who have a patient in their house to repair to the "scholar of the town", so that he shall "seek mercy" for the sufferer (*Y.D., cccxxxv.*10, gloss). The *New Testament* offers similar counsel: "Is there any sick among you? Let him call for the elders of the church; and let them pray over him, anointing him with oil in the name of the Lord. And the prayer of faith shall save the sick . . . ." (Epistle of James, *v.*14 and 15). Some scholars assume that these verses betoken a belief in the sufficiency of prayer and the rejection of all but theurgical cures, but we would scarcely be justified in inferring that ISSERLES's advice was meant to take the place of rational means of healing. He further adds: "It was also a custom to recite a blessing for the sick in the synagogue and to give them a new name therein; for a change of name tears up the [evil] decree against one" (*ib.*).

At the same time, the law severely limited the legitimate recourse to supernatural agencies. "He who whispers an incantation over a wound or over a sick person and expectorates and then recites a verse from the *Pentateuch* has no share in the world to come; if he does not expectorate, he still commits an offence; but in cases of danger to life, all is permitted" (*Y.D., clxxxix.*8), because, "although such charms are of no avail, the rabbis have allowed them when life is in danger, so as to prevent the distraction of the patient's mind (*ib.*, 6). To substitute faith-cures by prayer for rational healing is even more emphatically condemned in the following rule: "If a child is stricken, one must not read a scriptural verse, nor place a scroll of the Law, over it" (*ib.*, 9). For "the words of the *Torah*", explains MAIMONIDES, "are given not to heal the body, but to heal the soul". Scriptural passages may, however, always be recited for the protection of healthy persons from affliction and injury (*ib.*, 10). In this case, such readings serve merely a prophylactic, not therapeutic, purpose, and one is not tempted to trust their efficacy.

These laws indicate unmistakably that, while every encouragement was given for the sick to exploit their adversity for moral and religious ends and to strengthen their faith in recovery by prayer, confidence in the healing powers of God was never allowed to usurp the essential functions of the physician and of medical science. Judaism repudiates, therefore, as altogether incompatible with its religious teachings, the doctrine of "Christian Science" and similar movements, even when they are completely divorced from their Christological associations.

The frequency with which Jewish law consistently subscribes to medical measures to combat disease, and the long history of the rabbis' resort to medicine as their favorite profession, shows how wrong it is to speak with some historians of the "theurgical character of Jewish medicine", unless indeed the constant reminder of the physician's dependence on the "Healer of all flesh" can be construed to bear out such a claim. The wholly positive attitude to medicine evidenced in these pages must, moreover, decisively qualify the critical verdict on the rabbinic approach to science which finds that "... it is a special feature of Talmudic preoccupation that it tends to occupy the whole area of thought as do few other studies; for the Talmud is not only a subject of study, it is a habit of thought, a cast of mind, a way of life. The practical test lies in the historical record. Very few if any talmudists have made contributions to science. Why should this be? The answer must be in terms of Jewish sociology or psychology...." This thoughtful statement is substantially correct and yet incomplete. In the sphere of medicine, it is true, Jews have scarcely been noted for any outstanding discoveries or pioneering theories outside the modern period. But this lack of scientific creativeness was by no means restricted to students of the Talmud, and it cannot be ascribed exclusively to the effect of such studies. Moreover, this deficiency may well be more than offset by what is, perhaps, a far more momentous contribution to medical progress: the maintenance and uncompromising encouragement, throughout the Middle Ages, of an eminently sound approach to disease and its cure. It was in such soil, freed from its weeds of quackery and superstition, and fertilised in great measure by Talmudic traditions, that the seeds of enquiry and experiment eventually, in the period following the 16th century, bore such rewarding fruit.[12]

106. Filial Responsibility

LEVI MEIER

The tension between the need to care for a sick parent and the need to honor that same parent is one experienced with increasing frequency. Jewish legal thinking demonstrates how to keep these two duties in creative and productive tension. This essay is part of a book of essays on medical ethics edited by Rabbi Meier.

The guideline for interpersonal relations which cover life-cycle situations are a distinct aspect of Jewish law. For example, comforting the bereaved requires the comforter to be completely silent until the bereaved begins a conversation (Karo, *Shulhan Arukh, Yoreh Deah,* 376.1). Similarly, the laws for visiting the sick require certain behavior, such as saying words of encouragement and helping the sick to arrange their final affairs (*ibid.,* 335.7).

Under ordinary circumstances the behavior required for honoring one's father and mother is conceptually defined by two categories: honor *(kibbud)* and reverence *(morah). Honor* is defined as positive acts of personal service. Rabbinic examples include feeding and dressing one's parent (Talmud, *Kiddushin,* 31b). These examples illustrate that a child's relationship to the parent is comparable to that of a servant to the master. *Reverence* is defined as an avoidance of disrespectful acts. Rabbinic examples include not sitting in a parent's seat nor speaking before parents and never contradicting them (Talmud, *Kiddushin,* 31b). These examples demonstrate how, in general, a child should relate to superiors.

These child-parent obligations are applicable throughout the life cycle; when the parents are young, middle-aged, and in the late period of life. The purpose of this chapter is to analyze whether these obligations are similarly applicable when one's parent is senile.

"Senility" does not refer to forgetfulness or excessive reminiscing on the part of the aging parent. Senility, which is irreversible, is defined as chronic brain syndrome. Acute brain syndrome is reversible and does not fall in the category of senility. The mental status questionnaire devised by Kahn, Goldfarb, Pollack and Peck clearly differentiates between acute and chronic brain syndrome.

Acute brain syndrome (ABS) differs from chronic brain syndrome in the areas of causes, symptoms, and treatment. For purposes of this discussion, symptoms and treatment are the most significant considerations. Reversible brain syndrome involves a fluctuating level of awareness. The person typically is disoriented; recent memory is lost, while remote memory may be preserved. Restlessness or aggressiveness may appear in the behavior.

The clinical symptoms of chronic brain syndrome (CBS) differ significantly from those of reversible brain syndrome. There are two predominant types of chronic brain syndrome: *senile psychosis* and *psychosis associated with cerebral arteriosclerosis.* The symptoms of *senile psychosis* may appear insidiously without any abrupt changes. Gradually, small differences in physical, mental, and emotional functioning are noticed. Early symptoms may include errors in judgment and decline in personal care habits. Depression, anxiety, and irritability may also characterize the early stages of this syndrome. As the deterioration increases, the traditional five signs of organic dysfunction become more evident: (1) disturbance and impairment of memory; (2) impairment of intellectual functioning; (3) impairment of judgment; (4) impairment of orientation, and (5) shallow or labile affect.

The symptoms of *psychosis associated with cerebral arteriosclerosis* can either be gradual or sudden. With a slower onset, there is usually a gradual intellectual loss, and impairment of memory tends to be spotty rather than complete. The course is up and down rather than progressively downhill.

It appears that the reversible brain syndrome can result in complete recovery once the person survives the physical crisis which precipitated the psychiatric disorder. Treatment must be intensive but can often be short-term.

Senile psychosis is marked by steady and progressive deterioration and is eventually fatal. Emotional reactions may respond to treatment, and physical functioning can improve with proper support even though the physical loss is irreparable. Similarly, psychosis associated with cerebral arteriosclerosis can lead quickly to a fatal outcome or may produce an organic condition lasting a number of years....

In attempting to arrive at the Jewish law regarding care of a senile parent, one must rely not only on scientific definitions of brain syndromes, but also on the Talmudic treatment of mental dysfunction in a parent. An examination of pertinent Talmudic passages may be instructive in attempting to ascertain the *ha-*

lakhic differentiation between abnormal behavior and mental disturbance as well as the required behavior under Jewish law for dealing with one's senile parent.

The Talmud asks the question, "How far does the honor of parents extend?" (Talmud, *Kiddushin,* 31a). A few Talmudic anecdotes would appear to indicate that if a parent behaves abnormally, the child's responsibility to honor the father or mother is not altered. Rabbi Dimi gives this incident as an example:

> Once he [Dama the son of Metinah] was seated among the great men of Rome, dressed in a gold embroidered, silk garment, when his mother came and tore the garment from him, slapped him on the head, and spat in his face—but he did not shame her (Talmud, *Kiddushin,* 31a).

Rabbi Eliezer further asserts that even should the parent take the child's purse, and, in the child's presence, throw the purse into the sea, the child must still not shame the parent (*ibid.,* 32a).

These citations illustrate that even extreme deviations from normal parental behavior in no way alter the child's obligation to honor the parent, which remains an absolute, no matter what the difficulties of the child.

Maimonides codifies the two foregoing examples and establishes normative principles to guide people faced with similar circumstances.

> How far must one go to honor one's father and mother? Even if they took his wallet full of gold pieces and threw it into the sea before his very eyes, he must not shame them, show no pain before them or display anger to them; but he must accept the decree of scripture and keep his silence. And how far must one go in reverence? Even if he is dressed in precious clothes and is sitting in an honored place before many people, and his parents come and tear his clothes, hitting him in the head and spitting in his face, he may not shame them, but he must keep silent, and be in awe and fear of the King of Kings who commanded him thus. For if a king of flesh and blood had decreed that he do something more painful than this, he could not hesitate in its performance. How much more so, when he is commanded by Him who created the world at His will (Maimonides, *Mishneh Torah,* Laws of Mamrim [the Rebellious], 6.7).

Maimonides realizes the difficulties inherent in these events and in implementing these commandments. In his view, an additional motivation for the performance of these commandments, stems from one's awe and fear of the King of Kings.

From these Talmudic anecdotes and from Maimonides' analysis of them, it would appear, as previously assumed, that if a parent behaves abnormally, the child's responsibility to honor the father or mother is not altered. On the contrary, one finds that the child's responsibility increases in direct proportion to the specific needs of the parents. Also, as at any other time, personal service (honor) and the avoidance of disrespect (reverence) must characterize dealings with a parent in such a situation.

However, in addition to the codification of these two examples, Maimonides establishes a separate category for the conduct required in dealing with one's *mentally disturbed* parent. Maimonides writes:

> If one's father or mother should become mentally disordered, he should try to treat them as their mental state demands, until they are pitied [by God]. But if he finds he cannot endure the situation because of their extreme madness, let him leave and go away, assigning others to care for them properly (*Mishneh Torah,* Laws of Mamrim, 6.10).

Though there is no specific Talmudic statement upon which this view of Maimonides is based, the commentaries on Maimonides assume that the following anecdote is the basis for his statement:

> Rabbi Assi had an aged mother. Said she to him, "I want ornaments." So he made them for her.... "I want a husband as handsome as you." Thereupon he left her and went out to Palestine (Talmud, *Kiddushin,* 31b).

The departure of Rabbi Assi from Babylon has been interpreted as an acceptable response to the action of his senile mother. Rabbi Assi, unable to respond to his aged, senile mother in a constructive manner, leaves her in Babylon and makes his way to Palestine.

Maimonides clearly does more than codify this Talmudic event. He adds some interpretive dimensions. His codification accentuates three essential points, as Blidstein (1975) points out:

1. The parent is classified as mentally disturbed.

2. The child is exempt from personal service to the parent, but not from the responsibility to ensure that others attend to the parent.

3. The point of the child's exemption from personal service to the senile parent is the child's own evaluation of the situation.

The Rabad argues with Maimonides' conclusion. He asks, "If he leaves, whom will he assign to watch over his parents?" (*Mishneh Torah,* Laws of Mamrim, 6.10).

In Rabad's view, there is no limitation to the child's responsibility. Instructive here is the defense of Maimonides' view offered by Radvaz (*Mishneh Torah,* Laws of Mamrim, 6.10), who claims that the child is in a weakened position, unable to rebuke the parent and not able to command the respect necessary to effect some measure of stability. An outsider is unencumbered by these realities and is better able to restore the parent to a more functional level. The child's exemption from service to the parent is thus a perceptive clinical judgment.

The basic question arising from Maimonides' citations centers on his differentiation between a parent's acting abnormally and being mentally disturbed. Abnormal parental behavior must be withstood by the child, but care of a mentally disturbed parent may be delegated to others.

The examples of parental behavior given by the Talmud—throwing the son's wallet into the sea and tearing his clothes in front of dignitaries, in contrast to saying, "I want a husband as handsome as you"—are not, in themselves, sufficient for differentiating between abnormal behavior and mental disturbance.

The key issue in these situations is the halakhically acceptable response to these problems. The son must tolerate abnormal parental behavior, even abuse. However, Rabbi Assi, whose mother desired a husband as handsome as he, is allowed to depart for Palestine, leaving care of his aged mother to others.

One suggested explanation for these two distinct *halakhic* codifications by Maimonides may be that he equates Rabbi Assi's mother's condition with chronic, irreversible brain syndrome, while he regards the examples of parental abuse as cases of temporary abnormality.

According to Jewish law, the categories of *honor* and *reverence* apply in the cases of every normal and abnormal parent behavior, but honor may be suspended in cases of behavior which result from permanent mental disturbance. Even extreme deviations from the norm and totally illogical behavior on the part of parents must be tolerated when that behavior is the result of an acute condition, such as an acute brain syndrome. In these cases, filial responsibility increases according to parental needs and constructive responses can be expected, since the situation is reversible.

However, a chronic brain syndrome, an irreversible condition, falls into a different category. It is recognized that the child's tolerance may be overtaxed and the child is therefore exempted from direct personal service. However, the responsibility to ensure that someone else takes care of the parent is incumbent upon the child.

This hypothesis concerning the differentiation between acute and chronic brain syndrome in determining the applicable Jewish law is hinted at by Maimonides when he asserts that the child must try to treat the parent as the mental state demands, but if enduring the situation is no longer possible because the madness is extreme (chronic), the child *should* leave and assign others to care for the parent (*Mishneh Torah*, Laws of Mamrim, 6.10). That is, every mental disturbance must be initially dealt with until filial tolerance is exhausted due to the parent's extreme condition. This condition must be chronic and therefore, irreversible. An acute brain syndrome, although very taxing, will not worsen, but will indeed improve significantly when dealt with. In such a situation, filial responsibility is not suspended.

With an understanding of the distinction between these two types of brain syndrome, different filial responses toward abnormal parental behavior may be understood. Naturally, every deviation from the parental norm must initially be treated as acute until evidence indicates that the condition is in fact irreversible. Chronic brain syndrome may be a legitimate reason for transferring the obligation for attentiveness to a parent's needs to others. However, old age and the normal infirmities that may accompany it do not provide sufficient reason for transferring this obligation. Old age is expected to stimulate additional contact between parent and offspring rather than abandonment of the parent.[13]

107. The Healer's Fees

TALMUD

One who righteously practices medicine—without greed and with respect for each patient's humanity—earns greater eternal glory than even the greatest of sages.

Abba was a cupper and daily he would receive greetings from the Heavenly Academy. Abaye received greetings on every Sabbath eve, Raba on the eve of every Day of Atonement. Abaye felt dejected because of [the signal honour

shown to] Abba the Cupper. People said to him: This distinction is made because you cannot do what Abba does. What was the special merit of Abba the
Cupper? When he performed his operations he would separate men from
women, and in addition he had a cloak which held a cup [for receiving the
blood] and which was slit at the shoulder and whenever a woman patient came
to him he would put the garment on her shoulder in order not to see her [ex-
posed body]. He also had a place out of public gaze where the patients
deposited their fees there, and thus those who could not pay were not put to
shame. Whenever a young scholar happened to consult him not only would he
accept no fee from him but on taking leave of him he also would give him some
money at the same time adding, Go and regain strength therewith.[14]

108. The Jewish Patient

FRED ROSNER

> *Dr. Rosner demonstrates how one can balance the need for*
> *Jewish observance and modern medical care.*

The attitude toward healing in Judaism has always been a positive one. A physician is obligated to heal and is given divine license to do so. Physicians must
apply their skills for the benefit of the patient and be careful not to do harm. A
patient is also obligated to seek healing because one must be healthy in order to
serve the Lord by doing His will in the service of mankind.

Thus, while much of the modern secular ethical system is based on rights,
Judaism is an ethical system based on duties and responsibilities. Lord
Jakobovits eloquently articulates the Jewish view as follows:

> Now in Judaism we know of no intrinsic rights. Indeed there is no word for
> right in the very language of the Hebrew Bible and of the classic sources of
> Jewish law. In the moral vocabulary of the Jewish discipline of life we speak of
> human duties, not of human rights, of obligations, not entitlement. The Deca-
> logue is a list of Ten Commandments, not a Bill of Rights.

The Jewish patient's ability to carry on with daily life as a Jew while hospitalized is also important. The task of the healer is to help patients regain their
strength and confidence, as well as their physical well-being. Anything that

strengthens the will to live facilitates the patient's recovery. Consequently, during the trying period of illness, the religious needs of the patient may assume particular importance. For the observant Jewish patient, the provision of kosher food, Sabbath and Holy Day observance, and the general regard of others for the patient's religious dictates can be of inestimable help in the healing process. Although Judaism is a religion of obligations rather than rights, in our secular society, Jewish patients have the right to expect that hospital administrators and staff be sensitive to these needs. Observant Jewish patients have no automatic dispensation to suspend these precepts and practices, except in life-threatening situations. A patient who has always adhered to Judaic precepts and practices, and is suddenly thrust into a hospital environment that tempts or compels violation of these Judaic laws, may suffer severe emotional stress. Such a patient may feel harried and threatened, not only by the underlying disease, but also by hospital authority and personnel and may develop deep feelings of guilt if he or she succumbs to unwarranted violations.

Hospitalized Jewish patients have a Bill of Rights, which includes such things as being served kosher food, deferring advance payment until the end of the Sabbath or festival observance of Jewish rituals, refusing outpatient appointments scheduled for the Sabbath or festivals, and the right to consult with religious advisers before deciding whether to undergo medical procedures that might pose religious questions.

These problems and issues are either minimal or nonexistent for Reform or assimilated Jews who are less concerned with ritual and practice than with pure religious identification. Nevertheless, basic principles of Judaism regarding physician and patient transcend all denominations of Jews. These principles include the fact that a physician is given divine license to practice medicine. Jewish physicians are, in fact, obligated to heal the sick and are guilty of wrongdoing if they refuse. Similarly, the Jewish patient is obligated to seek healing from a physician. Judaism teaches that life is a gift from God to be held in trust. One is duty bound to care for one's life and health. Only God gives life, and hence only God can take it away. Humans do not possess absolute title to their life or to their body, which is given on loan to be used but not abused. We are charged with preserving, dignifying, and hallowing our life. For Jews of all denominations, consultation with their rabbi regarding medical ethical issues is helpful in the clinical setting in individual cases. Jewish physicians cannot and should not impose their moral values on non-Jewish patients but must respect the patient's own cultural and spiritual heritage. That is good and proper medical practice for any physician of any religion caring for patients of the same or any other religion. The basic principles and tenets of Judaism regarding the practice of medicine are presented in this essay to sensitive physicians and caregivers to fundamental axioms of medical ethics in general and Judaism in particular. Jewish medical ethical principles have broad applications whether or not the caregiver or patient is Jewish. Maleficence, nonmaleficence, autonomy, and justice are guiding principles for physicians and patients of all religious and ethnic backgrounds.[15]

109. The Patient as a Person

ABRAHAM J. HESCHEL

The patient-physician encounter is, at best, uncomfortable. Doctors see patients when patients are feeling their worst, when they are suffering from pain and anxiety, and feeling vulnerably undressed, no less. The physician, meanwhile, may or may not feel at ease touching a total stranger in ways that may help, but may hurt. The goal during these encounters is not to diminish these feelings, but to use them as a bridge to our common humanity. Theologian Abraham Joshua Heschel gave this impassioned address on the physician-patient relationship in 1963 to the American Medical Association. Rabbi Heschel and Rabbi Shulweis, whose selection follows, base their ethics of the physician-patient relationship on the concepts of covenant and I-thou relationship rather than traditional talmudic injunctions.

What is human about a human being?

Biologically man is properly classified as a type of mammal, and defined as an animal with a distinguishing attribute. And yet, such definitions prove to be meaningless when you stand with man face to face.

It is reported that after Plato had defined man to be a two-legged animal without feathers, Diogenes plucked a cock and brought it into the Academy.

The zoomorphic conceptions of man enables us to assign his place in the physical universe, yet it fails to account for the infinite dissimilarity between man and the highest animal below him. The gulf between the human and the non-human can be grasped only in human terms. The very question we ask: What is human about a human being? is not an animal problem but a human problem. What we seek to ascertain is not the animality but the humanity of man. The common definitions, for all the truths they contain, are both an over-simplification and an evasion.

Human being is being *sui generis.* The only adequate way to grasp its meaning is to think of man in human terms. Human is more than a concept of fact; it is a category of value, of the highest of all values available to us.

What is the worth of an individual man? According to a rabbinic dictum, "He who saves one man is regarded as if he saved all men; he who destroys one man is regarded as if he destroyed all men."

It is beyond my power to assess the worth of all of humanity. What should a Life Insurance Company charge for the insurance of the entire human race? It is just as staggering to ponder the worth of one human being.

In terms of statistics the individual man is an exceedingly insignificant specimen compared with the totality of the human species. So why should the life and dignity of an individual man be regarded as infinitely precious?

Because human being is not just being-around, being-here-too, a being to be assessed and classified in terms of quantity. Human being is a disclosure of the divine. The grandeur of human being is revealed in the power of being human.

What is the meaning of being human? In dealing with a particular man, I do not come upon a generality but upon an individuality, upon uniqueness, upon a person. I see a face, not only a body, a special situation, not typical case.

Most conspicuous is the variety and inner richness of the human species. Not only do individuals differ widely; the individual himself is not always the same. Look at a dog. Once a dog always a dog. Yet man may be a sinner today and a saint tomorrow. Perhaps the most amazing aspect about man is what is latent in him.

One thing that sets man apart from other animals is a boundless, unpredictable capacity for the development of an inner universe. There is more potentiality in his soul than in any other being known to us. Look at the infant and try to imagine the multitude of events it is going to engender. One child named Johann Sebastian Bach was charged with power enough to hold generations of men in his spell. But is there any potentiality to a claim or any surprise to expect in a calf or a colt? Indeed, the essence of a human being is not in what he is, but in what he is able to be.

What constitutes being human, personhood? The ability to be concerned for other human beings. Animals are concerned for their own instinctive needs; the degree of our being human stands in direct proportion to the degree in which we care for others. The word cure comes from the word care.

The truth of being human is gratitude, the secret of existence is appreciation, its significance is revealed in reciprocity. Mankind will not die for lack of information; it may perish for lack of appreciation.

Being human presupposes the paradox of freedom, the capacity to create events, to transcend the self. Being human is a surprise, a flash of light, a moment in time rather than a thing in space. It has no meaning, no genuine reality or validity within the context of the categories of space. It cannot be validated or kept alive within scientific empiricism.

The ultimate significance of human being as well as the ultimate meaning of being human may be wishful thinking, a ridiculous conceit in the midst of a world apparently devoid of ultimate meaning, a supreme absurdity.

It is part of the cure to trust in Him who cures.

Supreme meaning is therefore inconceivable without meaning derived from supreme being. Humanity without divinity is a torso. This is even reflected in the process of healing.

Without a sense of significant being, a sense of wonder and mystery, a sense of reverence for the sanctity of being alive, the doctor's efforts and prescriptions may prove futile.

I am born a human being; what I have to acquire is being human.

The contemporary man is bored, bitter, blasphemously disgruntled. His scientific goal is to quantify the soul. The human as a category is becoming meaningless, a linguistic aberration.

To be human we must know what humanity means, how to acquire, how to preserve it. Being human is both a fact and a demand, a condition and an expectation. Our being human is always on trial, full of risk, precarious; man is always in danger of forfeiting his humanity.

One of the most frightening prospects we must face is that this earth may be populated by a race of beings which, though belonging to the race of *homo sapiens* according to biology, will be devoid of the qualities by which man is spiritually distinguished from the rest of organic creatures.

Just as death is the liquidation of human being, dehumanization is the liquidation of being human.

America's problem number one is not the use of insecticide but the promotion of spiritual homicide, the systematic liquidation of man as a person.

Decay sets in inconspicuously, not dramatically. Is it not possible that we are entering a stage in history out of which we may emerge as morons, as an affluent society of spiritual idiots? Doctors will disappear, veterinarians may take over the practice of medicine.

A baby was born in the hospital, and the father's first chance to see his first-born child was after it was brought home and placed in the crib. His friends saw how he leaned over the crib, an expression of extreme bewilderment on his face. "Why do you look so bewildered?" "Impossible!" he answered. "How can they make such a fine crib for $29.50?"

We cannot speak about the patient as a person unless we also probe the meaning of the doctor as a person. You can only sense a person if you are a person. Being a person depends upon being alive to the wonder and mystery that surround us, upon the realization that there is no ordinary man. Every man is an extraordinary man.

Technology is growing apace. Soon the doctor may be obsolete. The data about the patient would be collected by camera and Dictaphone, arranged by typists, processed into a computer. Diagnosis and treatment would be established by a machine. Who, then, would need doctors?

The mother of medicine is not human curiosity but human compassion, and it is not good for medicine to be an orphan. Physics may be studied as a pure science, medicine must never be practiced for its own sake.

In contrast to times gone by, the doctor's role has broadened from healing the sick to serving all men, ill and well. However, I will limit myself to the role of the physician as a healer, a supreme test of his role in the life of society.

What manner of man is the doctor? Life abounds in works of achievement, in areas of excellence and beauty, but the physician is a person who has chosen to go to the areas of distress, to pay attention to sickness and affliction, to injury and anguish.

Medicine is more than a profession. Medicine has a soul, and its calling involves not only the applications of knowledge and the exercise of skill but also facing a human situation. It is not an occupation for those to whom a career is more precious than humanity or for those who value comfort and serenity about service to others. The doctor's mission is prophetic.

Humanity is an unfinished process, and so is religion. The law, the teaching, and the wisdom are here, yet without the outburst of prophetic men coming upon us again and again, religion may become fossilized. Nature has marvelous recuperative power, yet without the aid of the art of medicine the human species might degenerate.

There is a prophetic ingredient in the calling of the doctor. His vocation is to prevent illness, to cure disease, to lessen pain, to avert death. The doctor is a prophet, a watchman, a messenger, an assayer, a tester.

The weight of a doctor's burden is heavy and often grave. In other professions mistakes, inadvertency, blunders may be pardonable, even remediable; the doctor, however, is often like an acrobat, a ropewalker; precision and meticulousness are imperative; one mistake and the patient may be dead.

While medical science is advancing, the doctor-patient relationship seems to be deteriorating. In fairness to physicians, the relationship has changed because medicine has changed. The doctor of old may have had little more to offer the patient than understanding, sympathy, personal affection.

The great advances in medicine have made it necessary for men to specialize if they wish to remain abreast of any particular field of medicine, and this specialization has forced a change in the image of the practitioner. Yet there is no necessary clash between specialization and compassion, between the use of instruments and personal sensitivity.

Many of us fear a collapse of the old and traditional esteem for the character of the doctor, an increasing alienation between the healer and the sick. The doctor is alleged by many people to act like an executive, viewing the patient as only a consumer.

Generalizations are unfair. Such an image may apply to a minority of men in this great profession. Yet attitudes of some may reveal a condition of concern to many.

The crisis in the doctor-patient relationship is part of the ominous, unhealthy, livid condition of human relations in our entire society, a spiritual malaria, a disease of which high-powered commercialism and intellectual vulgarity are only premonitory symptoms. Let me offer an example of intellectual vulgarity.

According to the philosophy of a dog, to quote Bradley, what smells is, what does not smell is not real and does not exist. According to the philosophy of logical positivism, what is verifiable is meaningful; what is not verifiable is meaningless. Thus the term "person" should be regarded as a misnomer: unverifiable, indefinable, vague, mystical, and therefore both meaningless and worthless. Since we must think in terms which are both clear and exact, man must be regarded as a collection of tubes and cells, of pipes and wires. This is scientific fact, accessible to our instruments.

Strictly speaking, what is a patient? A human machine in need of repair; all else is accidental. Or, as has been suggested, man could best be defined as an ingenious assembly of portable plumbing.

As a patient, what do I see when I see a doctor? Since I am essentially a machine, I see the doctor as a plumber, whose task is to repair a tube in my system. What does the doctor encounter when he examines a patient? He sees a case, a urinary case, and intestinal case, but not a person. This, then would be philosophy: The world is a factory, man is a gadget, and the doctor is a plumber; all else is irrelevant.

While such a philosophy of medicine may seem plausible, it is being refuted by the grandeur and agony of man. And no one sees so much agony as you, gentlemen.

To accept such a philosophy would be to perpetrate euthanasia on the spirit of medicine itself. The mechanics of medicine must not be mistaken for the very essence of medicine, which is an art, not alone a science.

The human organism can accept an artificial leg or a transplanted kidney. But will a patient retain his identity if his brain is removed and a mechanized brain is put in instead? Will medicine retain its identity if reduced to engineering?

The doctor-patient relationship comes to pass in the dimension of personhood as it does in the dimension of time and space. There is no escape.

It is not true that the diagnosis or the treatment of a patient comes about in a way completely unaffected by religious and philosophical commitments. The doctor's commitments are as much a part of it as scientific knowledge and skill.

His attitudes are either sensitive or cruel, human or inhuman; there is no middle course. Indifference is callousness.

The doctor is not simply a dispenser of drugs, a computer that speaks. In treating a patient he is morally involved. What transpires between doctor and patient is more than a commercial transaction, more than a professional relationship between a specimen of the human species and a member of the A.M.A.; it is a profoundly human association, involving concern, trust, responsibility. The doctor is commander-in-chief in the battle for survival.

Disease has been defined by Spencer as a state which prevents an organism from relating itself to the condition of its environment. A doctor who lacks the ability to relate himself to a patient must be regarded as being in a condition of disease.

The doctor enters a covenant with the patient, he penetrates his life, affecting his mode of living, often deciding his fate. The doctor's role is one of royal authority, while the patient's mood is one of anxiety and helplessness. The patient is literally a sufferer, while the doctor is the incarnation of his hope.

The patient must not be defined as a client who contracts a physician for service; he is a human being entrusted to the care of a physician.

The physician is the trustee holding the patient's health in trust. In return, the patient's earnest is reliance, commitment. In other relationships trust may be replaceable by shrewdness or caution, in the doctor-patient relationship trust is the essence; distrust may spell disaster.

The work of a teacher is judged by a host of students. The books of a scholar are critically examined by reviews published in magazines. Yet the work of the practicing physician is seldom subject to public evaluation. The patient's reliance upon his doctor is often due to blind faith.

In our democratic society, where every individual insists upon being independent and authoritarianism is abhorrent, the doctor is the only person whose authority is accepted and even cherished and on whose judgment we depend. His position is formidable. He gives orders and demands strict obedience. The doctor is not alone in his effort to conquer disease. The patient is a partner not a bystander.

Disease is an assault, and healing is war. The doctor as an autocrat would be like a general without an army. The patient is both battlefield and soldier.

Chemistry supplies the weapons, but who will decide whether the enemy is defeated by strategy or valor?

The patient is a person. A person is not a combination of body and soul but rather body and soul as one.

Health is profoundly related to one's way of thinking, to one's sense of values. Physical well-being, the chemistry of the body, are not independent of the condition of the inner man. Sickness, like sin, indicates frailty, deficiency, scantiness in the make-up of man. The survival of the patient does not depend upon the pharmacist alone.

The doctor must find out the pressure of the blood and the composition of the urine, but the process of recovery also depends on the pressure of the soul and the composition of the mind.

Diet and physical exercise are important, but so are the capacity to praise, the power to revere, self-discipline and the taste of self-transcendence. All are qualities of being human.

Sickness, while primarily a problem of pathology, is a crisis of the total person, not only a physical disorder. There is a spiritual dimension to sickness. At a moment in which one's very living is called into question, the secretions of character, commitments of the heart, the modes of answering the ultimate question of what it means to be alive, are of supreme importance.

How to be sick gracefully? The process of healing is war, and the first casualty when war comes is moral pretentiousness. Peevishness, resentfulness, suspicion are not restrained by constipation. How to grow spiritually in distress?

Sickness ought to make us humble. In a world where recklessness and presumption are the style of living, and callousness dominates relationships between man and man, sickness is a reminder of our own need and extremity, an opportunity for the cynic to come upon the greatness of compassion.

Life is a mystery, the reflection of God's presence in His self-imposed absence. Jacob on his sickbed bowed his head (Genesis 47:31) in acknowledging the invisible presentness of the Lord. God's presence is at the patient's bed. His chief commandment is "Choose life" (Deuteronomy 30:19). The doctor is God's partner in the struggle between life and death. Religion is medicine in the form of prayer; medicine is prayer in the form of a deed. From the perspective of the love of God, the work of medicine and the work of religion are one. The body is a sanctuary, the doctor is a priest.

Medicine is a sacred art. Its work is holy. Yet the holy disappears when reverence is disused. Reverence for the doctor is a prerequisite for the sanity of all men. Yet we only revere a human being who knows to revere other human beings.

It is a grievous mistake to keep a wall of separation between medicine and religion. There is a division of labor but a unity of spirit. The act of healing is the highest form of *imitatio Dei*. To minister to the sick is to minister to God. Religion is not the assistant of medicine but the secret of one's passion for medicine.

No honor is adequate and no reward is too high for those who have chosen to live in the areas of distress, at the sickbeds, in the clinics. However, not all rewards are benign. Some are like narcotics, poisonous, habit-forming.

Acquisitiveness is an insidious disease. Among its effects are hardening of the arteries of love and understanding, perversion of one's sense of values. It poisons every vocation in our society, including those in which sensitivity to suffering humanity or dedication to the exercise of law and justice should be paramount.

The mortal danger faced by all of us is that of succumbing to the common virus of commercialism, the temptation to make a lot of money.

The motivation to dedicate one's life to the great calling of medicine has its source in the depth of the person. Yet a great calling, whether teaching, healing, or writing, is a jealous mistress; she requires complete devotion, supreme appreciation. Medicine, teaching and the ministry are not sinecures; nor are patients, students and parishioners shares to be traded at the stock exchange.

May I suggest a therapy for the virus of commercialism: a personal decision to establish a maximum level of income.

Luxuries are expensive, but making money is even more expensive. We pay for it dearly. Making money may cost us values that no money can buy.

The flesh is weak; temptations are strong. But the sign of intelligence is the capacity to delay the satisfaction of desire and above all to exercise preference, to make an option, when the integrity of one's vocation is in danger of being corrupted.

The doctor must realize the supreme nobility of his vocation, and cultivate a taste for the pleasures of the soul. There is no more thrilling adventure than to alleviate pain, no greater pleasure than to restore health. Perhaps no more beautiful life has ever been conceived than a life devoted to healing the sick.

Striving for personal success is a legitimate and wholesome ingredient of the person. The danger begins when personal success becomes a way of thinking, the supreme standard of all values. Success as the object of supreme and exclusive concern is both pernicious and demonic. Such passion knows no limit. According to my own medical theory, more people die of success than of cancer.

The goal is to protect or to restore the patient's health. But is it not a Sisyphus act if we cure him physically and destroy him economically? Is it a triumph when the appendix is removed and bitterness is imbued?

It is no secret that the image of the doctor in the mind of the public and in the profession itself is deteriorating. The compromise of our humanity is causing this to happen. The distortion of the image of the doctor is bound to affect the state of medicine itself. What should motivate a serious and dedicated student to commit himself to the study and practice of medicine?

Should the medical profession forfeit its nobility of purpose, the doctor becoming a status-seeker, it will lose its attraction, and only inspire gifted students to prepare themselves for better paid positions in business and industry. Is not the deplorable scarcity of nurses, and the poor quality of service in many hospitals, a foretaste of what may be expected?

Is dehumanization the price we must pay for technical progress? If medicine is not to lose its calling, it must be concerned with its own health. I invite you to understand your predicament a little better.

Let us think of the helpless and the poor languishing in the wards, in the clinics and dispensaries, or the private hospitals which refuse to admit a human being in agony unless cash is offered in advance.

The nightmare of medical bills, the high arrogance and callousness of the technicians, splitting fees, vested interests in promoting pharmaceutical products, suspicion that the physician is suggesting more surgery than absolutely necessary—all converge to malign the medical profession. Man is often sick, and medicine is indispensable for survival. But medicine today is believed to be afflicted with a *Sisyphus complex* and is itself in need of therapy.

Socialized medicine may be a dangerous thing. But what shall we think of socialized sickness, of socialized despair of the aged?

It is both sterile and dangerous to be involved in defensive and obsolete thinking. We must be open to the situation and seek to make available to all men the blessings that the genius of medicine has discovered.

It is not enough to battle socialism. What is needed is fresh creative thinking, openness to the situation.

We must not be enslaved to conceptual clichés, not remain in the rut of outworn ideas, not do what other people do, simply justifying our present economic practice.

The marvelous achievements of medicine must not make us blind to the problems that continue to arise as a result of the socio-economic revolution. It is terribly embarrassing to know that some individual doctors seem to think that it is highly improper for a patient to get sick during the weekends. (Night calls are as fashionable as horse and buggy.) The patient is haunted with fear, but some doctors are in a hurry, and above all impatient. They have something in common with God; they cannot be easily reached, not even at the golf-course.

A subject that requires most careful, dispassionate study is medical care for the aged. The expense of modern methods of therapy is high and often beyond the financial means of many citizens. The economics of medicine is a field about which I have no competence to speak. Yet it is certainly the obligation of the medical profession to see to it that every patient receives the care he needs. The task of the physician is to treat the whole man, the total individual. And is not the economic situation a part of the condition of the man? Can it be ignored in facing the patient as a person?

Doctors occupy a privileged position in society. It is their duty to rise above the standards of society and to herald a new ethical vision. The word "doctor" means teacher. We are in the midst of many revolutions. Above all, man's sense of the meaning of his being must change. This problem must become the doctor's concern. He has a stake in the battle against the decay of conscience.

Many of us, doctors and patients alike, are expecting the A.M.A. to serve as a major moral force in the life of our society. Whatever affects the health of man—care for the aged, the prevention of illness, the use of nuclear weapons—is within the scope of the A.M.A.

Physical vigor alone does not constitute total health. Nor is longevity the only purpose of living. Quality of living is as important as quantity of living. The achievement of personhood, being human, is as important for health as all medical invention put together.

For the doctor to carry out his part, he must be concerned with his own personhood. In addition to his efforts in enhancing his scientific knowledge and skill, his daily concern must be with enhancing his own qualities of living.

You might say that this is a task to be left to religion. Let the minister do it. No, I would not let him do it alone. Maintaining and conserving total health involves quality, and it is the doctor's duty to do it.

I feel humble in your presence. The least of you has to his credit the merit of soothing pain, or preventing grief and tears. All I can do is to labor in the mineworks where God and man are intermingled and to use the power of ideas to raise the mind, to unfreeze the heart. What I say in words, you proclaim in deeds.

To save human life is to do the work of God. There is nothing greater. The glory of God is reflected in the majesty of medicine. It is for this reason that we must strive for this majesty to remain immaculate, without fault, without blemish.

Moral sensitivity is neither inherent as grist in our bones, nor does it float in the air as an idea; it is radiant energy, waves of a divine light. Our moral substance depends upon the process of emission and absorption, upon the witnessing or receiving, upon the outpouring of the goodness done by human beings.

Eclipse of sensitivity is the mark of our age. Callousness expands at the rate of nuclear energy, while moral sensitivity subsides.

The calling and conduct of the doctor is care for others, and the meeting of doctor and patient is an occasion for being human. The doctor is a major source of moral energy affecting the spiritual texture and substance of the entire society.

Character is shaped by experiences of quality, particularly by what we come upon in times of anxiety. A patient is a person in crisis and anxiety. Few experiences have such a decisive impact upon our ability to understand the meaning of being human as the way in which the doctor relates himself to us at such times.

The doctor is not only a healer of disease; he is also a source of emanation about the spirit of concern and compassion. The doctor may be a saint without knowing it, and without pretending to be one.[16]

110. The Doctor in the Patient

HAROLD SHULWEIS

The physician is omnipotent, certain, well. The patient is passive, broken, and ill. These are the myths we carry into our encounters with illness. However, the Sages teach that everyone has something to teach another person:

> *Ben Azzai used to say: Do not despise any person*
> *and do not consider anything impossible; for there*
> *is no one who does not have his hour and there is*
> *nothing that does not have its place.*
> *(M. Avot 4:2).*

When patient and physician see each other in light of this wisdom, they are able to help each other. Rabbi Shulweis wrote this essay for the magazine Reconstructionist.

Mama encapsulated an entire world of Jewish values into two Yiddish words. If a glass were broken or money lost, or property robbed, Mama would respond, "*Abi gezint,*" as long as you have your health. And if I sneezed, which was frequent owing to my allergic reaction to cats, dust and pollen, Mama would rush in and with her hands pull both of my ears upwards while crying out, "*Gezuntheit.*" Years later when I observed the misshapen ears of *Star Trek*'s clever Mr. Spock, I concluded (a) that Spock must have suffered from allergy, and (b) that he must have been repeatedly blessed by a Jewish mother.

The primacy of health which entered the ethos of the family is rooted in the passionate Jewish affirmation of life. No matter the wretchedness of the human condition, life remains holy. And so the folk tale of Reb Moshe, a poor man gathering sticks of wood in the forest, placing them in a torn sack, throwing it over his bony shoulders and then stumbling. The sticks scatter to the earth and Reb Moshe cries out, "Ribbono Shel Olam—Master of the Universe—send the Angel of Death and take me from this earth." As if in response to his prayer, the Angel of Death appears out of nowhere. "You called for me Reb Moshe?" "Yes, yes," Reb Moshe stammers. "Would you help me gather these sticks?"

However frustrating our lot, health and life are sacred. "For a one-day-old child who is ill, the Sabbath may be violated. For a King David deceased it may not be desecrated" (B.T. *Shabbat* 151b). *"Hamira sakkanta meissura"* —violating one's health is a greater transgression than violating ritual. If health is sacred, the physician is endowed with a special measure of sanctity.

In medieval times, the physician was called to the Torah by no less a title than *moreinu*—our teacher. Jewish codes declared that a physician could pray his prayers before statutory time so as to be free to visit his patients. The doctor could shorten the days of his own mourning to attend to his patients, even if other doctors were available, since patients respond best to their own doctors.

The doctor and the patient are bound by a mystique. Between them there is more than an exchange of goods and services. Between them is health and sickness, life and death. Healing depends upon their intimate relationship. The patient enters the doctor's office prepared to reveal the most personal secrets of his body and soul. He stands naked before the physician exposing his private scars, blemishes, fears and anxieties. The doctor in turn has chosen to enter the gray world of complaints, screams and moans. It is no minor decision to assume the burdens of diagnosis and prognosis, to prescribe potent medicines and intrusive modalities. A medical misjudgment is not a grammatical mistake. It may prove to be an incorrigible and even fatal decision.

The rabbis knew how filled with anxiety the doctor's decisions must be. In a section of the codes (*Yoreh Deah* 336) they urged the physician not to despair. Let him not think, "Who needs the anguish of this practice? What if I err and cause the death of a patient?" They warned against the thinking which would lead the physician to argue, "God afflicts man with illness, shall I then interfere with His will and offer cures?" The rabbis interpreted Exodus 21:19, "He shall surely cause him to be healed," to counter the theology of human nonintervention. He who relieves suffering imitates the ways of the Faithful Physician. He who restrains his hand from healing the sick out of mistaken piety is deemed as one who sheds the blood of God's creation.

Ideally the doctor-patient relationship is a covenant of comradeship which shadows the covenant between God and the physician. But in fact, what has the patient in common with the physician? They each come from different stations and are endowed with different status. The doctor is healthy. He enters the hospital room dressed in a white, starched uniform, armed with charts and X-rays,

EEG's. He understands the undulating curves, the monitoring apparatus, the bizarre soundings of the mysterious beepings.

Etymology points to the difference. "Doctor" —teacher; patient—*patoir*—suffering. The patient is sick, frightened and ignorant, hanging on to every inflection, to every intonation of the doctor's voice. They place bracelets with the patient's name upon his wrist as with a newborn baby. He is infantilized, protected by iron rails attached to a mechanized bed. He lies obedient to every order issued by any uniformed authority.

The patient may revert to infancy and not simply because the system forces his regression. He is tempted, despite his occasional demurrers, to surrender his autonomy. He endows his physician with miraculous powers. He would transform the stethoscope into a magic wand and the illegible prescription into an *elixir vitae*. The doctor is apotheosized, made into a savior, redeemer, god.

With that surrender of self, the healing relationship is jeopardized. For therapy is a synergistic action, a cooperative venture between the healer and he who seeks to be healed. For the sake of therapy, the physician must guard against the seduction by the patient. He must resist the heady intoxication of the sick man's flattery. The patient would have him omnipotent, omniscient, ubiquitous. Every patient wishes to believe that his physician is the brightest and the best. Should he buy into the patient's adoration, the physician will be weighed down with unconscionable burdens. Should he prove fallible, or come late, or himself grow sick, it will be taken as betrayal and unforgivable failure. Shall the perfect healer stumble, falter, fall ill? Lionized yesterday, the physician will be demonized tomorrow.

Flattered by the omnipotent wish of the infantilized patient, the doctor may well grow aloof. His "coldness" stems less from conceit than from fear. Cast by the patient in the armor of infallibility, he turns impassible. Who can live up to the mystique of invulnerability without distancing himself from the idolatrous patient?

The doctor may enjoy the myth of his omnipotence, and the patient may find perverse comfort in his self-induced paralysis. The latter feels himself bathed in moral anesthesia. "I am helpless. I can do nothing. You, doctor, cure, heal, operate, excise, exorcise." The physician has lost the indispensable ally in the battle against disease. The patient has lost the curative powers breathed into his nostrils by the source of life. Will, hope, trust, and the vitality of his recuperative energy are abandoned. The healing is endangered, the relationship is injured.

Who knows where psyche ends and soma begins? Who knows how the spirit addresses the body? Jewish tradition is especially aware of the healing power of self-respect and the attitude of affirmation. When Hezekiah, the King, fell ill, God spoke to the prophet Isaiah: "Son of Amoz, go and tell the King, 'Set your affairs in order, for you are going to die. You will not live.'" Then Hezekiah, hearing Isaiah's message, rose and turned to the prophet. "The way of the world is for a person who is visiting the sick to say, 'May heaven have mercy upon you.' And the physician continues to tell him to eat this, to drink this and not that. Even when the physician realizes that his patient approaches death, he does not say: 'Arrange your affairs,' lest the patient's mind grow faint." This tradition of courage comes to us from King David. "Even if a sharp sword is placed against the throat of a man, let him not despair. As Job declared, 'Though He slay me, yet will I trust'" (*Ecclesiastes Rabbah; B.T. Berakhot*). In *articulo mortis,* in the teeth of death, the patient must not surrender to pitiless doom. Hope is no vain gesture. "Hope must never die too far ahead of the patient."

What have they in common, the doctor and the patient? Most important, the healing and liberating knowledge that in every doctor there is a patient and in every patient there is a doctor. The two comrades who struggle in common against pain and disease must release each other from the myths which tear the healing relationship apart. The patient must respect the doctor's competence and loyalty while acknowledging his fallibility and vulnerability. The physician must respect the patient's suffering while reminding him of his strength and curative powers. Healing is a dialogue of trust between the two. The doctor and the patient have this in common: They are persons. Persons in covenant, aware of the wonder of each other's humanity, may heal.[17]

The Sacredness of Health

My body's like a tree trunk in the woods—
It stretches to the sky with all its branches.
Rachel Korn, "My Body"

Introduction

*J*ewish society and literature have always valued and promoted healthfulness. As a result, asceticism, prolonged fasts, isolation, and self-denial have not been primary modes of Jewish spiritual expression.

In every era, Judaism has understood physical well-being to be closely bound with spiritual wholeness, each dependent upon and affecting the other. We will see in the selections of this chapter that in each era writers conceive that interdependence in different ways. They don't reject the formulations of prior periods but rather re-express them in different idioms and with different notions of the nature of physical and spiritual health.

Maimonides captured in words the classic Jewish attitude. Healthiness, he argued, had supreme spiritual importance because it freed the soul to pursue its highest purpose, the contemplation of God. In what has remained the most extensive statement in Jewish theology on the subject, Maimonides wrote that good health was never considered to be an end in itself, but, rather, was a necessary means to living according to God's commandments. Three centuries later, Joseph Caro incorporated Maimonides' philosophical overview, with little change, into the Shulḥan Arukh. Thereby healthiness is sacred and healthy living is a religious obligation in Jewish law.

111.   Laws of Purity

In the Torah, good health and long life seem to have been rewards for the Patriarchs and others favored by God. Many of the commandments, notably those dealing with sexuality, sanitation, quarantine, and the preparation of food, are said by some scholars to have an underlying purpose of promoting public health, but the intent of these rules was not explicit in the text and has long been a matter of debate. Conversely, illness is clearly depicted as a punishment from God, brought about by rebellion and sinfulness. Also, bodily deformities were a disqualification for the priesthood.

Four physical conditions are invariably marks of ritual "uncleanliness." These are vaginal bleeding, discharge after childbirth, penile discharge, and tsara'at, a set of skin blemishes as characterized in Leviticus. In all four, the person affected was not permitted to enter the Temple until the condition had ceased and only then after a ritual of purification. There was a special stigma attached to having tsara'at, for reasons unspecified in the Bible. In this case, the affected person was labeled "unclean" by a priest of the Temple and forced to live outside the community until the skin condition had disappeared. Then the priest conducted a rite of cleansing and reinstatement. It is of interest that the Hebrew priest in the Levitical rules was not given the power to heal or cure the illness.

These particular rituals in Leviticus are strange to us moderns, but rituals still exist in other guises. A medical anthropologist has written the following about hospital rituals:

> *When we arrived at the little hospital, the surgeon—a plump, middle-aged Irishman with no pretensions to the status of his teacher—guided me gently through the procedures of sterile technique. The hand washing was so methodical and repetitive, so exceedingly thorough,*

that it was like a ritual confirmation of the germ the-
ory, a self reteaching of that theory, every day. The
gowning and gloving were equally ritualistic but more
dramatic, since they involved nurses attending the
surgeon—and me, his new assistant—like priestesses
who, although subordinated, were responsible for the
purity of the ritual and who would pounce mercilessly
on a technical blemish. I had to put my hands and arms
into the gown without letting my fingers contact any
part of the front of it. Then I had to plunge my hands,
one at a time, into the tight rubber gloves without miss-
ing a finger or touching anything or ending up with the
fingers too loose. I did my best, as careful as if walking
on eggs, and I did not contaminate anything, but the
two nurses' pairs of eyes scrutinized me with an unre-
lenting critical gaze.[1]

Childbirth

The LORD spoke to Moses, saying: Speak to the Israelite people thus: When a woman at childbirth bears a male, she shall be unclean seven days; she shall be unclean as at the time of her menstrual infirmity.—On the eighth day the flesh of his foreskin shall be circumcised.—She shall remain in a state of blood purification for thirty-three days: she shall not touch any consecrated thing, nor enter the sanctuary until her period of purification is completed. If she bears a female, she shall be unclean two weeks as during her menstruation, and she shall remain in a state of blood purification for sixty-six days.

On the completion of her period of purification, for either son or daughter, she shall bring to the priest, at the entrance of the Tent of Meeting, a lamb in its first year for a burnt offering, and a pigeon or turtledove for a sin offering. He shall offer it before the LORD and make expiation on her behalf; she shall then be clean from her flow of blood. Such are the rituals concerning her who bears a child, male or female. If, however, her means do not suffice for a sheep, she shall take two turtledoves or two pigeons, one for a burnt offering and the other for a sin offering. The priest shall make expiation on her behalf, and she shall be clean.[2]

Tsaráat

The LORD spoke to Moses and Aaron, saying: When a person has on the skin of his body a swelling, a rash, or a discoloration, and it develops into a scaly affection on the skin of his body, it shall be reported to Aaron the priest or to one of his sons, the priests. The priest shall examine the affection on the skin of his body: if hair in the affected patch has turned white and the affection appears to be deeper than the skin of his body, it is a leprous affection; when the priest sees it, he shall pronounce him unclean.

As for the person with a leprous affection, his clothes shall be rent, his head shall be left bare, and he shall cover over his upper lip; and he shall call out, "Unclean! Unclean!" He shall be unclean as long as the disease is on him. Being unclean, he shall dwell apart; his dwelling shall be outside the camp.

The LORD spoke to Moses, saying: This shall be the ritual for a leper at the time that he is to be cleansed. When it has been reported to the priest, the priest shall go outside the camp. If the priest sees that the leper has been healed of his scaly affection, the priest shall order two live clean birds, cedar wood, crimson stuff, and hyssop to be brought for him who is to be cleansed. The priest shall order one of the birds slaughtered over fresh water in an earthen vessel; and he shall take the live bird, along with the cedar wood, the crimson stuff, and the hyssop, and dip them together with the live bird in the blood of the bird that was slaughtered over the fresh water. He shall then sprinkle it seven times on him who is to be cleansed of the eruption and cleanse him; and he shall set the live bird free in the open country. The one to be cleansed shall wash his clothes, shave off all his hair, and bathe in water; then he shall be clean. After that he may enter the camp, but he must remain outside his tent seven days. On the seventh day he shall shave off all his hair—of head, beard, and eyebrows. When he has shaved off all his hair, he shall wash his clothes and bathe his body in water; then he shall be clean. On the eighth day he shall take two male lambs without blemish, one ewe lamb in its first year without blemish, three-tenths of a measure of choice flour with oil mixed in for a meal offering, and one *log* of oil. These shall be presented before the LORD, with the man to be cleansed, at the entrance of the Tent of Meeting, by the priest who performs the cleansing.[3]

Penile Discharge

The LORD spoke to Moses and Aaron, saying: Speak to the Israelite people and say to them:

When any man has a discharge issuing from his member, he is unclean. The uncleanness from his discharge shall mean the following—whether his member runs with the discharge or is stopped up so that there is no discharge, his uncleanness means this: Any bedding on which the one with the discharge lies shall be unclean, and every object on which he sits shall be unclean.

When one with a discharge becomes clean of his discharge, he shall count off seven days for his cleansing, wash his clothes, and bathe his body in fresh water; then he shall be clean. On the eighth day he shall take two turtledoves or two pigeons and come before the LORD at the entrance of the Tent of Meeting and give them to the priest. The priest shall offer them, the one as a sin offering and the other as a burnt offering. Thus the priest shall make expiation on his behalf, for his discharge, before the LORD.[4]

Menstruation

When a woman has a discharge, her discharge being blood from her body, she shall remain in her impurity seven days; whoever touches her shall be unclean until evening. Anything that she lies on during her impurity shall be unclean; and anything that she sits on shall be unclean. Anyone who touches her bedding shall wash his clothes, bathe in water, and remain unclean until evening; and anyone who touches any object on which she has sat shall wash his clothes, bathe in water, and remain unclean until evening. Be it the bedding or be it the object on which she has sat, on touching it he shall be unclean until evening. And if a man lies with her, her impurity is communicated to him; he shall be unclean seven days, and any bedding on which he lies shall become unclean.

When she becomes clean of her discharge, she shall count off seven days, and after that she shall be clean. On the eight day she shall take two turtledoves or two pigeons, and bring them to the priest at the entrance of the Tent of Meeting. The priest shall offer the one as a sin offering and the other as a burnt offering; and the priest shall make expiation on her behalf, for her unclean discharge, before the LORD.[5]

112. Wise Sayings

BIBLE

The Book of Proverbs shows a keen understanding of the interconnections of body, mind, and spirit. Clearly, intellect could serve as an avenue for spiritual development.

Scattered throughout Proverbs are numerous aphorisms that express a perspective on health and illness that is distinct from that of the rest of the Bible. These aphorisms are observational, empathetic, naturalistic, and non-judgmental. They are even more noteworthy for their recognition of what we term "holism": the interconnections of body, mind, and spirit.

Pleasant words are like a honeycomb,
Sweet to the palate and a cure for the body.[6]

The heart alone knows its bitterness,
And no outsider can share in its joy.[7]

What brightens the eyes gladdens the heart;
Good news puts fat on the bones.[8]

A man's spirit can sustain him through illness;
But low spirits—who can bear them?[9]

Hope deferred sickens the heart,
But desire realized is a tree of life.[10]

A joyful heart makes for good health;
Despondency dries up the bones.[11]

My son, do not forget my teaching,
But let your mind retain my commandments;
For they will bestow on you length of days,
Years of life and well-being.[12]

Fear the Lord and shun evil.
It will be a cure for your body,
A tonic for your bones.[13]

A calm disposition gives bodily health;
Passion is rot to the bones.[14]

A healing tongue is a tree of life,
But a devious one makes for a broken spirit.[15]

113. In Its Time

BIBLE

> *Ecclesiastes gives expression to wisdom and a sense of balance.*
> *It differs from the rest of the Bible in its assertion that health,*
> *healing, and illness are part of a plan not knowable to us.*

To everything there is a season
A time to be born and a time to die;
A time to planting and a time to
pluck up that which is planted;
A time to kill, and a time to heal;
A time to break down, and a time
to build up;
A time to weep, and a time to laugh;
A time to mourn, and a time to dance;
A time to cast away stones, and
a time to gather stones together;
A time to embrace, and a time to
refrain from embracing;
A time to seek, and a time to lose;
A time to keep, and a time to cast
away;
A time to rend, and a time to sew;
A time to keep silenced, and a time to speak;
A time to love, and a time to hate....[16]

114. The Image of God

TALMUD

This story from the Mishnah about the great second-century Sage Hillel demonstrates the importance of caring for one's body.

"The merciful man doeth good to his own soul" (Prov. XI, 17). This applies to Hillel the Elder who once, when he concluded his studies with his disciples, walked along with them. His disciples asked him: "Master, whither are you bound?" He answered them: "To perform a religious duty." "What," they asked, "is this religious duty?" He said to them: "To wash in the bath-house." Said they: "Is this a religious duty?" "Yes," he replied; "if the statues of kings, which are erected in theatres and circuses, are scoured and washed by the man who is appointed to look after them, and who thereby obtains his maintenance through them—nay more, he is exalted in the company of the great of the kingdom—how much more I, who have been created in the Image and Likeness; as it is written, 'For in the image of God made he man'" (Gen. IX, 6)?[17]

115. The Merit of Good Health

BEN SIRA

Second Temple–period Jewish scholar Ben Sira cited good health as a virtue that each individual has the power to achieve.

Better the poor in vigorous health
than the rich with bodily ills.
I had rather sturdy health than gold
and a blithe spirit than coral.
No riches surpass a healthy body;
no happiness matches that of a joyful heart!
Rather death than a wretched life,
unending sleep than constant illness.
Dainties set before one who cannot eat

are like food offerings placed before a tomb.
Of what use is an offering to an idol
that can neither eat nor smell?
So it is with the one being punished by the Lord
who groans at the good things his eyes behold!

Do not give in to grief
or afflict yourself with brooding;
Gladness of heart is the very life of a person,
and cheerfulness prolongs his days.
Distract yourself, renew your courage,
drive resentment far away from you;
For grief has brought death to many,
nor is there aught to be gained from resentment.
Envy and anger shorten one's life;
anxiety brings on premature age.
One who is bright and cheery at table
benefits from his food.

Are you seated at a banquet table?
Bring to it no greedy gullet!
Say not, "What a spread this is!"
Remember, gluttony is a bad thing.[18]

116. Temperance and Health

PHILO

> *The first-century theologian Philo argued that healthfulness is*
> *a gift of God to all humanity.*

For by these the highest authority within us, reason, advances to sound health and well-being, and brings to nought the formidable menace to the body engineered in many a scene of drunkenness and gluttony and lewdness and the other insatiable lusts, the parents of that grossness of flesh which is the enemy of the quickness of mind.[19]

But we must speak of a sore personal matter, the blessings bestowed on the body. He promises that those who take pains to cultivate virtue and set the holy laws before them to guide them in all they do or say in their private or in their public capacity will receive as well the gift of complete freedom from diseases, and if some infirmity should befall them it will come not to do them injury but to remind the mortal that he is mortal, to humble his over-weaning spirit and to improve his moral condition. Health will be followed by efficiency of the senses and the perfection and completeness of every part, so that without impediment they may render the services for which it was made.[20]

God bestows health in the simplest way, preceded by no illness in our bodies, by Himself only, but health that comes by way of escape from illness he bestows both through medical science and through the physician's skill, letting both knowledge and practitioner enjoy the credit of healing, though it is He Himself that heals alike by these means and without them. Now His mode of dealing is the same in the case of the soul. The good things, the food, and He himself bestows with his own hand, but by the agency of Angels and Words such as involve riddance from ills.[21]

117. Warding Off Spirits

TALMUD

> There is enough advice in the Talmud on diet, health practices, and remedies to fill a small book. The tractate *Gittin*, for example, contains a virtual manual of medical care for skin rashes, headaches, toothaches, cough, and many other ailments, and is as lengthy as many ancient, medical treatises. Incantations and amulets were intended to expel the evil eye and pervasive illness spirits.

Our Rabbis taught: A man must not drink water either on the nights of the fourth days [Wednesdays] or on the nights of a Sabbath, and if he does drink, his blood is on his own head, because of the danger. What is the danger? An evil spirit. Yet if he is thirsty what is his remedy? Let him recite the seven "voices" which David uttered over the water then drink, as it is said: *The voice of the*

Lord is upon the waters; the God of glory thundereth, even the Lord upon many waters. The voice of the Lord is powerful; the voice of the Lord is full of majesty. The voice of the Lord breaketh the cedars; yea, the Lord breaketh in pieces the cedars of the Lebanon . . . The voice of the Lord heweth out flames of fire. The voice of the Lord shaketh the wilderness; the Lord shaketh the wilderness of Kadesh. The voice of the Lord maketh the hinds to calve, and strippeth the forests bare; and in His temple all say: "Glory." But if [he does] not [say this], let him say thus: *"Lul shafan anigron anirdafin,* I dwell among the stars, I walk among lean and fat people." But if [he does] not [say this], if there is a man with him, he should rouse him and say to him, "So-and-so the son of So-and-so, I am thirsty for water," and then he can drink. But if not, he knocks the lid against the pitcher, and then he can drink. But if not, let him throw something into it and then drink.

Our Rabbis taught: A man should not drink water from rivers or pools at night, and if he drinks, his blood is on his own head, because of the danger. What is the danger? The danger of blindness. But if he is thirsty, what is his remedy? If a man is with him he should say to him, "So-and-so the son of So-and-so, I am thirsty for water," and then he can drink. But if not, let him say to himself, "O So-and-so, my mother told me, 'Beware of shabrire': Shabrire, berire, rire, ire re. I am thirsty for water in a white glass."[22]

118. *Morning Bread*

TALMUD

> *The Sage's intent was plain: to warn and protect people against what they understood to be the causes of disease.*

Our Rabbis taught: Thirteen things were said of the morning bread: It is an antidote against heat and cold, winds and demons; instills wisdom into the simple, causes one to triumph in a lawsuit, enables one to study and teach the Torah, to have his words heeded, and retain scholarship; he [who partakes thereof] does not perspire, lives with his wife and does not lust after other women; and it kills the worms in one's intestines. Some say, it also expels jealousy and induces love.[23]

119. The Sacredness of Health

MAIMONIDES

Maimonides elevated the study of hygiene and medicine to an "act of worship" in his commentary on the Mishnah.

Man needs to subordinate all his soul's powers to thought, in the way we set forth in the previous chapter, and to set his sight on a single goal; the perception of God (may He be glorified and magnified), I mean, knowledge of Him, in so far as that lies within man's power. He should direct all his actions, both when in motion and at rest, and all his conversation toward this goal so that none of his actions is in any way frivolous, I mean, an action not leading to this goal. For example, he should make his aim only the health of his body when he eats, drinks, sleeps, has sexual intercourse, is awake, and is in motion or at rest. The purpose of his body's health is that the soul find its instruments healthy and sound in order that it can be directed toward the sciences and toward acquiring the moral and rational virtues, so that he might arrive at that goal.

On the basis of this reasoning, he would not aim at pleasure alone, choosing the most pleasant food and drink, and similarly with the rest of his conduct. Rather, he would aim at what is most useful. If it happens to be pleasant, so be it; and if it happens to be repugnant, so be it. Or he would aim at what is most pleasant in accordance with medical theory. For example, if his desire for food subsides, it should be stimulated by agreeable, pleasant, good foods. Similarly, if the humor of black bile agitates him, he should make it cease by listening to songs and various kinds of melodies, by walking in gardens and fine buildings, by sitting before beautiful forms, and by things like this which delight the soul and make the disturbance of black bile disappear from it. In all this he should aim at making his body healthy, the goal of his body's health being that he attain knowledge. Similarly, if he bestirs himself and sets out to acquire money, his goal in accumulating it should be to spend it in connection with the virtues and to use it to sustain his body and to prolong his existence, so that he perceives and knows of God what is possible for him to know.

On the basis of this reasoning, the art of medicine is given a very large role with respect to the virtues, the knowledge of God, and attaining true happiness. To study it diligently is among the greatest acts of worship.[24]

120. Preserving Health

MAIMONIDES

Maimonides elaborated on the theme of the sacred nature of healthfulness in his code, the Mishneh Torah. *He captured in elegant and concise language the belief of the Sages that good health would enable one to live spiritually, which for him was a life of enlightenment. For Maimonides, who experienced severe illness himself, disease corrodes our capacity to achieve the highest level of spirituality, which in the words of Moses, is our capacity "to love God, to walk in His ways, and to keep His commandments, His laws, and His regulations." The details of hygiene that he included in the* Mishneh Torah *came from ancient Greek and contemporary Islamic medical texts.*

Perhaps a man will say: "Since desire, honor, and the like constitute a bad way and remove a man from the world, I shall completely separate myself from them and go to the other extreme." So he does not eat meat, nor drink wine, nor take a wife, nor live in a decent dwelling, nor wear decent clothing, but sack-cloth, coarse wool, and so on, like the priest of Edom. This, too is a bad way and it is forbidden to follow it.

Whoever follows this way is called a sinner. Indeed, He [God] says about the Nazirite: "He [the priest] shall make atonement for him because he sinned against the soul." The wise men said: "If the Nazirite who only abstained from wine needs atonement, how much more does one who abstains from every thing [need atonement]."

Those who fast continually are in this class; they do not follow the good way. The wise men prohibited a man from tormenting himself by fasting. Concerning all these things and others like them, Solomon commanded, saying: "Do not be overly righteous and do not be excessively wise; why should you destroy yourself?"

Man needs to direct every single one of his deeds solely toward attaining knowledge of the Name, blessed be He. His sitting down, his standing up, and his speech, everything shall be directed toward this goal. How so? When he conducts business or works to receive a wage, his heart shall not only be set upon taking in money, but he shall do these things in order to acquire what the body needs, such as food, drink, shelter, and a wife.

Likewise when he eats, drinks, and has sexual intercourse, his purpose shall not be to do these things only for pleasure, eating and drinking only what is sweet to the palate and having sexual intercourse only for pleasure. Rather his only purpose in eating and drinking shall be to keep his body and limbs healthy. Therefore he shall not eat everything that the palate desires, like a dog or an ass, but he shall eat things that are useful for him, whether bitter or sweet, and he shall not eat things bad for the body, even if they are sweet to the palate.

How so? Whoever has warm flesh shall not eat meat or honey, nor drink wine. As Solomon, for example said: "It is not good to eat much honey, etc." He shall drink chicory water, even though it is bitter. Since it is impossible for a man to live except by eating and drinking, he shall eat and drink only in accordance with the directive of medicine, in order that he become healthy and remain perfect. Likewise when he has sexual intercourse, he shall do so only to keep his body healthy and to have offspring. Therefore he shall not have sexual intercourse every time he has the desire, but whenever he knows that he needs to discharge sperm in accordance with the directive of medicine, or to have offspring.

If one conducts himself in accordance with the [art of] medicine and sets his heart only upon making his body limbs perfect and strong, and upon having sons who will do his work and labor for his needs, this is not a good way. Rather, he shall set his heart upon making his body perfect and strong so that his soul will be upright to know the Lord. For it is impossible for him to understand and reflect upon wisdom when he is sick or when one of his limbs is in pain. He shall set his heart upon having a son who perhaps will be a wise and great man in Israel. Whoever follows this way all his days serves the Lord continuously, even when he engages in business and even when he has sexual intercourse, because his thought in everything is to fulfill his needs so that his body will be perfect to serve the Lord.

Even when he sleeps, if he sleeps with the intention of resting his mind and his body so that he does not become sick—for he is unable to serve the Lord when he is sick—his sleep shall become a service of the Lord, blessed be He.

Concerning this subject, the wise men commanded, saying: "Let all your deeds be for the sake of Heaven." That is what Solomon said in his wisdom: "In all your ways know Him, and He will make your paths straight."

[1] Since preserving the body's health and strength is among the ways of the Lord—for to attain understanding and knowledge is impossible when one is sick—a man needs to keep away from things that destroy the body and to accustom himself to things that make him healthy and vigorous. They are as follows. A man should eat only when he is hungry and drink only when he is thirsty. Whenever he needs to urinate or defecate, he should do so at once; he should not delay for even a single moment.

[2] A man should not eat until his stomach is full, but about one-fourth less than would make him sated. He should not drink water with the food, except a little mixed with wine. When the food begins to be digested in his intestines, he should drink what he needs to drink. He should not drink an excessive amount of water even when the food is being digested. He should not eat until he has examined himself very well, lest he needs to ease himself.

A man should not eat unless he first takes a walk so that his body becomes heated, or he should work or exert himself in some other way. The general rule is that he should afflict his body and exert himself every day in the morning until his body starts to become hot. Then he should rest a little until his soul is tranquil, and then eat. If he washes with warm water after his exertion, that is good. Afterward, he should wait a little and then eat.

[3] While he is eating, a man should always sit at his place or incline to the left, and should neither walk nor ride. He should not exert himself nor shake his body nor take a long walk until all the food in his intestines is digested. Anyone who takes long walks or exerts himself immediately after eating brings bad and severe illnesses upon himself.

[4] Day and night have altogether twenty-four hours. It suffices for a man to sleep one-third of them, i.e., eight hours, at the end of the night, so that there be eight hours from the beginning of his sleep until the sun rises. He should stand up from his bed before the sun rises.

[5] A man should not sleep upon his face, nor upon his back, but upon his side; at the beginning of the night, on the left side, and at the end of the night, on the right side. He should not go to sleep shortly after eating. He should not sleep during the day.[25]

121. The Regimen of Health: Body, Emotions, and Spirit

MAIMONIDES

Maimonides' Regimen of Health is a letter that he wrote to a personal acquaintance, an Arab prince who had requested his advice about physical and emotional problems. In this selection, Maimonides argues that religious study, and more broadly, the study of philosophy benefits health. He advocates the study of the Law and disciplined living according to its instructions. Note that he expresses the belief that it was not the role of the physician to teach religion, but only to treat physical ailments and to alleviate emotional distress. By implication, a spiritual counselor should complement the efforts of the physician.

It is known to our Master, may God prolong his days, that passions of the psyche produce changes in the body, that are great, evident and manifest to all. As evidence thereof, you can see a man of robust build, ringing voice, and glowing face, when there reaches him, unexpectedly, news that afflicts him greatly. You will observe, that all of a sudden his color dims, the brightness of his face departs, he loses stature, his voice becomes hoarse, and even if he strives to raise his voice he cannot, his strength diminishes and often he trembles from the magnitude of the weakness, his pulse diminishes, his eyes sink, his eyelids become too heavy to move, the surface of his body cools, and his appetite subsides. The cause of all these signs is the recall of the natural heat and the blood into the interior of the body.

The state of the timorous and anxious, and the confident and sanguine, is known; so also, the state of the vanquished and the victorious is clear. The vanquished is so disheartened that he may not notice things because of the lessening of the visual spirit and its dispersal, whereas the light of the vision of the victorious is so greatly augmented that it seems as though the light of the day has increased and grown. This subject is so clear that it is unnecessary to dilate on it.

On this account, the physicians have directed that concern and care should always be given to the movements of the psyche; these should be kept in balance in the state of health as well as in disease, and no other regimen should be given precedence in any wise. The physician should make every effort that all the sick, and all the healthy, should be most cheerful of soul at all times, and that they should be relieved of the passions of the psyche that cause anxiety. Thereby the health of the healthy will persist. This is also foremost in curing the sick, and especially those whose disease is psychic, like those who harbor hypochondria and morbid melancholy, because solicitude for the emotions in these is obligatory. It is the same for someone who is overcome by grief and obsessions, or by terror of whatever is unnatural to fear, or by the diminution of satisfaction in what is natural for him to enjoy. In all of these, the skillful physician should place nothing ahead of rectifying the state of the psyche by removing these passions. Nonetheless, the physician, inasmuch as he is a physician, should not insist upon his own art as the rationale for the stratagem in removing these passions, for truly this virtue is to be attained from practical philosophy, and from the admonitions and disciplines of the Law.

Indeed, just as the philosophers have composed books in the various sciences, so have they composed many books about the rectification of morals and the discipline of the psyche so that it acquires a virtuous nature, until nothing comes from it but good actions. They inveigh against moral imperfections, and teach the way to remove them from the psyche of whoever finds any of these in himself, until all those tendencies that incline to evil actions depart. Likewise, the disciplines of the Law and the admonitions and laws received from the prophets, peace be with them, or from their followers, and the knowledge of their virtuous ways, will rectify the disposition of the psyche until it acquires a virtuous state, so that nothing comes from it but good actions. You find, therefore, that these passions make strong impressions only on persons who were not taught the philosophy of morals or the disciplines and admonitions of the Law, such as children, women, and the ignorant. These, because of the softness of their spirit, are irresolute and fearful, and you find that when some harm comes to them, and there falls upon them a calamity from the adversities of the world, their grief is great, and they cry out and weep, slap their cheeks, and beat their breasts, and often the affliction is so great upon them that some die, either suddenly or after a time, from the grief and the distress that possessed them. Likewise, when these people acquire something from the good of this world, their joy in it is magnified, and they suppose, for the want of discipline and psyche, that they have indeed acquired a very great good. Their conceit grows, their delight exaggerates what they have acquired. They become greatly affected by this, their laughter and senseless gaiety increase, so that some of them die in the vehemence of their exultation because of the dissolution of the spirit through the intensity of its sudden deflection to the outside, as Galen has mentioned. The cause of all this is softness of the spirit and ignorance of the truth of things.

But people nurtured in the philosophy of the morals, or in the disciplines and admonitions of the Law, acquire strength of mind, and they are the truly strong. Their psyche does not change and is affected as little as possible. The more a person is disciplined, the less is his agitation in both these states, namely, in the state of prosperity and in the state of adversity. So, when acquiring a great good from the good of this world, and this is what the philosophers call imaginary good, he is not affected by it, and this good is not magnified within him. Likewise, when there falls upon him a great evil from the evils of this world, and this is what the philosophers call imaginary evil, he is neither dismayed nor disheartened, but bears it in good spirit.

Indeed, this quality of spirit will develop in man through consideration of the truths of things and recognition of the nature of reality, because the best of the good of this world, even though it endures with a man all his life, is a very minor thing and a perishable thing, and what is there in this for man who must die like other animals? Likewise, when the greatest of the evils of this world is compared with death, from which there is no escape, all such evil is less than death, without doubt. One should therefore moderate his reaction to such evil, for indeed it is less than that from which there is no escape.

In truth the philosophers have called the good of this world, and its evil, imaginary good and imaginary evil, because how often something of its good is supposed to be good, yet in truth is evil, and how often one of its evils is supposed to be evil, yet is good in truth. How often has much wealth befallen a man and how often has he acquired vain possessions, and this has become the cause of the corruption of his body, the warping of his soul with vices of character, the shortening of his life, his alienation from the Most High God, and an estrangement between him and his Creator? Indeed, what is there in it for him but eternal misery? How often has a man been deprived of wealth, or property torn from him, yet this has become the cause of the improvement of his body, the adornment of his soul with virtues of character, and the prolongation of his life, drawing him near his Creator and turning his face toward His worship? Indeed, herein lies eternal happiness for him. What this servant has said about the lengthening or shortening of life is only said upon the opinion of the physicians, and the philosophers, and some masters of the Law that have preceded Islam.

On the whole, most of what the public supposes to be good fortune, is in truth misfortune, and most of what they suppose to be misfortune is in truth good fortune. It is not the intention of this treatise to expound the truth of this subject, or to explain it and to teach its way, for much has already been compiled about this in all times and in all learned nations that have studied the sciences. This servant has only meant by these references to suggest training the psyche to restrain the passions by studying books on morals, the disciplines of the Law and the admonitions and the laws spoken by the sages. Thus the psyche will be strengthened and will see the true as true and the false as false. The passions will diminish, the evil thoughts will depart, the depressions will lift, and the psyche will dilate in whatever situation a man might encounter.

Here, contemplation is very good; it will reduce evil thoughts, anxiety, and distress. Often they will cease altogether if a person holds the following consideration before his mind's eye. If one reflects on something and becomes distressed by the thought, and grief, sorrow, and sadness arise in him, this can come from one of two things. Either he thinks about something that has passed, like thinking about what has befallen him from the loss of wealth that was his or the death of someone for whom he grieves, or he thinks of things that might yet happen and fears their coming, like thinking and dwelling upon what might result from the coming of adversity. Yet it is known through rational observation, that thought regarding what has come and passed is of no value at all, and that sorrow and gloom about things that have come and passed are the occupation of fools. There is no difference between a man who is gloomy because of wealth that has perished, and its like, and one who grieves because he is a man and not an angel, or a star, or similar thoughts that are impossibilities.

As for obsession with thoughts about what might befall in the future that lead to anxiety, these ought also to be relinquished with the consideration that everything that one might anticipate lies in the realm of possibility; it might happen or it might not happen. And just as one might grieve and sorrow over what he anticipates might occur, so it behooves him to dilate his spirit and hope, and with this hope he might perhaps obtain the opposite of what he anticipates. Indeed, that which is anticipated and its opposite are both possible.[26]

122. The Importance of Medicine to Man

MAIMONIDES

Maimonides offered sage advice to an acquaintance with
asthma about choosing the right physician.

It should be clear that medicine is a science essential to man, at any time, anywhere; not only in times of illness but in health as well. It may truly be said that medicine (the medical man) should be a man's constant companion. To be sure, this holds good only in the case of a consummate physician with a complete mastery of theoretical and practical knowledge, so that a man may safely lodge himself in his hands, body and soul, to be guided by his directions. Such physicians are encountered in all countries and in all times. On the other hand, if only uncultured (imperfect) physicians are available, who unfortunately comprise the bulk of the profession, it is best not to rely upon them in the same that a man might make shift with bad food when no good food was available. Though he cannot do without food, he can certainly manage without placing his body and soul in the hands of one who has not the slightest notion of science.[27]

123. Rules Concerning Physical Well-Being

SHULḤAN ARUKH

The Shulḥan Arukh codified permanently into Jewish law vir-
tually unchanged the advice of Maimonides about the impor-
tance of health, and it took his lead on the details of diet.

Since it is the will of the Almighty that man's body be kept healthy and strong, because it is impossible for a man to have any knowledge of his Creator, when ill, it is, therefore, his duty to shun anything which may waste his body, and to strive to acquire habits that will help him to become healthy. Thus it is written (Deuteronomy 4:15): "Take you, therefore, good heed of your souls."

The Creator, blessed be He, and blessed be His name, created man and gave him the natural warmth which is the essence of life, for, if the natural warmth of the body should be cooled off, life would cease. This warmth of the body is maintained by means of the food which the man consumes. Just as in the case of fire, if wood is not added to it, it will be extinguished, so it is with man, if he would stop eating, the heat within him would cool off, and he would die. The food is first ground between the teeth and becomes mixed with juice and saliva. From there it goes down into the stomach where it is likewise ground and mixed with juices, the juice of the stomach and the juice of the gall, and is reduced to dregs, and it is boiled by means of the heat and the juice, and thus becomes digested. The limbs are nourished by the pure parts of the food, and this sustains the life of the man, and the impure substance which is unnecessary, is pushed towards the outside. And concerning this process, we say in the benediction *Asher yatzar (who formest), the following: Umafli la'asot (and doest wonderfully),* which means that the Holy One, blessed be He, has endowed the man with the nature to select the good part of the food, and every limb selects for itself the nourishment that is suitable for it, and rejects the waste out of the body; for, if the waste should remain in the body, it would cause many diseases, God forbid. Therefore, the good health of the body depends upon the digestion of the food; if it is easily digested, the man is healthy and vigorous, but if the digestive system does not function properly, the man becomes weak, and this may cause a dangerous state of health, God forbid.[28]

124. Fatherly Advice

JUDAH IBN TIBBON

Medieval Jews often drew up "ethical wills" during their lifetimes to give moral instruction to their children. In his will, Judah ibn Tibbon is particularly concerned about what his son should eat.

Thou knowest what I suffered in bringing thee up. Thou hast seen what the learned R. Moses, son of R. Judah, did. He had four sons, and he dispersed them here and there, and went and left them, to marry again. But I, from out of my compassion towards thee, did not wish to bring thee into the hand of another woman. But I bore all the anxiety, and great it was, of rearing and caring for thee. Thou knowest this, and all men know it, for, but for my great devotion thou wouldst have died, or lived deformed. Remember these things, my son! And take it to thy heart to hear and perform my instructions. Very important is it that thou shouldst fulfil my commands regarding thy diet. Slay me not before my time! For thou knowest my distress, my soul's sorrow, my fear for thee in thy sickness. Better death to me than life, that I look not on my wretchedness. Yearly, as thou knowest, thou art visited with sickness (for my sins!), and the cause of thy complaints is unwholesome food. Ben Mishle says:

Dost thou desire thy health to hold,
O'er thy lust make long thy furrow;
Wage war against thyself as though
Opposed to archer or to spearman!

And now, O my son! By the God of heaven, by the obedience to me imposed by His law, by the gratitude due for my rearing and educating thee, I adjure thee to abstain, with all thy resolution, from noxious food! Experience has taught thee how much thou has suffered from carelessness in this regard. Be content with little and good, and beware of hurtful sweets. "Eat no eating that prevents thee from eatings." What is the use of all thy wisdom if "thou layest a snare for my life, to cause me to die?" Art thou not ashamed before thyself and the world when all know that thou art periodically sick because of thy injurious diet?[29]

125. Chicken Soup

FRED ROSNER

Chicken soup has been the Jewish tonic through the ages, as we learn from Dr. Fred Rosner.

A hen was once combined with leek and given to a man bitten by a snake. A special food described in the Talmud was the chicken of Rabbi Abba. The therapeutic efficacy of chicken, chicken soup and other fowl is extensively described in the medical writings of Moses Maimonides in his book *On the Causes of Symptoms.* He recommends the meat of hens or roosters (or chicken or pullets) and their broth because this type of fowl has the property of rectifying corrupted humors, especially the black humor (i.e., black bile, an excess of which was thought to cause melancholy), so much so that physicians mention that chicken broth is beneficial in leprosy. The type of chicken to be used is described by Maimonides as follows:

> One should not use the too large, that is of more than two years of age; nor the too small, that is those in whom the mucus still prevails; neither the too lean, nor those who through feeding become obese; but those that are fat by nature without being stuffed.

The chicken or pullet can be broiled or stewed or steamed or boiled with fresh coriander, or with some green fennel added to the soup. This dish is especially suitable in winter. The soup, however, where lemon juice or citron juice or lemon slices are added to the broth, is better suited for summertime. The method of breeding and feeding the chickens is also discussed in some detail.

Maimonides' conclusion is that "these procedures have been verified and their usefulness is clear." He does not state, however, whether or not he conducted a double-blind randomized study. In the chapter on diet in his *Medical Aphorisms,* Maimonides states that boiled chicken soup neutralizes body constitution. Chicken soup is both an excellent food, as well as a medication for the beginning of leprosy, and fattens the body substance of the emaciated and those convalescing from illness. Turtle doves increase memory, improve intellect and sharpen the senses. The consumption of fowl, continues Maimonides, is beneficial for feebleness, hemiplegia, facial paresis and the pain of edema. It also increases sexual potential. House pigeons that graze in the streets increase natural body heat. Soup made from the bird called *kanaber* loosens the cramps of colic. The quail helps the healthy, as well as those convalescing from illness; its flesh is fine, it dissolves a kidney stone and it stimulates urine flow. Maimonides further states that chicken testicles provide excellent nourishment. They are especially useful to nourish a weakened or convalescent individual. Testicles of all living creatures are warming and moistening in their action and aid the libido in a strongly perceptible manner. Pigeon eggs are good aphrodisiacs. Similarly, all eggs help the libido, especially if they are cooked with onion or turnip. Finally, baby chicks that are separated from their mother alleviate heat that occurs in the stomach. Soup made from an old chicken is of benefit against chronic fevers that develop from white bile and also aids the cough which is called asthma.

In his *Treatise on Asthma* Maimonides advises the consumption of chicken meat that is not fat for sufferers of asthma. Other small fowl, such as the turtle dove, are also useful. The soup of chickens or fat hens is said to be an effective remedy for asthma. The method of preparation of the chicken soup and the ingredients are also described. An enema with sap of linseed and fenugreek or both, with oil and chicken fat, with an admixture of beet juice, is strongly endorsed for the treatment of asthma.

In the recent medical literature, chicken soup has been reported to be efficacious for pneumonia, and inhibits the growth of pneumococci in vitro. Chicken fat is also said to cure male impotence and relieves frustration and anxiety. With the recent demonstration that chicken soup mobilizes nasal mucous better than other hot liquids, scientific respectability has now been obtained to prove what the proverbial Jewish mother has always known,—that chicken soup can help cure an upper respiratory infection.

As with all medical agents, however, the consumption of fowl is not without occasional side effects. Maimonides states that pigeon sucklings may produce migraine headaches, partridge and quail cause constipation and obstruct bowels, and geese and duck produce thick juices which are harmful to digestion. The physician is thus cautioned against the indiscriminate application of chicken and chicken soup for the therapy of all ailments, abiding by the *dictum primum non nocere*. However, the judicious use of chicken soup as an important element of the therapeutic approach to upper and lower respiratory tract infections seems to be fully justified.[30]

126. Visualization

TEHILLA LICHTENSTEIN

Visualization is a technique promoted by mind-body therapists to facilitate mental relaxation and to reduce anger and bitterness. Tehilla Lichtenstein, a founder of Jewish Science, an early twentieth-century movement that placed healing in a Jewish context, advocated visualization to maintain emotional health.

We have said that visualization of a goal brings into action, or initiates the action on the part of the body, on the part of man's physical, mental and spiritual forces, which will achieve that goal; this is true in the field of material attainment, and it is equally, and even more true, in the evoking of divine action within man for the good of man. Therefore, along with your affirmation for health or healing, practice *visualization* of health or healing; affirm, "The Divine Mind is filling my being—my heart, if that is the organ that is suffering ill-health—with perfect health and renewed strength;" then see a stream, a stream of health, flowing from a divine fount, within or outside of yourself, for God is both without and within yourself, see that stream pouring into your heart and filling it, every nook and cranny and fiber of it, with renewed health and strength; see that stream clearly, hold it devotedly, knowing that that image is your prayer for the evocation of God's healing power, just as the Psalmist evoked God's strength in his behalf when he declared God to be his fortress and his high tower. We do not know whether renewed health comes in a stream or a force or a current like that flowing through an electric wire, but seeing it as a stream is a visualization of God's healing powers, just as seeing a tower is a visualization of God's strength; that image of a stream of health, stirs into action the divine forces of health within you, just as the image of a Divine fortress evoked in the Psalmist a surge of strength, and just as the visualization of rays of serenity will evoke within you the blessed experience of calmness and peace.[31]

127. Emotional Wellness

MARCIA GLAUBMAN HAIN

Marcia Glaubman Hain wrote the following introduction to her book of poetry, Twice Chai, *which was inspired by Hebrew religious sayings.*

> As I became more and more involved with putting together this volume, I realized that we are all in recovery from something. Each of us is faced at one time or another with some sort of awesome burden. It is at such times that we must make a conscious decision to "choose life," instead of allowing ourselves to be overwhelmed by our particular situation. . . . I chose to use various selections and concepts inherent in Judaism as an inspiration. These ideas and prayers form the basis for new poems and thoughts, which then combined the beauty of our heritage with the experiences, I, and others around me, were living through.

"He Giveth Strength to the Weary" (Isaiah XL, 29)

There is a tiredness
that sleep can't reach,
an all-consuming weariness
that makes it
difficult to do the simplest things . . .
It comes of resignation
and despair,
and of trying times
and all the times we didn't try
enough . . .

It comes of drifting when
the current seems too rough,
when swimming's not an option
nor drowning either.
It comes from knowing and
not knowing
and yet half remembering the
spark of light and life
that made that state a challenge
long ago . . .

There is a tiredness
that sleep can't reach
and yet wakefulness is filled
with faded dreams
replaying endlessly
in sepia tones,
blurred and formless
and never quite in focus.
And then one day there is the first awakening
a gentle stirring
not unlike the first faint
signs of spring . . .

A whispered word, a quiet hope,
a sharper image
and a small resolve.
Day by day
and almost imperceptibly
it grows and blossoms,
an unseen energy,
a new awareness
as the numbness disappears.

And with the feeling comes
the pain,
but in perspective now,
it takes its place
as we take ours
The healing has begun . . .[32]

Addenda

Additional Reading

This sourcebook on illness and health in Jewish literature is the first collection with a wide scope. Consequently, there is no simple path through all the sources.

The article "Medicine" in the *Encyclopaedia Judaica,* 1972, is a good place to start, as it touches on a variety of subjects and ranges from biblical to modern times. Its assertion that many of the Bible's commandments are intended to promote health and hygiene represents a school of thought among medical historians earlier in this century, but that concept is disputed by contemporary scholars of the Bible and Talmud.

Medicine in ancient Jewish texts has been the subject of a number of books. The classic source is Julius Preuss's *Biblical and Talmudic Medicine,* translated and edited by Fred Rosner (Sanhedrin Press, 1978). It deals with ancient conceptions about the human body, diseases, and therapies. Unfortunately Preuss treats Bible and Talmud together, as if they were of one mind. Consequently it takes some probing to focus on one or the other. Fred Rosner's *Medicine in the Bible and the Talmud* (Ktav, 1977) is made up of a number of essays that explore the early antecedents of Jewish medical ethics. A related subject is a study of references to medicine by a first-century Jewish historian, which is titled *Medicine and Hygiene in the Works of Flavius Josephus* by Samuel S. Kottek (E. J. Brill, 1994). Some general textbooks on the history of medicine have a chapter on the Bible and Talmud. One such medical history text, adorned by classic art, is *Medicine: An Illustrated History* by Albert S. Lyons and R. Joseph Petrucelli (Abrams, 1978). For a discussion of ancient herbals, see *The Healing Past: Pharmaceuticals in the Biblical and Rabbinic World,* edited by Irene and Walter Jacob (E. J. Brill, 1993).

Maimonides has long been an icon to Jewish physicians. All ten of Maimonides' medical treatises have been translated into English. The *Treatise on Asthma,* edited by Simon Muntner (Lippincott, 1963) was the first of a recent series. The remainder have been completed by his protégé, Fred Rosner, and his colleague, Uriel S. Barzel, in the five-volume series *Maimonides' Medical Writings* (Maimonides Research Institute). Dr. Rosner has provided an overview of each of the ten treatises in the introductions to volumes one and five as well as an extensive, invaluable bibliography of periodical literature. The five treatises that were letters to Maimonides' correspondents, entitled the two "Regimens of

Health," "Asthma," "Poisons," and "Cohabitation," are easy to understand. The other five were intended for professional readers and demand knowledge of medicine as it was understood in the early Middle Ages. Fred Rosner's *Medicine in the Mishneh Torah of Maimonides* (Ktav, 1984) is indispensable to understand the references to health in Maimonides' great compendium of Jewish Law. *The Medical Legacy of Moses Maimonides* by Fred Rosner (Ktav, 1998) is a collection of Dr. Rosner's essays for medical journals, in which he presents still relevant, even prescient clinical comments by the Rambam, who is considered by historians to have been among the greatest of medieval physicians.

A subject of great pride for Jews, especially physicians, has been the prodigious involvement of Jews in the healing professions. Harry Friedenwald, an ophthalmologist at Johns Hopkins Medical School, devoted his life to research on the lives and careers of Jewish physicians in the Middle Ages. His collected writings, now a classic, is *The Jews and Medicine: Essays* (Ktav, 1967). It contains a large number of brief biographies and some historical essays. Other compilations of prominent Jewish physicians are Solomon Kagan's *Jewish Medicine* (Medico-Historical Press, 1952) and *Jewish Contributions to Medicine in America, 1656–1934* (Boston Medical Publishing Co., 1934); two books by Harry A. Savitz, *Profiles of Erudite Jewish Physicians and Scholars* (Spertus College of Judaica Press, 1973) and *A Jewish Physician's Harvest* (Ktav, 1979); and Michael Nevins's *The Jewish Doctor* (Jason Aronson, 1996), which is aimed at the general reader. *Three Jewish Physicians of the Renaissance: The Marriage of Science and Ethics* by Aaron J. Feingold (American Friends of Beth Hatefutsoth, 1994) presents several medieval treatises on medical ethics.

Our knowledge of medicine among Jews in the Middle Ages has been advanced in two recently published scholarly works. *Kabbalah, Magic, and Science: The Cultural Universe of a Sixteenth Century Physician* by David B. Ruderman (Harvard University Press, 1988) explores through the writings of its subject how a late medieval physician thinks about patients, diseases, and the world in general. Through painstaking analysis of institutional archives, Joseph Shatzmiller's *Jews, Medicine and Medieval Society* (University of California, 1994) documents the importance of Jewish physicians in medieval Jewish and Christian society.

Jewish medical ethics is a field that continues to develop. The subject has been summarized in a number of modern books, notably Immanuel

Jakobovits' *Jewish Medical Ethics* (Bloch, 1959), Abraham S. Abraham's *The Comprehensive Guide to Medical Halakah* (Feldheim, 1990), and J. David Bleich's *Judaism and Healing: Halakhic Perspectives* (Ktav, 1981). Compilations of essays on problematic contemporary ethical issues, such as end-of-life care, abortion, and the physician-patient relationship, include Fred Rosner's *Modern Medicine and Jewish Ethics* (Ktav, 1991), *Medicine and Jewish Law, Volumes I and II* (Jason Aronson, 1990 and 1993), and Levi Meier's *Jewish Values in Bioethics* (Human Sciences, 1986) and *Jewish Values in Health and Medicine* (Lanham). *Matters of Life and Death: A Jewish Approach to Modern Medical Ethics* by Elliot N. Dorff (Jewish Publication Society, 1998) presents a Conservative point of view on matters that are currently contentious among Jewish ethicists, particularly modern methods of treating fertility, genetic screening and engineering, abortion, homosexual unions, assisted suicide, and prolongation of life. David M. Feldman's *Health and Medicine in the Jewish Tradition* (Crossroad, 1986) gives an overview of Jewish medical ethics for the general, non-Jewish reader. Rabbinic responsa on health from the twelfth to nineteenth centuries is the subject of H. J. Zimmel's *Magicians, Theologians, and Doctors* (Goldston, 1952). *Halachah and Medicine Today,* edited by Dr. Mordechai Koenigsberg (Feldheim, 1997), contains translations of selected essays from *Halachah Refuah* (edited by Rabbi Moshe Hershler) and deals with topics of concern to an Orthodox Jewish physician and health care worker, topics that are encountered in everyday medical practice.

Jewish folklore in medieval times is treated in a chapter of Jewish *Magic and Superstition* by Joshua Trachtenberg (Behrman's, 1939) and in *The Folklore of the Jews* by Angelo Rapaport (Soncino, 1937). Folk medicine in modern Israel is the subject of a chapter in *Jews and Medicine: Religion, Culture, Science* (see below).

For further considerations of the rabbi's role in caring for the sick, see the books from which excerpts are taken in part five. Of particular interest are Joseph Ozarowski's *To Walk in God's Ways* (Jason Aronson, 1995), Avraham Greenbaum's *The Wings of the Sun* (Breslov Research Institute, 1995), and the Hasidic publication *How to Perform the Great Mitzvah of Bikkor Cholim* by Aaron Levine (Zichron, 1987).

Responses to Suffering in Classical Rabbinic Literature by David Kraemer (Oxford, 1995) is a scholarly exegesis of the various explanations given to the existence of suffering, focusing on rabbinic literature. Rabbi Harold S. Kushner's *When Bad Things Happen to Good People* (Avon, 1981), which is excerpted in this anthology, is a personal response to the theological dilemma of evil, in this instance the disease of his child. A traditional rabbinical view of the subject is found in *Judaism on Illness and Suffering* by Reuven P. Bulka (Jason Aronson, 1998).

Jews and Medicine: Religion, Culture, Science (Beth Hatefutsoth, 1995; Jewish Publication Society, 1997) is a compilation of essays on the involvement of Jews in the healing professions. It was published to accompany an exhibit on the subject at the Museum of the Diaspora in Tel Aviv and has been re-published for wider circulation by the Jewish Publication Society.

Jewish insights on the subject of emotional and spiritual healing are the subjects of *In Sickness and in Health: How to Cope When Your Loved One is Ill* (Beacon, 1980) by Earl Grollman, *Twice Chai: A Jewish Road to Recovery* by Marcia Glaubman Hain (Block, 1991), and *Healing of Soul, Healing of Body: Spiritual Leaders Unfold the Strength and Solace of the Psalms,* edited by Rabbi Simkha Y. Weintraub (Jewish Lights Publishing, 1994).

Many Jewish fiction writers have explored drama and metaphor in illness. The general subject of illness in literature has been of interest to scholars only in very recent times, and virtually nothing has been written about illness in Jewish literature. We have come across a number of fascinating stories, beside the two included here, Sholom Aleichem's *At the Doctor's,* and Sholem Asch's *East River. The Old Man* by I. B. Singer, *The Healer* by Aharon Appelfeld, *The Silver Crown* by Bernard Malamud, *To the Doctor* by S. Y. Agnon, and *Open Heart* by A. B. Yehoshua all explore with biting irony and skepticism the ambiguities of spiritual and physical healing, arrogant pretensions of professionals, and the ultimate powerlessness of all human endeavor to avoid death.

Several Internet websites deal with the linkage of Judaism and medical practice. Judaism and Medicine on the Web, a resource of the Albert Einstein Synagogue (http://shamash.org/einstein/medlinks.html) provides links to hospitals, Jewish health care organizations, research facilities, and medical-ethical essays. The website of the Institute for Jewish Medical Ethics, located in San Francisco (http://www.ijme.org), lists the mission of the Institute, its conferences, recordings of lectures from previous annual international conferences on Jewish medical ethics, and also bibliographies of books and articles that can be purchased via the Internet. The website of the National Institute of Judaism and Medicine in New York City (http://www.nijm.org) offers tapes of discussion of Jewish bioethics from its series of annual international conferences.

Historical Background

What can Judaism offer to a person who is ill, or to a person involved with someone going through an illness? Not surprisingly, over centuries of existence, Judaism has developed texts and practices that address the physical, emotional, intellectual, and spiritual issues raised by illness and healing. These texts give us the skills to cope, while simultaneously allowing us to give meaning to our suffering, to experience illness's unfairness, and to express our concomitant anger. Judaism can show us how to value medicine and other forms of healing as well as giving us a sound basis for ethical decision-making when we are in sorest need of level-headed advice. Understanding some key facts of Jewish history and the development of Jewish texts is necessary to best appreciate the works included herein.

Survey of Jewish History and Its Documents

Judaism began in the Patriarchal era, when Mesopotamia (modern Iraq) was the dominant power. Abraham, the founder of Judaism, came from Mesopotamia to the Land of Israel. From there, the Hebrews migrated to Egypt, became enslaved, were liberated, and returned to Israel. The Land of Israel was eventually settled and came to be ruled by one king: first Saul, then David, and finally Solomon. The First Temple was constructed under Solomon's rule, and the priesthood, descendants of Aaron, Moses' brother, officiated in that cult while other members of the tribe of Levi helped in the Temple service and provided musical accompaniment to it. It was during the period of the united monarchy that one of the founding documents of the Torah, the first five books of the Jewish Bible, was produced. After the kingdom of Israel split into two—Judea in the south and Israel in the north—more component parts of the Torah were created.

The section of the Tanakh called Prophets begins with the history of the conquest of Israel by Joshua and extends through the periods of the united and the divided monarchies as well as including the prophecies generated in these eras by Isaiah, Jeremiah, and others. The prophets provided the counterpoint to the worldly viewpoints of the kings and spoke to them in God's words.

The Writings include a diverse set of works: Psalms, Proverbs, short novellas (e.g., the Books of Ruth and Esther), and sustained poems (e.g., Job and the

Song of Songs) as well as a retelling of the story of Israel during the monarchy (Chronicles) and how the Temple was rebuilt (Ezra and Nehemiah).

If we had to say, in the broadest terms, what the different parts of the Tanakh were about, we might say that the Torah is the template for Israel's place in the universe and for how it could become a monotheistic faith in a world of idolatry. The section of the Prophets concerns itself with how to transform the theory presented in the Torah into a living reality and the struggle to adhere to the ideal faith the Israelites developed in the wilderness. The Writings are a textbook for diverse views on life, suffering, sin, repentance, prayer, and history. Views are expressed in Writings that conflict with basic motifs of the Torah (e.g., Deuteronomy's vision of God working through history versus Job's inscrutable Deity), yet all these works were included in the canon. This ability of Judaism to contain within itself diverse views will also be seen in rabbinic literature.

In the Second Temple period (516 B.C.E.–70 C.E.), great changes enveloped the Jews in the Land of Israel. Alexander the Great conquered the Persians in Israel in 332 B.C.E., and Jewish culture thereafter fell under Greek, and later, Roman, rule and cultural influence. Under Seleucid rule, Jews came to be more and more oppressed until they rebelled against Antiochus IV Epiphanes and liberated Jerusalem in 164 B.C.E., an event celebrated by the holiday Hanukkah ever since. The Hasmonean dynasty, which led the revolution, ruled Jewish life until 63 B.C.E. when independent Hasmonean rule came to an end. Judea was thereafter ruled by Rome. A turbulent political period followed, culminating in the revolt against Rome beginning in 66 C.E. and ending with the destruction of the Temple in 70 C.E. When a decision was made to establish a Roman colony on Jerusalem's ruins, the Bar Kokhba revolt ensued in 132 C.E. By 135 C.E., when the revolt ended, the Jewish population in the Land of Israel was decimated through death, enslavement, and emigration.

The literature produced during the Second Temple period was vast and varied. The surviving texts from this era consist of testaments, apocalyptic literature, biblical exegesis by Philo (c. 20 B.C.E.–50 C.E.), and the Dead Sea scrolls. One of the best known of these works was written by Ben Sira (second century B.C.E.) and is known as Ecclesiasticus. Josephus (c. 38–after 100 C.E.), a Jerusalem-born Jew who eventually moved to Rome, wrote works in this era about the conquest of the Land of Israel. Though some Jews had lived in Babylonia since the First Temple's destruction in 586 B.C.E., and throughout the whole Second Temple period, diaspora communities became more populous, prosperous, and important after the Second Temple's fall.

When the Temple was destroyed in 70 C.E. by the Romans, a new form of Judaism gradually came into being, based on continuing interpretation of the Tanakh. While the synagogue had existed in some form during the Second Temple period, it became more important after the Temple's destruction. In time, this culture of study, text development, and worship services within the synagogue came to replace the Temple. The replacements, though, were generally considered to be second best, and a lingering nostalgia for the Temple permeates Jewish texts and worship to the present day. The Sages who promulgated the "Oral Torah," i.e., interpretations of the "Written Torah" as the Tanakh came to be called, engaged in persuasive creativity to convince Jews to follow their vision of a Judaism without a Temple. In time, this vision was accepted, but the Sages who composed this rabbinic literature never operated from a base of easy authority and universally-accepted symbolism as did the priests in the Temple.

The foundation document of rabbinic literature is the Mishnah. Its component parts, called mishnayot, were composed after the destruction of the Temple in 70 C.E. These mishnayot, oral teachings, were promulgated in many schools and were finally culled, organized, and codified by Rabbi Judah ha-Nasi in c. 200 C.E. These teachings, which became the Mishnah, might have been collected to provide a binding code of law or to be a textbook of laws that were not necessarily binding. At this point, we can probably never know, conclusively, which sort of document the redactors of the Mishnah intended to produce.

Various commentaries on the Mishnah—Tosefta and Gemara—as well as commentaries on the Torah were created and passed on by the Sages of the rabbinic era. The Talmud of the Land of Israel, called the Yerushalmi, appears to have been redacted in the early fifth century. The commentary to the Mishnah, i.e., the Gemara of the Babylonian Talmud, also known as the Bavli, was completed as early as 427 or as late as 700 C.E.

Just as the Tanakh and rabbinic literature considered legal, religious, and symbolic aspects of illness and healing, so these factors were important in later Jewish sources, as well. Moses Maimonides, also called Rambam and Moses ben Maimon, systematized Jewish law in his fourteen-volume work, the Mishneh Torah (The Second Torah). It covers every aspect of Jewish law, including areas that were no longer practiced. The rules governing the Temple, the complicated laws of ritual purity, and the Jewish laws that were observed in Rambam's day such as how to pray, observe kashrut, transact a valid wedding and divorce, and so forth are all outlined in this comprehensive work.

Joseph ben Efrayim Caro (1488–1575), a well-respected authority of his day, was able to unify Jewish law. He created the Shulḥan Arukh (The Set Table), which eventually came to be accepted as the standard book of Jewish law.

Halakhic works were not the sole type of Jewish creativity produced in this era. Ethical wills, such as the ones written by the Spaniard Judah Ibn Tibbon (b. 1120), and memoirs, such as those of Gluckel of Hameln (1646–1719), offer more personal perspectives on Jewish life and values in the medieval world. In addition, The Zohar (The Book of Splendor) was produced by Moses de Leon during this era. It is a collection of several mystical works, loosely organized as a commentary to the Torah, and is one of Judaism's most important mystical documents.

One of the most popular forms of mysticism is that of the Hasidic movement. This form of Judaism emphasized joy and simplicity in worship and in following the commandments. The Mitnagdim, those who were opposed to Hasidism, favored scholarship over simplicity. Hasids and the heirs of the Mitnagdim still practice their forms of Judaism to this day. They are but two of the major bands of light within the spectrum of Jewish thought, practice, and literary creativity.

The Reform Movement, begun in the mid-1800s in Germany, sought to embrace modernity while remaining within Jewish spirituality. The Conservative Movement emphasizes the importance of Jewish law but insists on continuing the creative process that brought it forth. The Reconstructionist and Renewal Movements have developed relatively recently and also focus on creativity, responding to modernity, and the importance of Jewish culture and spirituality.

Of course, the establishment of the State of Israel in the Land of Israel (1948), and the Holocaust of European Jews that preceded it, continue to shape Judaism and Jewish ethics today. Well-known, contemporary authorities on Jewish medical and legal issues are Immanuel Jakobovits, J. David Bleich, and Fred Rosner among many, many others.

Jewish literary, ethical, and spiritual development will likely continue as long as Judaism and Jews exist. Judaism, and Jews, are living, collective entities whose creativity is a source of strength.

Notes and Credits

PART I

[1] 2 Samuel 12:15–23. All biblical selections are from *Tanakh, The Holy Scriptures* (Philadelphia: Jewish Publication Society, 1985) with the exception of Psalm 23 and Ecclesiastes 3:1–8, which are from *The Holy Scriptures* (Philadelphia: Jewish Publication Society, 1956).

[2] Psalm 41:1–4.

[3] Erubin 54a. All Talmud selections are from the Babylonian Talmud, ed. I. Epstein (London: Soncino, 1936). Reprinted by permission of the Soncino Press, Ltd., New York.

[4] Gluckel, *Gluckel of Hameln,* trans. Marvin Lowenthal (New York: Schocken, 1977), 47–56.

[5] Ibid., 4–5.

[6] Adin Steinsaltz, *The Thirteen Petalled Rose* (New York: Basic, 1980), 60–61. Reprinted by permission of Rabbi Adin Steinsaltz.

[7] Michael Swirsky, ed., *At the Threshold: Jewish Meditations on Death* (Northvale, NJ: Jason Aronson Inc., 1996), 112. Reprinted by permission of the publisher, Jason Aronson, Inc., Northvale, NJ, © 1996.

[8] Kadya Molodowsky, "And Yet," trans. Seymour Levitan, in *Voices Within the Ark: The Modern Jewish Poets,* eds. Howard Schwartz and Anthony Rudolph (New York: Avon, 1980), 319. Reprinted by permission of Seymour Levitan.

[9] Sholem Asch, *East River,* trans. A. H. Gross (New York: G. P. Putnam's Sons, 1946), 428–438. Reprinted by permission of the Sholem Asch Literary Estate.

[10] Hirshel Jaffe, James Rudin, and Marcia Rudin, *Why Me? Why Anyone?* (New York: St. Martin's Press, 1986), 12–14, 83–86, 90–91, 115–116, 133–135. Reprinted by permission of Rabbi James A. Rudin.

[11] Max Lerner, *Wrestling with the Angel: A Memoir of My Triumph Over Illness* (New York: W. W. Norton, 1990), 168-176. Reprinted by permission of W. W. Norton & Company, Inc.

[12] William Cutter, "Growing Sick: Thoughts on Months as a Heart Patient, Years as a Rabbi," in *Jewish Values in Health and Medicine,* ed. Levi Meier (Lanham, MD: University Press of America, 1991), 29–35. Reprinted by permission of Cedars-Sinai Medical Center and Rabbi Levi Meier.

[13] Viktor Frankl, *Man's Search for Meaning: An Introduction to Logotherapy* (New York: Simon and Schuster, 1984), 74–78, 81–86. Reprinted by permission of Beacon Press, Boston.

PART II

[1] Deuteronomy 32:39.

[2] Exodus 15:26.

[3] Deuteronomy 28:1–6.

[4] Deuteronomy 28:15–22.

[5] Leviticus 26:14–17.

[6] Genesis 18:1–15.

[7] Numbers 21:4–9.

[8] 2 Kings 4:8–37.

[9] Isaiah 53.

[10] Psalm 38.

[11] Job 2:1–10; 16:6–13; 30:15–30; 40:1–9; 42:1–6.

[12] Baba Mezia 85a.

[13] Shabbath 31b.

[14] Shabbath 33a.

[15] H. Freedman and Maurice Simon, ed., "Genesis Rabbah XCVII (Vayechi)," in *Midrash Rabbah: Genesis* (London: Soncino, 1939), 932. Reprinted by permission of The Soncino Press, Ltd., New York.

[16] Isaiah Tishby, ed., *The Wisdom of the Zohar: An Anthology of Texts* (Washington: Littman Library of Jewish Civilization, 1991), 840–841. Reprinted by permission of The Littman Library of Jewish Civilization, Oxford.

[17] Sholom Aleichem, "At the Doctor's," in *Stories and Satires,* trans. Curt Leviant (New York: Thomas Yoseloff, 1959), 175–181. Reprinted by permission of Curt Leviant.

[18] Rachel Cowan, "From Anger to Anguish to Healing and Wholeness," in *Healing of the Soul, Healing of the Body: Spiritual Leaders Unfold the Strength and Solace in Psalms,* ed. Simkha Weintraub (Woodstock, VT: Jewish Lights Publishing, 1994), 41–45. Reprinted by permission of Jewish Lights Publishing, Woodstock, VT.

[19] Mordecai Kaplan, *Questions Jews Ask: Reconstructionist Answers* (New York: Reconstructionist Press, 1956), 119–120. Reprinted by permission of Reconstructionist Press, Wyncote, PA.

[20] Harold S. Kushner, *When Bad Things Happen to Good People* (New York: Avon, 1981), 134–142. Reprinted by permission of Schocken Books, distributed by Pantheon Books, a division of Random House, Inc.

[21] Esther Goshen-Gottstein, *Recalled to Life: The Story of a Coma* (New Haven: Yale, 1988), 20–21, 49–50. Reprinted by permission of Schocken Publishing House Ltd., Tel Aviv.

[22] Leslie What, "What God Takes," *Lilith* (Fall, 1995): 22–24. Reprinted by permission of Leslie What.

[23] "That I Might Do Great Things," Anonymous.

[24] Eric J. Cassell, *The Nature of Suffering and the Goals of Medicine* (New York: Oxford University Press, 1991), 44–45. Reprinted by permission of Oxford University Press, Inc.

PART III

[1] Marcia Falk, trans., *Selected Poems of Zelda* (unpublished). © by Marcia Falk. Reprinted by permission of Marcia Falk.

[2] Numbers 12:1–15.

[3] Psalm 103.

[4] Psalm 23.

[5] Psalm 6.

[6] *Mi Shebeirakh*, traditional Jewish prayer.

[7] Isaiah 38:1–6, 9–21.

[8] 1 Samuel 2:1–10.

[9] Geza Vermes, *The Complete Dead Sea Scrolls in English* (New York: Penguin, 1997), 281–282. Reprinted by permission of Penguin Books Ltd.

[10] Berakoth 54b.

11 Shabbath 61a.

12 Joseph H. Hertz, *The Authorized Daily Prayer Book* (New York: Bloch Publishing Company, 1959), 141. Reprinted by permission of Block Publishing Company, New York.

13 Nathan Glatzer, ed., "Thou Givest All, Taking Nought," in *Language of Faith* (New York: Schocken, 1975), 186–188. Reprinted by permission of Schocken Books, distributed by Pantheon Books, a division of Random House, Inc.

14 Isaiah Tishby, *The Wisdom of the Zohar: An Anthology of Texts,* vol. 1 (Washington: Littman Library of Jewish Civilization, 1991), 848. Reprinted by permission of The Littman Library of Jewish Civilization, Oxford.

15 Central Conference of American Rabbis, *Rabbi's Manual* (New York: CCAR, 1988), 108. Reprinted by permission of the Central Conference of American Rabbis.

16 Adapted from Union of American Hebrew Congregations Biennial Havdalah Service.

17 Marcia Falk, *The Book of Blessings* (San Francisco: Harper, 1996), 272, 276, 483. Reprinted by permission of HarperCollins Publishers and Marcia Falk.

18 Chava Weissler, "Mitzvot Built into the Body," in *People of the Body: Jews and Judaism from an Embodied Perspective,* ed. Howard Eilberg-Schwartz (Albany: SUNY, 1992), 107. Reprinted by permission of the State University of New York Press, New York.

19 Ibid., 109.

20 Nina Beth Cardin, "Prayer for Those Having Difficulty Conceiving," in *Lifecycles: Jewish Women on Life Passages and Personal Milestones,* ed. Debra Orenstein (Woodstock, VT: Jewish Lights Publishing, 1994), 44–45. Reprinted by permission of Jewish Lights Publishing, Woodstock, VT.

21 Sandy Eisenberg Sasso, "Prayer after a Miscarriage or Stillbirth," in Orenstein, 45. Reprinted by permission of Jewish Lights Publishing, Woodstock, VT.

22 Fanny Neuda, "Prayer after Safe Delivery," in *Four Centuries of Jewish Women's Spirituality: A Sourcebook,* eds. Ellen M. Umansky and Dianne Ashton (Boston: Beacon, 1992), 99–100. Reprinted by permission of Beacon Press, Boston, and Ellen Umansky.

23 Laura Levitt and Sue Ann Wasserman, "*Mikveh* Ceremony for Laura," in Umansky and Ashton, 321–323. Reprinted by permission of Sue Ann Wasserman, Laura Levitt, and Ellen Umansky.

24 Penina V. Adelman, "A Fertility Ritual," in Umansky and Ashton, 247–250. Reprinted by permission of Beacon Press, Boston, Penina Adelman, and Ellen Umansky.

25 Vicki Hollander, "After a Miscarriage," in Orenstein, 446–447. Reprinted by permission of Jewish Lights Publishing, Woodstock, VT.

26 Earl A. Grollman, *In Sickness and in Health; How to Cope When Your Loved One is Ill* (Boston: Beacon, 1987), 117–119. Reprinted by permission of Rabbi Earl A. Grollman.

PART IV

1 1 Samuel 16:14–23.

2 2 Chronicles 16:11–14.

3 Patrick W. Skehan, trans., *The Wisdom of Ben Sira* (New York: Doubleday, 1987), chap. 38:1–15, 438–439. Reprinted by permission of Doubleday, a division of Bantam Doubleday Dell Publishing Group, Inc.

4 Josephus, "The Wars of the Jews VI: 3" in *The Complete Works of Josephus,* trans. William Whiston (Grand Rapids: Kregel, 1981), 595.

5   Ibid., "Antiquities of the Jews VIII: 2," 173.

6   Abodah Zarah 55a.

7   Fred Rosner, trans., *Julius Preuss's Biblical and Talmudic Medicine* (New York: Sanhedrin, 1978), 144–146. Reprinted by permission of the publisher, Jason Aronson Inc., Northvale, NJ © 1996.

8   Mishnah Kiddushin 82a.

9   Berakot 60a.

10 Midrash Temurah, in *Otzar Midrashim Vol. II*, ed. J. D. Eisenstein (New York: Reznick, 1915), 580–581.

11 Yoma 82b.

12 Warren T. Reich, ed., *Encyclopedia of Bioethics* (New York: Free Press, 1978), 1733–1734.

13 Isaac Israeli, "Propaedeudic for Physicians," trans. Martin Levy, in "Medical Ethics of Medieval Islam with Special Reference to Al-Ruhawis' 'Practical Ethics of the Physician,'" *American Philosophical Society* 57, no. 3 (May 1967): 95–97. Reprinted by permission of the American Philosophical Society, Philadelphia, PA.

14 Leon Stitskin, trans., *Letters of Maimonides* (New York: Yeshiva, 1977), 134–135. Reprinted by permission of Yeshiva University Press.

15 Ibid., 72–73.

16 Ariel Bar Sela, Hebbel E. Hoff, and Elias Farias, "Moses Maimonides: Two Treatises on the Regimen of Health," *American Philosophical Society* 54, no. 4 (1964), 24–27. Reprinted by permission of the American Philosophical Society, Philadelphia, PA.

17 Joseph Shatzmiller, *Jews, Medicine, and Medieval Society* (Berkeley: University of California Press, 1994), 1.

18 David B. Ruderman, *Jewish Thought and Scientific Discovery in Early Modern Europe* (New Haven: Yale, 1995), 286–287. Reprinted by permission of Yale University Press, New Haven, CT.

19 David B. Ruderman, *Kabbalah, Magic, and Science: The Cultural Universe of a Sixteenth-Century Jewish Physician* (Cambridge: Harvard, 1988), 25–31, 36–39. Reprinted by permission of the publisher. Copyright © 1988 by the President and Fellows of Harvard College.

20 Aaron J. Feingold, *Three Jewish Physicians of the Renaissance: The Marriage of Science and Ethics* (Tel Aviv: American Friends of Beth Hatefutsoth, 1994), 14–16.

21 "Daily Prayer of a Physician" in Reich, *Encyclopedia of Bioethics,* 1737–1738.

22 Chaim M. Denburg, trans., Code of Hebrew Law, Shulhan 'Aruk, Yorah Deah #335-404 (Montreal: Montreal Jurisprudence, 1954), 8–9. Reprinted by permission of the family of Rabbi Chaim Denburg.

23 Harry Friedenwald, *The Jews and Medicine: Essays* (New York: Ktav, 1967), 79–80. Reprinted by permission of Ktav Publishing House, Inc.

24 Samuel S. Kottek, "The Jewish Hospice," *Review of Infectious Diseases* 3 (July-August 1981): 636–639. Reprinted by permission of the University of Chicago Press.

25 HaRav Y. Halberstam, "Principles of Administration of the Hospital," in *Pathways in Medicine: A Journal of Topics in Medicine in the Spirit of Halacha and Jewish Thought,* trans. Paltiel Roodyn (Kiryat Sanz, Netanya: Laniado Hospital, 1995), 23–25. Reprinted by permission of Laniado Hospital, Israel.

26 Myron Winick, ed., *Hunger Disease: Studies by the Jewish Physicians in the Warsaw Ghetto* (New York: John Wiley, 1979), 3–5. Reprinted by permission of John Wiley & Sons, Inc., New York.

27 Shimon M. Glick, "Unlimited Human Autonomy: A Cultural Bias," *New England Journal of Medicine* 336, no. 13 (March 27, 1997): 954–956. Copyright 1997 Massachusetts Medical Society. All rights reserved.

PART V

1 James H. Charlesworth, *The Old Testament Pseudoepigrapha* (New York: Doubleday, 1983), 977–978. Reprinted by permission of Doubleday, a division of Bantam Doubleday Dell Publishing Group, Inc.

2 Negaim 1:4.

3 Gittin 69a.

4 Baba Mezia 85b.

5 Hayem Saye, "Medical Excerpts from Sefer Mif'Alot Elokim," *Bulletin of the History of Medicine* 4 (1936), 301–302. Reprinted by permission of Johns Hopkins University Press, Baltimore, MD.

6 Jerome R. Mintz, *Legends of the Hasidim: An Introduction to Hasidic Culture and Oral Tradition in the New World* (Chicago: University of Chicago Press, 1968), 324. Reprinted by permission of Mrs. Jerome Mintz.

7 Avraham Greenbaum, *The Wings of the Sun* (Jerusalem: Breslov Research Institute, 1995), 123–124. Reprinted by permission of Breslov Research Institute, Jerusalem.

8 Aaron Levine, *How to Perform the Great Mitzvah of Bikkur Cholim, Visiting the Sick* (Willowdale, Canada: Zichron Meir Publications, 1987), 18–19. Reprinted by permission of Rabbi Aaron Levine.

9 Levi Meier, "Visiting the Sick, An Authentic Encounter," in *Jewish Values in Bioethics*, ed. Levi Meier (New York: Human Sciences Press, 1986), 183–188. Reprinted by permission of Plenum Publishing Corporation and Rabbi Levi Meier.

10 Roland B. Gittelsohn, *Here I Am—Harnessed to Hope* (New York: Vantage, 1988), 51–55. Reprinted by permission of Mrs. Roland Gittelsohn.

11 Hirshel Jaffe, James Rudin, and Marcia Rudin, *Why Me? Why Anyone?* (New York: St. Martin's Press, 1980), 1–11. Reprinted by permission of Rabbi James A. Rudin.

12 Joseph S. Ozarowski, *To Walk in God's Ways: Jewish Pastoral Perspectives on Illness and Bereavement* (Northvale, NJ: Jason Aronson, Inc., 1995), 43–45. Reprinted by permission of the publisher, Jason Aronson Inc., Northvale, NJ © 1995.

13 Sidney Greenberg, "Oriental Rugs," in *A Treasury of the Art of Living*, ed. Sidney Greenberg (Hartford: Hartmore House, 1963), 289. Reprinted by permission of Hartmore House, New York.

14 Chaim Stern, "It is a fearful thing," unpublished. Copyright © by Chaim Stern. Reprinted by permission of Rabbi Chaim Stern.

PART VI

1 Shabbath 147a-148a.

2 Midrash Rabbah Song of Songs 11.16.2.

3 Berakoth 5b.

4 Midrash Rabbah Leviticus XXXIV.1.

5 Nedarim 39a-41b.

6 B. Shabbat 127a.

[7] Maimonides, *Code of Maimonides, Book 4* (New Haven: Yale University Press, 1949), 201. Reprinted by permission of Yale University Press. Copyright © by Yale University Press.

[8] Chaim M. Denburg, trans., *Code of Hebrew Law, Shulhan 'Aruk,* Yorah Deah #335-403 (Montreal: Montreal Jurisprudence, 1954), 2, 4, 6. Reprinted by permission of the family of Rabbi Chaim M. Denburg.

[9] Rachel Cowan, "Learning to Cheer the Sick," *Lilith* (Winter 1991): 32. Reprinted by permission of *Lilith Magazine,* the independent Jewish feminist quarterly, and Rabbi Rachel Cowan.

[10] Basil F. Herring, ed., *Jewish Ethics and Halakah for Our Time* (New York: Ktav, 1984), 72. Reprinted by permission of Ktav Publishing House, Inc., Hoboken, NJ, and Rabbi Basil Herring.

[11] Ibid.

[12] Immanuel Jakobovits, *Jewish Medical Ethics* (New York: Bloch Publishing Co., 1959), 19–23. Reprinted by permission of Block Publishing Co., New York.

[13] Levi Meier, "Filial Responsibility," in *Jewish Values in Bioethics,* ed. Levi Meier (New York: Human Sciences Press, 1986), 75–83. Reprinted by permission of Plenum Publishing Corporation, New York, and Rabbi Levi Meier.

[14] Taanith 21b.

[15] Fred Rosner, "Principles of Practice Concerning the Jewish Patient," *Journal of General Internal Medicine* 11 (August 1996): 486–489. Reprinted by permission of Blackwell Science, Inc., Malden, MA.

[16] Abraham J. Heschel, "The Patient as a Person," *Conservative Judaism* (Fall 1964, vol. XIX): 1–20. Reprinted by permission of *Conservative Judaism.*

[17] Harold M. Shulweis, "The Doctor in the Patient, the Patient in the Doctor," *Reconstructionist* (April-May 1984, vol. XLIX, no. 6): 13–32. Reprinted by permission of Reconstructionist Press, Wyncote, PA.

PART VII

[1] Melvin Konner, *Becoming a Doctor: A Journey of Initiation in Medical School* (New York: Viking Penguin, 1988), 37.

[2] Leviticus 12:1–8.

[3] Leviticus 13:1–3; 13:45–46; 14:1–11.

[4] Leviticus 15:1–4, 13–15.

[5] Leviticus 15:19–23, 28–30.

[6] Proverbs 16:24.

[7] Proverbs 14:10.

[8] Proverbs 15:30.

[9] Proverbs 18:14.

[10] Proverbs 13:12.

[11] Proverbs 17:22.

[12] Proverbs 3:1–3.

[13] Proverbs 3:7–8.

[14] Proverbs 14:30.

[15] Proverbs 15:4.

16 Ecclesiastes 3:1–3.

17 Midrash Rabbah Leviticus XXXIV.3.

18 Patrick Skehan, trans., *The Wisdom of Ben Sira* (New York: Doubleday, 1987), 378–379, 384. Reprinted by permission of Doubleday, a division of Bantam Doubleday Dell Publishing Group, Inc., New York.

19 F. H. Colson, trans., *Philo,* vol. 6, (Cambridge: Harvard University Press, 1966), 541. Reprinted by permission of the publishers and the Loeb Classical Library. Copyright © Harvard University Press, 1935, 1937.

20 Ibid., 385.

21 Philo, "Allegorical Interpretation," III 178, in *Philo,* vol. 1, 421. Reprinted by permission of the publishers and the Loeb Classical Library. Copyright © Harvard University Press 1929, 1935, 1937.

22 Pesahim 112a.

23 Baba Mezia 107b.

24 Raymond L. Weiss and Charles Butterworth ed., *Ethical Writings of Moses Maimonides* (New York: Dover Publications Inc., 1975), 75. Reprinted by permission of Dover Publications, Inc., Mineola, NY.

25 Ibid., 34–36.

26 Ariel Bar Sela, Hebbel E. Hoff, and Elias Farias, "Moses Maimonides: Two Treatises on the Regimen of Health," *American Philosophical Society* 54, no. 4 (1964): 24–27. Reprinted by permission of the American Philosophical Society, Philadelphia, PA.

27 Suessman Muntner, trans., *Maimonides' Treatise on Asthma* (New York: Lippincott, 1963), 8–9.

28 Hyman E. Goldin. trans., *Code of Jewish Law, Kitzur Shulhan Aruh: A Compilation of Jewish Laws and Customs by Rabbi Solomon Ganzfried* (New York: Hebrew Publishing Co., 1928), 101–102. Reprinted by permission of Hebrew Publishing Co., Rockaway Beach, NY. Copyright © 1961, 63, renewed 1989, 91.

29 Israel Abrahams, ed., *Hebrew Ethical Wills* (Philadelphia: Jewish Publication Society, 1976), 75–76. Reprinted by permission of Jewish Publication Society.

30 Fred Rosner, "Pharmacology and Dietetics," in *The Healing Past,* eds. Irene and Walter Jacob (Leiden: E. J. Brill, 1993), 21–23. Reprinted by permission of Brill Publishing, Inc., Kinderhook, NY.

31 Tehilla Lichtenstein, "Believing is Seeing," in *Four Centuries of Jewish Women's Spirituality,* eds. Ellen M. Umansky and Dianne Ashton (Boston: Beacon, 1992), 183. Reprinted by permission of Beacon Press, Boston.

32 Marcia Glaubman Hain, *Twice Chai: A Jewish Road to Recovery* (New York: Bloch Publishing Co., 1991), 53–54. Reprinted by permision of the Coordinating Council on Bikur Cholim of Greater New York.